RELATIVITY

Stories and Essays

Robert J. Sawyer

Introduction by Mike Resnick

Critical Article by Valerie Broege

ISFiC PRESS
Deerfield, 2004

RELATIVITY

Published by ISFiC Press
707 Sapling Lane
Deerfield, Illinois 60015

ISFiC Press Logo Design: Todd Cameron Hamilton

Book Design by Robert T. Garcia
Garcia Publishing Services
919 Tappan Street, Woodstock, Illinois 60098
www.garciapublishingservices.com

10 9 8 7 6 5 4 3 2 1

ISBN: 0-9759156-0-6

PRINTED IN THE UNITED STATES OF AMERICA
by Thomson-Shore, 7300 West Joy Road, Dexter, Michigan 48130-9701
www.tshore.com

For Peter Halasz

Contents

ABOUT ROB

Introduction
by Mike Resnick

Rob Sawyer hit the ground running. One day he hadn't published a word of science fiction, and (it seemed) the next day he was atop the field, turning out one award-caliber novel after another. I was present at Long Beach when he won his first Best Novel Nebula, and I was applauding him at Toronto when he pulled off the unprecedented double of winning the Hugo for one novel and the Seiun (the Japanese Hugo) for a different one.

But you know all that, or you probably wouldn't have picked up the book you now hold in your hands. Anyone can tell you about Rob Sawyer the Superstar Writer; I'd like to tell you about the Rob Sawyer I know – the Superstar Fan and Friend.

If Rob has ever refused a request for anything – an autograph, a word of encouragement or advice, a speech, a non-paying fanzine article, a few moments of his increasingly valuable time to someone he barely knows – it's not only escaped my notice, but just about everyone else's. I've often said that Robert Bloch is my role model, not as a writer, but as a professional – and especially as a professional who interacts with fans. Rob is simply the Canadian version.

An exceptionally gracious man, when he won his Nebula he thanked me for my help and encouragement – neither of which had anything to do with his success – in his acceptance speech. I still remember turning to Carol with an excrement-eating grin on my face after hearing that and bragging, "I got to hold the hero's horse!"

And a hero he is. He remains to this day the only winner of the Best Novel Hugo to remember to thank not only his editor and publisher, but his American and Canadian distributors. I mean, hell, we'd all be starving to death without our book distributors, but only Rob ever thought to thank them publicly.

I don't remember quite when we first met in person – we already knew each other through the Internet – but it must have been at a convention in the 1980s or early 1990s, and we've been friends ever since. It's pretty hard not to be Rob's friend; once you get past being dazzled by his talent, you find yourself equally dazzled by his quick intellect, his wide-ranging knowledge, his humor, and his always good-natured personality.

And I like to think that I had a little something to do with one other bit of dazzling Rob does on occasion – the short story. It's an unhappy fact that if you want to make a living writing short stories in this field and your name isn't Ray or Harlan, you're going to wind up in the poorhouse. So if you have any skill as a novelist, you go where the money is, and if you're as skilled as Rob, you are contracted many books and many years in advance.

But along with novels, I happen to like writing and editing short stories, and I also happen to know that Rob has an incredibly difficult, almost impossible, time saying No to his friends. So over the years I have frequently asked him to contribute stories for anthologies I was editing, and, being Rob, he has yet to turn me down. Or hand in a story that was anything less than stellar in quality. One of them won an award; others were nominated. When Rob says Yes, it's never a half-hearted Yes; he gives it his best.

And some of his best are right here in this volume. I'm proud to say I was responsible for a pair of them – "Immortality" and "Relativity." But there are some other gems that I had nothing to do with (except, like you, to enjoy as a reader), gems like "Ineluctable" and "The Hand You're Dealt." And to show his versatility, Rob has also included a dozen how-to-write columns that he's done for *On Spec* – the Canadian equivalent of my "Ask Bwana" columns for *Speculations* (or maybe my stuff is the American equivalent of Rob's) – plus several speeches, and a touching tribute to Judy Merril.

I read somewhere that Rob recently made his 200th television appearance, which must be close to a record for anyone not named Isaac; and I know he's been very active promoting science fiction on radio, too. And when I say promoting, I don't mean just his own work; he always goes out of his way to find competitors and newcomers to praise and promote. As they say, you can't pay back (although I wouldn't mind if he'd loan me $67,084.22 until payday), so you pay forward – and Rob pays those dues about as well and generously as anyone.

And now that I've told you a little about Rob Sawyer and a little about what awaits you in the pages up ahead, let me simply point out that this book can be considered Essence of Sawyer: fiction, non-fiction, how-to pieces, tributes, speeches. If you buy it – and why would you be reading this if you weren't going to buy it? – and Rob is anywhere around, hunt him up and ask him to sign it. I guarantee he'll be happy to. And if he's not around, take it with you to the next convention he'll be attending; you'll not only get a signature, but you'll get a chance to meet a real *mensch* as well.

A *mensch*? You don't know?

Well, it means a lot of things. In the Fandango dialect of western Botswana, it means a tuskless elephant with three testicles and a bad attitude. In Barsoomian, it means A Foul Perpetrator of a Fate Worse Than Death. In ancient Egyptian, it means He Who Does Vile Things To Mummies Under Cover of Night.

But where I come from, it means a man's man and a writer's writer – in other words, Robert J. Sawyer.

RELATIVITY

Stories and Essays

Fiction

Just Like Old Times

In 1987, I gave up writing short fiction: the pay rates were a tiny fraction of what I was getting for non-fiction, response times from SF magazines were ridiculously long, and I was mightily discouraged by having been unable to sell "Lost in the Mail." Five years went by during which the only fiction I wrote was novel-length.

And then came Mike Resnick.

In July 1992, Mike asked me if I'd agree to write a story for the anthology Dinosaur Fantastic *he and Martin H. Greenberg were putting together.*

Note what Mike was doing: he was commissioning *a story. My work wouldn't have to languish for the better part of a year in a magazine's slush pile.*

This was a very appealing notion. Throughout the 1980s, I had made my living as a freelance non-fiction writer, specializing in high technology and personal finance. I'd done over 200 articles for Canadian and American magazines and newspapers, almost all of which were commissioned in advance of my writing them . . . and I liked it that way.

I accepted Mike's offer, but with trepidation. I hadn't written a short story for half a decade now. What if I'd forgotten how? Or, even worse, what if, as the apparent failure of "Lost in the Mail" had demonstrated, I never really knew how in the first place?

"Just Like Old Times" turned out to be quite a success: Mike and Marty used it as the lead story in Dinosaur Fantastic, *and I also sold it to* On Spec: The Canadian Magazine of Speculative Writing. *The* On Spec *people*

reprinted it in their "best-of" anthology, On Spec: The
First Five Years; *Marty Greenberg scooped it up for his
unrelated hardcover anthology* Dinosaurs; *Jack Dann and
Gardner Dozois reprinted it in their* Dinosaurs II; *and
David G. Hartwell and Glenn Grant bought it for their
anthology* Northern Stars.

*After that, there was no turning back: I knew writing
short fiction would always be a part of my life. Still, since
that day in 1992, I haven't written any short fiction without
a specific commission; I just don't seem to find the time for
short work otherwise.*

———•+•———

The transference went smoothly, like a scalpel slicing into skin.

Cohen was simultaneously excited and disappointed. He was
thrilled to be here – perhaps the judge was right, perhaps this was
indeed where he really belonged. But the gleaming edge was
taken off that thrill because it wasn't accompanied by the usual
physiological signs of excitement: no sweaty palms, no racing
heart, no rapid breathing. Oh, there was a heartbeat, to be sure,
thundering in the background, but it wasn't Cohen's.

It was the dinosaur's.

Everything was the dinosaur's: Cohen saw the world now
through tyrannosaur eyes.

The colors seemed all wrong. Surely plant leaves must be the
same chlorophyll green here in the Mesozoic, but the dinosaur
saw them as navy blue. The sky was lavender; the dirt underfoot
ash gray.

Old bones had different cones, thought Cohen. Well, he could
get used to it. After all, he had no choice. He would finish his life
as an observer inside this tyrannosaur's mind. He'd see what the
beast saw, hear what it heard, feel what it felt. He wouldn't be able
to control its movements, they had said, but he would be able to
experience every sensation.

The rex was marching forward.

Cohen hoped blood would still look red.

It wouldn't be the same if it wasn't red.

"And what, Ms. Cohen, did your husband say before he left
your house on the night in question?"

"He said he was going out to hunt humans. But I thought he was making a joke."

"No interpretations, please, Ms. Cohen. Just repeat for the court as precisely as you remember it, exactly what your husband said."

"He said, 'I'm going out to hunt humans.'"

"Thank you, Ms. Cohen. That concludes the Crown's case, my lady."

The needlepoint on the wall of the Honorable Madam Justice Amanda Hoskins's chambers had been made for her by her husband. It was one of her favorite verses from *The Mikado*, and as she was preparing sentencing she would often look up and re-read the words:

> *My object all sublime*
> *I shall achieve in time –*
> *To let the punishment fit the crime –*
> *The punishment fit the crime.*

This was a difficult case, a horrible case. Judge Hoskins continued to think.

It wasn't just colors that were wrong. The view from inside the tyrannosaur's skull was different in other ways, too.

The tyrannosaur had only partial stereoscopic vision. There was an area in the center of Cohen's field of view that showed true depth perception. But because the beast was somewhat wall-eyed, it had a much wider panorama than normal for a human, a kind of saurian Cinemascope covering 270 degrees.

The wide-angle view panned back and forth as the tyrannosaur scanned along the horizon.

Scanning for prey.

Scanning for something to kill.

The *Calgary Herald*, Thursday, October 16, 2042, hardcopy edition:

Serial killer Rudolph Cohen, 43, was sentenced to death yesterday.

Formerly a prominent member of the Alberta College of Physicians and Surgeons, Dr. Cohen was convicted in August of thirty-seven counts of first-degree murder.

In chilling testimony, Cohen had admitted, without any signs of remorse, to having terrorized each of his victims for hours before slitting their throats with surgical implements.

This is the first time in eighty years that the death penalty has been ordered in this country.

In passing sentence, Madam Justice Amanda Hoskins observed that Cohen was "the most cold-blooded and brutal killer to have stalked Canada's prairies since *Tyrannosaurus rex . . .*"

From behind a stand of dawn redwoods about ten meters away, a second tyrannosaur appeared. Cohen suspected tyrannosaurs might be fiercely territorial, since each animal would require huge amounts of meat. He wondered if the beast he was in would attack the other individual.

His dinosaur tilted its head to look at the second rex, which was standing in profile. But as it did so, almost all of the dino's mental picture dissolved into a white void, as if when concentrating on details the beast's tiny brain simply lost track of the big picture.

At first Cohen thought his rex was looking at the other dinosaur's head, but soon the top of other's skull, the tip of its muzzle and the back of its powerful neck faded away into snowy nothingness. All that was left was a picture of the throat. Good, thought Cohen. One shearing bite there could kill the animal.

The skin of the other's throat appeared gray-green and the throat itself was smooth. Maddeningly, Cohen's rex did not attack. Rather, it simply swiveled its head and looked out at the horizon again.

In a flash of insight, Cohen realized what had happened. Other kids in his neighborhood had had pet dogs or cats. He'd had lizards and snakes – cold-blooded carnivores, a fact to which expert psychological witnesses had attached great weight. Some kinds of male lizards had dewlap sacks hanging from their necks. The rex he was in – a male, the Tyrrell paleontologists had believed – had looked at this other one and seen that she was smooth-throated and therefore a female. Something to be mated with, perhaps, rather than to attack.

Perhaps they would mate soon. Cohen had never orgasmed except during the act of killing. He wondered what it would feel like.

"We spent a billion dollars developing time travel, and now you tell me the system is useless?"

"Well —"

"That is what you're saying, isn't it, professor? That chronotransference has no practical applications?"

"Not exactly, Minister. The system *does* work. We can project a human being's consciousness back in time, superimposing his or her mind overtop of that of someone who lived in the past."

"With no way to sever the link. *Wonderful.*"

"That's not true. The link severs automatically."

"Right. When the historical person you've transferred consciousness into dies, the link is broken."

"Precisely."

"And then the person from our time whose consciousness you've transferred back dies as well."

"I admit that's an unfortunate consequence of linking two brains so closely."

"So I'm right! This whole damn chronotransference thing is useless."

"Oh, not at all, Minister. In fact, I think I've got the perfect application for it."

The rex marched along. Although Cohen's attention had first been arrested by the beast's vision, he slowly became aware of its other senses, too. He could hear the sounds of the rex's footfalls, of twigs and vegetation being crushed, of birds or pterosaurs singing, and, underneath it all, the relentless drone of insects. Still, all the sounds were dull and low; the rex's simple ears were incapable of picking up high-pitched noises, and what sounds they did detect were discerned without richness. Cohen knew the late Cretaceous must have been a symphony of varied tone, but it was as if he was listening to it through earmuffs.

The rex continued along, still searching. Cohen became aware of several more impressions of the world both inside and out, including hot afternoon sun beating down on him and a hungry gnawing in the beast's belly.

Food.

It was the closest thing to a coherent thought that he'd yet detected from the animal, a mental picture of bolts of meat going down its gullet.

Food.

The Social Services Preservation Act of 2022: Canada is built upon the principle of the Social Safety Net, a series of entitlements and programs designed to ensure a high standard of living for every citizen. However, ever-increasing life expectancies coupled with constant lowering of the mandatory retirement age have placed an untenable burden on our social-welfare system and, in particular, its cornerstone program of universal health care. With most taxpayers ceasing to work at the age of 45, and with average Canadians living to be 94 (males) or 97 (females), the system is in danger of complete collapse. Accordingly, all social programs will henceforth be available only to those below the age of 60, with one exception: all Canadians, regardless of age, may take advantage, at no charge to themselves, of government-sponsored euthanasia through chrono-transference.

There! Up ahead! Something moving! Big, whatever it was: an indistinct outline only intermittently visible behind a small knot of fir trees.

A quadruped of some sort, its back to him/it/them.

Ah, there. Turning now. Peripheral vision dissolving into albino nothingness as the rex concentrated on the head.

Three horns.

Triceratops.

Glorious! Cohen had spent hours as a boy poring over books about dinosaurs, looking for scenes of carnage. No battles were better than those in which *Tyrannosaurus rex* squared off against *Triceratops,* a four-footed Mesozoic tank with a trio of horns projecting from its face and a shield of bone rising from the back of its skull to protect the neck.

And yet, the rex marched on.

No, thought Cohen. Turn, damn you! Turn and attack!

• • •

Cohen remembered when it had all begun, that fateful day so many years ago, so many years from now. It should have been a routine operation. The patient had supposedly been prepped properly. Cohen brought his scalpel down toward the abdomen, then, with a steady hand, sliced into the skin. The patient gasped. It had been a *wonderful* sound, a beautiful sound.

Not enough gas. The anesthetist hurried to make an adjustment.

Cohen knew he had to hear that sound again. He had to.

The tyrannosaur continued forward. Cohen couldn't see its legs, but he could feel them moving. Left, right, up, down.

Attack, you bastard!

Left.

Attack!

Right.

Go after it!

Up.

Go after the *Triceratops.*

Dow –

The beast hesitated, its left leg still in the air, balancing briefly on one foot.

Attack!

Attack!

And then, at last, the rex changed course. The ceratopsian appeared in the three-dimensional central part of the tyrannosaur's field of view, like a target at the end of a gun sight.

"Welcome to the Chronotransference Institute. If I can just see your government benefits card, please? Yup, there's always a last time for everything, heh heh. Now, I'm sure you want an exciting death. The problem is finding somebody interesting who hasn't been used yet. See, we can only ever superimpose one mind onto a given historical personage. All the really obvious ones have been done already, I'm afraid. We still get about a dozen calls a week asking for Jack Kennedy, but he was one of the first to go, so to speak. If I may make a suggestion, though, we've got thousands of Roman legion officers cataloged. Those tend to be very satisfying deaths. How about a nice something from the Gallic Wars?"

• • •

The *Triceratops* looked up, its giant head lifting from the wide flat gunnera leaves it had been chewing on. Now that the rex had focussed on the plant-eater, it seemed to commit itself.

The tyrannosaur charged.

The hornface was sideways to the rex. It began to turn, to bring its armored head to bear.

The horizon bounced wildly as the rex ran. Cohen could hear the thing's heart thundering loudly, rapidly, a barrage of muscular gunfire.

The *Triceratops*, still completing its turn, opened its parrot-like beak, but no sound came out.

Giant strides closed the distance between the two animals. Cohen felt the rex's jaws opening wide, wider still, mandibles popping from their sockets.

The jaws slammed shut on the hornface's back, over the shoulders. Cohen saw two of the rex's own teeth fly into view, knocked out by the impact.

The taste of hot blood, surging out of the wound . . .

The rex pulled back for another bite.

The *Triceratops* finally got its head swung around. It surged forward, the long spear over its left eye piercing into the rex's leg . . .

Pain. Exquisite, beautiful pain.

The rex roared. Cohen heard it twice, once reverberating within the animal's own skull, a second time echoing back from distant hills. A flock of silver-furred pterosaurs took to the air. Cohen saw them fade from view as the dinosaur's simple mind shut them out of the display. Irrelevant distractions.

The *Triceratops* pulled back, the horn withdrawing from the rex's flesh.

Blood, Cohen was delighted to see, still looked red.

"If Judge Hoskins had ordered the electric chair," said Axworthy, Cohen's lawyer, "we could have fought that on Charter grounds. Cruel and unusual punishment, and all that. But she's authorized full access to the chronotransference euthanasia program for you." Axworthy paused. "She said, bluntly, that she simply wants you dead."

"How thoughtful of her," said Cohen.

Axworthy ignored that. "I'm sure I can get you anything you want," he said. "Who would you like to be transferred into?"

"Not who," said Cohen. "What."

"I beg your pardon?"

"That damned judge said I was the most cold-blooded killer to stalk the Alberta landscape since *Tyrannosaurus rex.*" Cohen shook his head. "The idiot. Doesn't she know dinosaurs were warm-blooded? Anyway, that's what I want. I want to be transferred into a *T. rex.*"

"You're kidding."

"Kidding is not my forte, John. *Killing* is. I want to know which was better at it, me or the rex."

"I don't even know if they can do that kind of thing," said Axworthy.

"Find out, damn you. What the hell am I paying you for?"

The rex danced to the side, moving with surprising agility for a creature of its bulk, and once again it brought its terrible jaws down on the ceratopsian's shoulder. The plant-eater was hemorrhaging at an incredible rate, as though a thousand sacrifices had been performed on the altar of its back.

The *Triceratops* tried to lunge forward, but it was weakening quickly. The tyrannosaur, crafty in its own way despite its trifling intellect, simply retreated a dozen giant paces. The hornface took one tentative step toward it, and then another, and, with great and ponderous effort, one more. But then the dinosaurian tank teetered and, eyelids slowly closing, collapsed on its side. Cohen was briefly startled, then thrilled, to hear it fall to the ground with a *splash* – he hadn't realized just how much blood had poured out of the great rent the rex had made in the beast's back.

The tyrannosaur moved in, lifting its left leg up and then smashing it down on the *Triceratops*'s belly, the three sharp toe claws tearing open the thing's abdomen, entrails spilling out into the harsh sunlight. Cohen thought the rex would let out a victorious roar, but it didn't. It simply dipped its muzzle into the body cavity, and methodically began yanking out chunks of flesh.

Cohen was disappointed. The battle of the dinosaurs had been fun, the killing had been well engineered, and there had certainly been enough blood, but there was no *terror*. No sense that the *Triceratops* had been quivering with fear, no begging for mercy.

No feeling of power, of control. Just dumb, mindless brutes moving in ways preprogrammed by their genes.

It wasn't enough. Not nearly enough.

Judge Hoskins looked across the desk in her chambers at the lawyer.

"A *Tyrannosaurus*, Mr. Axworthy? I was speaking figuratively."

"I understand that, my lady, but it was an appropriate observation, don't you think? I've contacted the Chronotransference people, who say they can do it, if they have a rex specimen to work from. They have to back-propagate from actual physical material in order to get a temporal fix."

Judge Hoskins was as unimpressed by scientific babble as she was by legal jargon. "Make your point, Mr. Axworthy."

"I called the Royal Tyrrell Museum of Paleontology in Drumheller and asked them about the *Tyrannosaurus* fossils available worldwide. Turns out there's only a handful of complete skeletons, but they were able to provide me with an annotated list, giving as much information as they could about the individual probable causes of death." He slid a thin plastic printout sheet across the judge's wide desk.

"Leave this with me, counsel. I'll get back to you."

Axworthy left, and Hoskins scanned the brief list. She then leaned back in her leather chair and began to read the needlepoint on her wall for the thousandth time:

> *My object all sublime*
> *I shall achieve in time* –

She read that line again, her lips moving slightly as she subvocalized the words: "I shall achieve *in time* . . ."

The judge turned back to the list of tyrannosaur finds. Ah, that one. Yes, that would be perfect. She pushed a button on her phone. "David, see if you can find Mr. Axworthy for me."

There had been a very unusual aspect to the *Triceratops* kill – an aspect that intrigued Cohen. Chronotransference had been performed countless times; it was one of the most popular forms of euthanasia. Sometimes the transferee's original body would give an ongoing commentary about what was going on, as if talking during sleep. It was clear from what they said that transferees couldn't exert any control over the bodies they were transferred into.

Indeed, the physicists had claimed any control was impossible. Chronotransference worked precisely because the transferee could exert no influence, and therefore was simply observing things that had already been observed. Since no new observations were being made, no quantum-mechanical distortions occurred. After all, said the physicists, if one could exert control, one could change the past. And that was impossible.

And yet, when Cohen had willed the rex to alter its course, it eventually had done so.

Could it be that the rex had so little brains that Cohen's thoughts *could* control the beast?

Madness. The ramifications were incredible.

Still . . .

He had to know if it was true. The rex was torpid, flopped on its belly, gorged on ceratopsian meat. It seemed prepared to lie here for a long time to come, enjoying the early evening breeze.

Get up, thought Cohen. *Get up, damn you!*

Nothing. No response.

Get up!

The rex's lower jaw was resting on the ground. Its upper jaw was lifted high, its mouth wide open. Tiny pterosaurs were flitting in and out of the open maw, their long needle-like beaks apparently yanking gobbets of hornface flesh from between the rex's curved teeth.

Get up, thought Cohen again. *Get up!*

The rex stirred.

Up!

The tyrannosaur used its tiny forelimbs to keep its torso from sliding forward as it pushed with its powerful legs until it was standing.

Forward, thought Cohen. *Forward!*

The beast's body felt different. Its belly was full to bursting.

Forward!

With ponderous steps, the rex began to march.

It was wonderful. To be in control again! Cohen felt the old thrill of the hunt.

And he knew exactly what he was looking for.

• • •

"Judge Hoskins says okay," said Axworthy. "She's authorized for you to be transferred into that new *T. rex* they've got right here in Alberta at the Tyrrell. It's a young adult, they say. Judging by the way the skeleton was found, the rex died falling, probably into a fissure. Both legs and the back were broken, but the skeleton remained almost completely articulated, suggesting that scavengers couldn't get at it. Unfortunately, the chronotransference people say that back-propagating that far into the past they can only plug you in a few hours before the accident occurred. But you'll get your wish: you're going to die as a tyrannosaur. Oh, and here are the books you asked for: a complete library on Cretaceous flora and fauna. You should have time to get through it all; the chronotransference people will need a couple of weeks to set up."

As the prehistoric evening turned to night, Cohen found what he had been looking for, cowering in some underbrush: large brown eyes, long, drawn-out face, and a lithe body covered in fur that, to the tyrannosaur's eyes, looked blue-brown.

A mammal. But not just any mammal. *Purgatorius*, the very first primate, known from Montana and Alberta from right at the end of the Cretaceous. A little guy, only about ten centimeters long, excluding its ratlike tail. Rare creatures, these days. Only a precious few.

The little furball could run quickly for its size, but a single step by the tyrannosaur equaled more than a hundred of the mammal's. There was no way it could escape.

The rex leaned in close, and Cohen saw the furball's face, the nearest thing there would be to a human face for another sixty million years. The animal's eyes went wide in terror.

Naked, raw fear.

Mammalian fear.

Cohen saw the creature scream.

Heard it scream.

It was beautiful.

The rex moved its gaping jaws in toward the little mammal, drawing in breath with such force that it sucked the creature into its maw. Normally the rex would swallow its meals whole, but Cohen prevented the beast from doing that. Instead, he simply had it stand still, with the little primate running around, terrified, inside the great cavern of the dinosaur's mouth, banging into the giant teeth and great fleshy walls, and skittering over the massive, dry tongue.

Cohen savored the terrified squealing. He wallowed in the sensation of the animal, mad with fear, moving inside that living prison.

And at last, with a great, glorious release, Cohen put the animal out of its misery, allowing the rex to swallow it, the furball tickling as it slid down the giant's throat.

It was just like old times.

Just like hunting humans.

And then a wonderful thought occurred to Cohen. Why, if he killed enough of these little screaming balls of fur, they wouldn't have any descendants. There wouldn't ever be any *Homo sapiens*. In a very real sense, Cohen realized he *was* hunting humans – every single human being who would ever exist.

Of course, a few hours wouldn't be enough time to kill many of them. Judge Hoskins no doubt thought it was wonderfully poetic justice, or she wouldn't have allowed the transfer: sending him back to fall into the pit, damned.

Stupid judge. Why, now that he could control the beast, there was no way he was going to let it die young. He'd just –

There it was. The fissure, a long gash in the earth, with a crumbling edge. Damn, it *was* hard to see. The shadows cast by neighboring trees made a confusing gridwork on the ground that obscured the ragged opening. No wonder the dull-witted rex had missed seeing it until it was too late.

But not this time.

Turn left, thought Cohen.

Left.

His rex obeyed.

He'd avoid this particular area in future, just to be on the safe side. Besides, there was plenty of territory to cover. Fortunately, this was a young rex – a juvenile. There would be decades in which to continue his very special hunt. Cohen was sure that Axworthy knew his stuff: once it became apparent that the link had lasted longer than a few hours, he'd keep any attempt to pull the plug tied up in the courts for years.

Cohen felt the old pressure building in himself, and in the rex. The tyrannosaur marched on.

This was *better* than old times, he thought. Much better.

Hunting all of humanity.

The release would be *wonderful.*

He watched intently for any sign of movement in the under-brush.

Immortality

Janis Ian is a wonderfully popular folk singer, best known for "Society's Child" and "At Seventeen." Turns out, though, that she's also a big science-fiction fan, and she began attending World Science Fiction Conventions in 2001. Soon, she and Mike Resnick hatched the idea of having all of Janis's favorite SF authors write stories inspired by her song lyrics. The resulting anthology, Stars, *turned out to be one of the major books of 2003, and I was very honored, and very proud, to be asked to contribute to it.*

Still, I found this a very difficult story to write, since my point-of-view character was obviously, and presumptuously, based at least in part on Janis. Although I had finished a draft of this story on the day I left Toronto for the 2002 Worldcon in San Jose, I'd actually planned to tell Janis that I hadn't been able to come up with anything – I just wasn't comfortable with the story. But Janis greeted me with a big hug and told me how much she was looking forward to my submission. With great trepidation, I polished it up and sent it in after the Worldcon, and, to my infinite relief, Janis loved it. Whew!

> *Baby, I'm only society's child*
> *When we're older, things may change*
> *But for now this is the way they must remain*
> *— Janis Ian*

Sixty years.

Sweet Jesus, had it been that long?

But of course it had. The year was now 2023, and then –
Then it had been 1963.
The year of the march on Washington.
The year JFK had been assassinated.
The year I –
No, no, I didn't want to think about that. After all, I'm sure *he* never thinks about it . . . or about me.

I'd been seventeen in 1963. And I'd thought of myself as ugly, an unpardonable sin for a young woman.

Now, though . . .

Now, I was seventy-seven. And I was no longer homely. Not that I'd had any work done, but there was no such thing as a homely – or a beautiful – woman of seventy-seven, at least not one who had never had treatments. The only adjective people applied to an unmodified woman of seventy-seven was *old*.

My sixtieth high-school reunion.

For some, there would be a seventieth, and an eightieth, a ninetieth, and doubtless a mega-bash for the hundredth. For those who had money – real money, the kind of money I'd once had at the height of my career – there were pharmaceuticals and gene therapies and cloned organs and bodily implants, all granting the gift of synthetic youth, the gift of time.

I'd skipped the previous reunions, and I wasn't fool enough to think I'd be alive for the next one. This would be it, my one, my only, my last. Although I'd once, briefly, been rich, I didn't have the kind of money anymore that could buy literal immortality. I would have to be content knowing that my songs would exist after I was gone.

And yet, today's young people, children of the third millennium, couldn't relate to socially conscious lyrics written so long ago. Still, the recordings would exist, although . . .

Although if a tree falls in a forest, and no one is around to hear it, does it make a sound? If a recording – digitized, copied from medium to medium as technologies and standards endlessly change – isn't listened to, does the song still exist? Does the pain it chronicled still continue?

I sighed.

Sixty years since high-school graduation.

Sixty years since all those swirling hormones and clashing emotions.

Sixty years since Devon.

It wasn't the high school I remembered. My Cedar Valley High had been a brown-and-red brick structure, two stories tall, with large fields to the east and north, and a tiny staff parking lot.

That building had long since been torn down — asbestos in its walls, poor insulation, no fiber-optic infrastructure. The replacement, larger, beige, thermally efficient, bore the same name but that was its only resemblance. And the field to the east had become a parking lot, since every seventeen-year-old had his or her own car these days.

Things change.

Walls come down.

Time passes.

I went inside.

"Hello," I said. "My name is . . ." and I spoke it, then spelled the last name — the one I'd had back when I'd been a student here, the one that had been my stage name, the one that pre-dated my ex-husbands.

The man sitting behind the desk was in his late forties; other classes were celebrating their whole-decade anniversaries as well. I suspected he had no trouble guessing to which year each arrival belonged, but I supplied it anyway: "Class of Sixty-Three."

The man consulted a tablet computer. "Ah, yes," he said. "Come a long way, have we? Well, it's good to see you." A badge appeared, printed instantly and silently, bearing my name. He handed it to me, along with two drink tickets. "Your class is meeting in Gymnasium Four. It's down that corridor. Just follow everyone else."

They'd done their best to capture the spirit of the era. There was a US flag with just fifty stars — easy to recognize because of the staggered rows. And there were photos on the walls of Jack and Jackie Kennedy, and Martin Luther King, and a *Mercury* space capsule bobbing in the Pacific, and Sandy Koufax with the Los Angeles Dodgers. Someone had even dug up movie posters for the hits of that year, *Dr. No* and *Cleopatra*. Two video monitors were silently playing *The Beverly Hillbillies* and *Bonanza*. And

"Easier Said Than Done" was coming softly out of the detachable speakers belonging to a portable stereo.

I looked around the large room at the dozens of people. I had no idea who most of them were – not at a glance. They were just old folks, like me: wrinkled, with gray or white hair, some noticeably stooped, one using a walker.

But that man, over there . . .

There had only been one black person in my class. I hadn't seen Devon Smith in the sixty years since, but this had to be him. Back then, he'd had a full head of curly hair, buzzed short. Now, most of it was gone, and his face was deeply lined.

My heart was pounding harder than it had in years; indeed, I hadn't thought the old thing had that much life left in it.

Devon Smith.

We hadn't talked, not since that hot June evening in '63 when I'd told him I couldn't see him anymore. Our senior prom had only been a week away, but my parents had demanded I break up with him. They'd seen Governor George Wallace on the news, personally blocking black students – "coloreds," we called them back then – from enrolling at the University of Alabama. Mom and Dad said their edict was for my own safety, and I went along with it, doing what society wanted.

Truth be told, part of me was relieved. I'd grown tired of the stares, the whispered comments. I'd even overheard two of our teachers making jokes about us, despite all their posturing about the changing times during class.

Of course, those teachers must long since be dead. And as Devon looked my way, for a moment I envied them.

He had a glass of red wine in his hand, and he was wearing a dark gray suit. There was no sign of recognition on his face. Still, he came over. "Hello," he said. "I'm Devon Smith."

I was too flustered to speak, and, after a moment, he went on. "You're not wearing your nametag."

He was right; it was still in my hand, along with the drink chits. I thought about just turning and walking away. But no, no – I couldn't do that. Not to him. Not again.

"Sorry," I said, and that one word embarrassed me further. I lifted my hand, opened my palm, showing the nametag held within.

He stared at it as though I'd shown him a crucifixion wound.

"It's you," he said, and his gaze came up to my face, his brown eyes wide.

"Hello, Devon," I said. I'd been a singer; I still had good breath control. My voice did not crack.

He was silent for a time, and then he lifted his shoulders, a small shrug, as if he'd decided not to make a big thing of it. "Hello," he replied. And then he added, presumably because politeness demanded it, "It's good to see you." But his words were flat.

"How have you been?" I asked.

He shrugged again, this time as if acknowledging the impossibility of my question. How has anyone been for six decades? How does one sum up the bulk of a lifetime in a few words?

"Fine," he said at last. "I've had . . ." But whatever it was he'd had remained unsaid. He looked away and took a sip of his wine. Finally, he spoke again. "I used to follow your career."

"It had its ups and downs," I said, trying to keep my tone light.

"That song . . ." he began, but didn't finish.

There was no need to specify which song. The one I'd written about him. The one I'd written about what I *did* to him. It was one of my few really big hits, but I'd never intended to grow rich off my – off *our* – pain.

"They still play it from time to time," I said.

Devon nodded. "I heard it on an oldies station last month." *Oldies.* I shuddered.

"So, tell me," I said, "do you have kids?"

"Three," said Devon. "Two boys and a girl."

"And grandkids?"

"Eight," said Devon. "Ages two through ten."

"Immortality." I hadn't intended to say it out loud, but there it was, the word floating between us. Devon had his immortality through his genes. And, I suppose, he had a piece of mine, too, for every time someone listened to that song, he or she would wonder if it was autobiographical, and, if so, who the beautiful young black man in my past had been.

"Your wife?" I asked.

"She passed away five years ago." He was holding his wineglass in his left hand; he still wore a ring.

"I'm sorry."

"What about you?" asked Devon. "Any family?"

I shook my head. We were quiet a while. I was wondering what color his wife had been.

"A lot has changed in sixty years," I said, breaking the silence.

He looked over toward the entrance, perhaps hoping somebody else would arrive so he could beg off. "A lot," he agreed. "And yet . . ."

I nodded. And yet, there still hadn't been a black president or vice-president.

And yet, the standard of living of African-Americans was still lower than that of whites – not only meaning a shorter natural life expectancy, but also that far fewer of them could afford the array of treatments available to the rich.

And yet, just last week, they'd picked the person who would be the first to set foot on Mars. *Of course it was a man,* I'd thought bitterly when the announcement was made. Perhaps Devon had greeted the news with equal dismay, thinking, *Of course he's white.*

Suddenly I heard my name being called. I turned around, and there was Madeline Green. She was easy to recognize; she'd clearly had all sorts of treatments. Her face was smooth, her hair the same reddish-brown I remembered from her genuine youth. How she'd recognized me, though, I didn't know. Perhaps she'd overheard me talking to Devon, and had identified me by my voice, or perhaps just the fact that I *was* talking to Devon had been clue enough.

"Why, Madeline!" I said, forcing a smile. "How good to see you!" I turned to Devon. "You remember Devon Smith?"

"How could I forget?" said Madeline. He was proffering his hand, and, after a moment, she took it.

"Hello, Madeline," said Devon. "You look fabulous."

It had been what Madeline had wanted to hear, but I'd been too niggardly to offer up.

Niggardly. A perfectly legitimate word – from the Scandinavian for "stingy," if I remembered correctly. But also a word I never normally used, even in my thoughts. And yet it had come to mind just now, recalling, I supposed, what Madeline had called Devon behind his back all those years ago.

Devon lifted his wineglass. "I need a refill," he said.

The last time I'd looked, he'd still had half a glass; I wondered if he'd quickly drained it when he saw Madeline approaching, giving him a way to exit gracefully, although whether it was me or Madeline he wanted to escape, I couldn't say. In any event, Devon was now moving off, heading toward the cafeteria table that had been set up as a makeshift bar.

"I bought your albums," said Madeline, now squeezing my hand. "Of course, they were all on vinyl. I don't have a record player anymore."

"They're available on CD," I said. "And for download."

"Are they now?" replied Madeline, sounding surprised. I guess she thought of my songs as artifacts of the distant past.

And perhaps they were – although, as I looked over at Devon's broad back, it sure didn't feel that way.

"Welcome back, class of Nineteen Sixty-Three!"

We were all facing the podium, next to the table with the portable stereo. Behind the podium, of course, was Pinky Spenser – although I doubt anyone had called him "Pinky" for half a century. He'd been student-council president, and editor of the school paper, and valedictorian, and on and on, so he was the natural MC for the evening. Still, I was glad to see that for all his early success, he, too, looked old.

There were now perhaps seventy-five people present, including twenty like Madeline who had been able to afford rejuvenation treatments. I'd had a chance to chat briefly with many of them. They'd all greeted me like an old friend, although I couldn't remember ever being invited to their parties or along on their group outings. But now, because I'd once been famous, they all wanted to say hello. They hadn't had the time of day for me back when we'd been teenagers, but doubtless, years later, had gone around saying to people, "You'll never guess who *I* went to school with!"

"We have a bunch of prizes to give away," said Pinky, leaning into the mike, distorting his own voice; part of me wanted to show him how to use it properly. *"First, for the person who has come the farthest . . ."*

Pinky presented a half-dozen little trophies. I'd had awards enough in my life, and didn't expect to get one tonight – nor did I. Neither did Devon.

"And now," said Pinky, *"although it's not from 1963, I think you'll all agree that this is appropriate . . ."*

He leaned over and put a new disk in the portable stereo. I could see it from here; it was a CD-ROM that someone had burned at home. Pinky pushed the play button, and . . .

And one of my songs started coming from the speakers. I recognized it by the second note, of course, but the others didn't until the recorded version of me started singing, and then Madeline Green clapped her hands together. "Oh, listen!" she said, turning toward me. "It's you!"

And it was – from half a century ago, with my song that had become the anthem for a generation of ugly-duckling girls like me. How could Pinky possibly think I wanted to hear that now, here, at the place where all the heartbreak the song chronicled had been experienced?

Why the hell had I come back, anyway? I'd skipped even the fiftieth reunion; what had driven me to want to attend my sixtieth? Was it loneliness?

No. I had friends enough.

Was it morbid curiosity? Wondering who of the old gang had survived?

But, no, that wasn't it, either. That wasn't why I'd come.

The song continued to play. I was doing my guitar solo now. No singing; just me, strumming away. But soon enough the words began again. It was my most famous song, the one I'm sure they'll mention in my obituary.

To my surprise, Madeline was singing along softly. She looked at me, as if expecting me to join in, but I just forced a smile and looked away.

The song played on. The chorus repeated.

This wasn't the same gymnasium, of course – the one where my school dances had been held, the ones where I'd been a wallflower, waiting for even the boys I couldn't stand to ask me to dance. That gym had been bulldozed along with the rest of the old Cedar Valley High.

I looked around. Several people had gone back to their conversations while my music still played. Those who had won the little trophies were showing them off. But Devon, I saw, was listening intently, as if straining to make out the lyrics.

We hadn't dated long – just until my parents found out he was black and insisted I break up with him. This wasn't the song I'd written about us, but, in a way, I suppose it was similar. Both of them, my two biggest hits, were about the pain of being dismissed because of the way you look. In this song, it was me – homely, lonely. And in that other song . . .

I had been a white girl, and he'd been the only black – not *boy*, you can't say boy – anywhere near my age at our school. Devon had no choice: if he were going to date anyone from Cedar Valley, she would have had to be white.

Back then, few could tell that Devon was good-looking; all they saw was the color of his skin. But he had been *fine.* Handsome, well muscled, a dazzling smile. And yet he had chosen me.

I had wondered about that back then, and I still wondered about it now. I'd wondered if he'd thought appearances couldn't possibly matter to someone who looked like me.

The song stopped, and –

No.

No.

I had a repertoire of almost a hundred songs. If Pinky was going to pick a second one by me, what were the chances that it would be *that* song?

But it was. Of course it was

Devon didn't recognize it at first, but when he did, I saw him take a half-step backward, as if he'd been pushed by an invisible hand.

After a moment, though, he recovered. He looked around the gym and quickly found me. I turned away, only to see Madeline softly singing this one, too, *la-la-ing* over those lyrics she didn't remember.

A moment later, there was a hand on my shoulder. I turned. Devon was standing there, looking at me, his face a mask. "We have some unfinished business," he said, softly but firmly.

I swallowed. My eyes were stinging. "I am so sorry, Devon," I said. "It was the times. The era." I shrugged. "Society."

He looked at me for a while, then reached out and took my pale hand in his brown one. My heart began to pound. "We never got to do this back in '63," he said. He paused, perhaps wondering whether he wanted to go on. But, after a moment, he did, and there was no reluctance in his voice. "Would you like to dance?"

I looked around. Nobody else was dancing. Nobody had danced all evening. But I let him lead me out into the center of the gym.

And he held me in his arms.

And I held him.

And as we danced, I thought of the future that Devon's grand-children would grow up in, a world I would never see, and, for the first time, I found myself hoping my songs wouldn't be immortal.

The Stanley Cup Caper

The 2003 World Science Fiction Convention was in Toronto, where I live. The Toronto Star, Canada's largest-circulation newspaper, decided to commemorate that fact – and my then-current Hugo nomination for Hominids *– by commissioning a short story from me predicting the future of Toronto some thirty years down the road.*

I'd just finished reading Dan Brown's runaway bestseller The Da Vinci *code, and puzzles and mysteries were very much on my mind. I'm not a hockey fan – sacrilege for a Canadian, I know – but somehow hit on this premise.*

"She shoots! She scores! For the first time in sixty-seven years, the Toronto Maple Leafs have won the Stanley Cup! Captain Karen Lopez and her team have skated to victory as the 2031 NHL champions. The hometown crowd here is going wild, and – wait! Wait! Ladies and gentlemen, this is incredible . . . we've just received word that the Stanley Cup trophy is missing!"

Detectives Joginder Singh and Trista Chong let their car drive them east along the Gardiner Expressway. At Bathurst, the vehicle headed down into the tunnel. Jo shuddered; he hated the underground portion of the Gardiner. Sadly, his fear of tunnels also kept him from using the subway, even though it now ran all the way from Pearson Airport to the Pickering Solar Power Plant.

Still, the one tolerable thing about going underground here was that he didn't have to lay eyes on the spire of the Quebec Consulate; Trista, fifteen years his junior, didn't really remember a united Canada, but Jo certainly did.

At Yonge, their car resurfaced. South of them was the *Toronto Sun-Star* building. But they were going north: their car let them out across the street from the Hockey Hall of Fame. Of course, there was no place to park; the car would just keep driving around the block until they signaled it to pick them up.

Jo and Trista had spent most of yesterday fruitlessly examining the crime scene at the JetsGo Centre. Today, they were going to start by having a look at the duplicate Stanley Cup – the mockup that was on public display at the Hall of Fame – just to get a feel for the dimensions of the stolen object.

Once inside, Jo stood in front of the glass case containing the duplicate, while Trista walked around the case, taking pictures of the duplicate's engraved surface with her pocketbrain. When she was finished, something apparently caught her eye. "Look!" she crowed, pointing to the adjacent glass case. "There it is – taken apart, but there it is!"

Jo glanced at the other case and laughed. "Those are just retired bands."

Trista made a perplexed frown. "Like the Barenaked Ladies?"

"No. Bands from the original trophy. It always consists of the cup on top and five circular bands forming the cylindrical body." He pointed back at the mockup. "See? Each of the five bands has room for listing the members of thirteen winning teams. When they fill the last spot on the bottom band, they retire the top one, slide the other four up, and add a new band. Those bands in that other case are the ones that have already been removed."

Karen took some pictures of the retired bands, then looked back at the mockup, peering at its base. "But the last band on the trophy is already full," she said.

Jo nodded. "That's right. They're going to have to retire the top band this year and start a new one." He paused. "Seen enough?"

Trista nodded. They exited, crossed the street, and waited for their car to come get them. With the Gardiner buried, it was easy to see the Central Nanotechnology Tower on the lakeshore, but there was no point going up to the observation deck anymore. Jo shook his head; he was old enough to remember when the city's nickname had been Hogtown, not Smogtown.

The car took them north on Yonge Street, the toll being debited automatically. It had been ten years since GTA amalgamation, combining Toronto with everything from Mississauga to

Oshawa. Still, the stolen trophy had to be somewhere inside the supercity's borders; like every other North American metropolis, T.O. was surrounded by security checkpoints, and something as big as the Stanley Cup couldn't have been smuggled out.

On their left now was the Eaton Centre. Jo's sister had a condominium there, in what had once been a Grand & Toy store; with most people shopping online these days, there was little need for big malls. As they continued up Yonge, the towers of Ryerson – "the Harvard of the North," as CNNMSNBC had recently dubbed it – were visible off to the right. Jo watched the landscape going by–a succession of Krispy Kreme donut shops, pot bars, and licensed bordellos. Karen, meanwhile, had her pocketbrain out and was staring at its screen, studying the pictures she'd taken earlier.

Their car turned right onto Carleton, heading towards Maple Leaf Gardens – a historic site, which perhaps might hold a clue – when suddenly Trista looked up from her screen. "No! Car, turn around – head to University Avenue, and then go south."

Jo looked at his partner. "What's up?"

"I think I know where the Stanley Cup is."

"Where?"

Trista brought up a map of downtown Toronto on her pocketbrain and showed it to him. "Right there," she said, tapping a spot on the screen.

"Oh, come on!" said Jo. "Why would they want it?"

"Did you see what was on that band they're going to retire this year?"

"Thirteen old winning teams," said Jo.

"Yes – but which teams?"

"I have no idea."

She brought up one of the images she'd taken of the duplicate trophy. "The winners from 1953 to 1965."

"So?"

"So I've read what's on all the bands now, including the retired ones. The band they're about to remove lists the only five-wins-in-a-row Stanley Cup champions."

"Really?"

"Yes. See? From 1956 through 1960, Montreal won the Stanley Cup every single year, and –"

Jo got it in a flash. "And there's no way a sovereign Quebec would let the band commemorating that be archived at the Hockey Hall of Fame, which is on Canadian soil. But the Quebec Consulate –"

"Exactly!" said Trista. "The Quebec Consulate is technically Quebecois soil."

Jo frowned. "But we don't have any jurisdiction on the consulate grounds."

"I know," said Trista. "It'll take some political wrangling between Ottawa and Quebec."

"Plus ca change, plus c'est la meme chose," said Jo.

"What's that mean?" asked Trista. She was young enough that she hadn't had to study French in school.

Jo looked out the car's window as they turned onto University, passing the statue of Mel Lastman. "The more things change," he said, "the more they stay the same."

Relativity

Mike Resnick edits a lot of anthologies, and I'm always thrilled when he asks me to contribute to one of them. In 2003, he did a pair of fascinating books for DAW entitled Men Writing Science Fiction as Women *and* Women Writing Science Fiction as Men. *Mike said I could only be in the first, as I was "biologically disqualified" from the second.*

I've always been fascinated by time dilation and relationships (one of my all-time favorite SF stories is John Varley's "The Pusher") and so "Relativity" – the title piece for this collection – was born.

I'm rather happy with the way the story turned out, but whenever I look at the anthology it originally appeared in, I feel a pang of sadness. One of my best writing friends, Robyn Herrington, contributed to Women Writing Science Fiction as Men. *She had been mentored through her career by both me and Mike, and we both loved her a lot. Sadly, though, on May 3, 2004, shortly after her story was published, she passed away after a two-year battle with cancer. I'll always miss her.*

You can't have brothers without being familiar with *Planet of the Apes.* I'm not talking about the "re-imaging" done by Tim Burton, apparently much ballyhooed in its day, but the Franklin J. Schaffner original – the one that's stood the test of time, the one that, even a hundred years after it was made, boys still watch.

Of course, one of the reasons boys enjoy it is it's very much a guy film. Oh, there had been a female astronaut along for the ride with Chuck Heston, but she died during the long space voyage, leaving just three macho men to meet the simians. The woman ended up a hideous corpse when her suspended-animation chamber failed, and even her name – "Stewart" – served to desexualize her.

Me, I liked the old *Alien* films better. Ellen Ripley was a survivor, a fighter. But, in a way, those movies were a cheat, too. When you got right down to it, Sigourney Weaver was playing a man – and you couldn't even say, as one of my favorite (female) writers does, that she was playing "a man with tits and hips" – 'cause ole Sigourney, she really didn't have much of either. Me, I've got not enough of one and too much of the other.

I'd had time to watch all five *Apes* films, all four *Alien* films, and hundreds of other movies during my long voyage out to Athena, and during the year I'd spent exploring that rose-colored world. Never saw an ape, or anything that grabbed onto my face or burst out of my chest – but I did make lots of interesting discoveries that I'm sure I'll be spending the rest of my life telling the people of Earth about.

And now, I had just about finished the long voyage home. Despite what had happened to *Apes*'s Stewart, I envied her her suspended-animation chamber. After all, the voyage back from Athena had taken three long years.

It was an odd thing, being a spacer. My grandfather used to talk about people "going postal" and killing everyone around them. At least the United States Postal Service had lasted long enough to see that term retired, in favor of "going Martian."

That had been an ugly event. The first manned – why isn't there a good non-sexist word for that? Why does "crewed" have to be a homonym for "crude"? Anyway, the first manned mission to Mars had ended up being a bloodbath; the ebook about it – *The Red Planet* – had been the most popular download for over a year.

That little experiment in human psychology finally taught NASA what the reality-television shows of a generation earlier had failed to: that you can't force a bunch of alpha males – or alpha females, for that matter – together, under high-pressure circumstances, and expect everything to go fine. Ever since then, manned – that damn word again – spaceflight had involved only individual astronauts, a single human to watch over the dumb robotic probes and react to unforeseen circumstances.

When I said "single human" a moment ago, maybe you thought I meant "unmarried." Sure, it would seem to make sense that they'd pick a loner for this kind of job, some asocial bookworm – hey, do you remember when books were paper and worms weren't computer viruses?

But that didn't work, either. Those sorts of people finally went stir-crazy in space, mostly because of overwhelming regret. They'd never been married, never had kids. While on Earth, they could always delude themselves into thinking that someday they might do those things, but, when there's not another human being for light-years around, they had to face bitter reality.

And so NASA started sending out – well, color me surprised: more sexism! There's a term "family man" that everyone understands, but there's no corresponding "family woman," or a neutral "family person." But that's what I was: a family woman – a woman with a husband and children, a woman devoted to her family.

And yet . . .

And yet my children were grown. Sarah was nineteen when I'd left Earth, and Jacob almost eighteen.

And my husband, Greg? He'd been forty-two, like me. But we'd endured being apart before. Greg was a paleoanthropologist. Three, four months each year, he was in South Africa. I'd gone along once, early in our marriage, but that was before the kids.

Damn ramscoop caused enough radio noise that communication with Earth was impossible. I wondered what kind of greeting I'd get from my family when I finally returned.

"You're going *where?*" Greg always did have a flair for the dramatic.

"Athena," I said, watching him pace across our living room. "It's the fourth planet of –"

"I know what it is, for Pete's sake. How long will the trip take?"

"Total, including time on the planet? Seven years. Three out, one exploring, and three back."

"Seven years!"

"Yes," I said. Then, averting my eyes, I added, "From my point of view."

"What do you mean, 'From your point . . .?' Oh. Oh, crap. And how long will it be from *my* point of view?"

"Thirty years."

"*Thirty!* Thirty! Thirty . . ."

"Just think of it, honey," I said, getting up from the couch. "When I return, you'll have a trophy wife, twenty-three years your junior."

I'd hoped he would laugh at that. But he didn't. Nor did he waste any time getting to the heart of the matter. "You don't seriously expect me to wait for you, do you?"

I sighed. "I don't expect anything. All I know is that I can't turn this down."

"You've got a family. You've got kids."

"Lots of people go years without seeing their kids. Sarah and Jacob will be fine."

"And what about me?"

I draped my arms around his neck, but his back was as stiff as a rocket. "You'll be fine, too" I said.

So am I a bad mother? I certainly wasn't a bad one when I'd been on Earth. I'd been there for every school play, every soccer game. I'd read to Sarah and Jacob, and taught Sarah to cook. Not that she needed to know how: instant food was all most people ever ate. But she *liked* to cook, and I did, too, and to hell with the fact that it was a traditional female thing to do.

The mission planners thought they were good psychologists. They'd taken holograms of Jacob and Sarah just before I'd left, and had computer-aged them three decades, in hopes of preparing me for how they'd look when we were reunited. But I'd only ever seen such things in association with missing children and their abductors, and looking at them – looking at a Sarah who was older now than I myself was, with a lined face and gray in her hair and angle brackets at the corners of her eyes – made me worry about all the things that could have happened to my kids in my absence.

Jacob might have had to go and fight in some goddamned war. Sarah might have, too – they drafted women for all positions, of course, but she was older than Jacob, and the president always sent the youngest children off to die first.

Sarah could have had any number of kids by now. She'd been going to school in Canada when I left, and the ZPG laws – the *zed-pee-gee* laws, as they called them up there – didn't apply in that country. And *those* kids –

Those kids, my grandkids, could be older now than my own kids had been when I'd left them behind. I'd wanted to have it all: husband, kids, career, the stars. And I'd come darn close – but I'd almost certainly missed out on one of the great pleasures of life, playing with and spoiling grandchildren.

Of course, Sarah and Jacob's kids might have had kids of their own by now, which would make me their . . .

Oh, my.

Their *great-grandmother*. At a biological age of 49 when I return to Earth, maybe that would qualify me for a listing in *Guinness eBook of Solar System Records*.

Just what I need.

There's no actual border to the solar system – it just sort of peters out, maybe a light year from the sun, when you find the last cometary nucleus that's gravitationally bound to Sol. So the official border – the point at which you were considered to be within solar space, for the purpose of Earth's laws – was a distance of 49.7 AU from the sun, the maximal radius of Pluto's orbit. Pluto's orbit was inclined more than 17 degrees to the ecliptic, but I was coming in at an even sharper angle. Still, when the ship's computer informed me that I'd passed that magic figure – that I was now less than 49.7 times the radius of Earth's orbit from the sun – I knew I was in the home stretch.

I'd be a hero, no doubt about that (and, no, not a heroine, thank you very much). I'd be a celebrity. I'd be on TV – or whatever had replaced TV in my absence.

But would I still be a wife? A mother?

I looked at the computer-generated map. Getting closer all the time . . .

You might think the idea of being an old-fashioned astronaut was an oxymoron. But consider history. John Glenn, he was right out of Norman Rockwell's U. S. of A., and he'd gone into space not once but twice, with a sojourn in Washington in between. As an astronaut, he'd been on the cutting edge. As a man, he was conservative and family-centered; if he'd run for the presidency, he'd probably have won.

Well, I guess I'm an old-fashioned astronaut, too. I mean, sure, Greg had spent months each year away from home, while I raised the kids in Cocoa Beach and worked at the Kennedy Space Center (my whole CV could be reduced to initials: part-time jobs at KFC while going to university, then full-time work at KSC: from finger-lickin' good to giant leaps for . . . well, for you know who).

When Greg was in South Africa, he searched for *Australo-pithecus africanus* and *Homo sterkfonteinensis* fossils. Of course, a succession of comely young coeds (one of my favorite Scrabble words – nobody knew it anymore) had accompanied him there. And Greg would argue that it was just human nature, just his genes, that had led him to bed as many of them as possible. Not that he'd ever confessed. But a woman could tell.

Me, I'd never strayed. Even with all the beefcake at the Cape – my cape, not his – I'd always been faithful to him. And he had to know that I'd been alone these last seven – these last thirty – years.

God, I miss him. I miss everything about him: the smell of his sweat, the roughness of his cheek late in the day, the way his eyes had always watched me when I was undressing.

But did he miss me? Did he even remember me?

The ship was decelerating, of course. That meant that what had been my floor up until the journey's halfway point was now my ceiling – my world turned upside down.

Earth loomed.

I wasn't going to dock with any of the space stations orbiting Earth. After all, technology kept advancing, and there was no reason for them to keep thirty-year-old adapter technology around just for the benefit of those of us who'd gone on extrasolar missions. No, my ship, the *Astarte* – "Ah-star-tee," as I kept having to remind Greg, who found it funny to call it the *Ass Tart* – had its own planetary lander, the same one that had taken me down to Athena's surface, four years ago by my calendar.

I'd shut down the ramjet now and had entered radio communication with Houston, although no one was on hand that I knew; they'd all retired. Still, you would have thought someone might have come by especially for this. NASA put Phileas Fogg to shame when it came to keeping on schedule (yeah, I'd had time to read all the classics in addition to watching all those movies). I could have asked about my husband, about my daughter and son, but I didn't. Landing took all my piloting skills, and all my concentration. If they weren't going to be waiting for me at Edwards, I didn't want to know about it until I was safely back on mother Earth.

I fired retros, deorbited, and watched through the lander's sheet-diamond windows as flames flew past. All of California was still there, I was pleased to see; I'd been worried that a big hunk of it might have slid into the Pacific in my absence.

Just like a big hunk of my life might have –

No! Concentrate, Cathy. Concentrate. You can worry about all that later.

And, at last, I touched down vertically, in the center of the long runway that stretched across Roger's Dry Lake.

I had landed.

But was I home?

Greg looked *old.*

I couldn't believe it. He'd studied ancient man, and now he'd become one.

Seventy-two.

Some men still looked good at that age: youthful, virile. Others – apparently despite all the medical treatments available in what I realized with a start was now the 22nd century – looked like they had one foot in the grave.

Greg was staring at me, and – God help me – I couldn't meet his eyes.

"Welcome back, Cath," he said.

Cath. He always called me that; the robot probes always referred to me as *Cathy.* I hadn't realized how much I'd missed the shorter version.

Greg was no idiot. He was aware that he hadn't aged well, and was looking for a sign from me. But he was still Greg, still putting things front and center, so that we could deal with them however we were going to. "You haven't changed a bit," he said.

That wasn't quite true, but, then again, everything is relative.

Einstein had been a man. I remember being a student, trying to wrap my head around his special theory of relativity, which said there was no privileged frame of reference, and so it was equally true to claim that a spaceship was at rest and Earth was moving away from it as it was to hold the more obvious inter-pretation, that the ship was moving and Earth was stationary.

But for some reason, time always passed slower on the ship, not on Earth.

Einstein had surely assumed it would be the men who would go out into space, and the women who would stay at home, that the men would return hale and youthful, while the women had stooped over and wrinkled up.

Had that been the case, the women would have been tossed aside, just as Einstein had divorced his own first wife, Mileva. She'd been vacationing with their kids – an older girl and a younger boy, just like Greg and I had – in Switzerland when World War I broke out, and had been unable to return to Albert in Berlin. After a few months – only months! – of this forced separation, he divorced her.

But now Greg and my separation was over. And my husband – if indeed he still *was* my husband; he could have gotten a unilateral divorce while I was away – was an old man.

"How are Sarah and Jacob?" I asked.

"They're fine," said Greg. His voice had lost much of its strength. "Sarah – God, there's so much to tell you. She stayed in Canada, and is running a big hypertronics company up there. She's been married, and divorced, and married again. She's got four daughters and two grandsons."

So I *was* a great-grandmother. I swallowed. "And Jacob?"

"Married. Two kids. One granddaughter, another due in April. A professor at Harvard – astronautics, if you can believe that. He used to say he could either follow his dad, looking down, or his mom, looking up." Greg shrugged his bony shoulders. "He chose the latter."

"I wish they were here," I said.

"I asked them to stay away. I wanted to see you first, alone. They'll be here tomorrow." He reached out, as if to take my hand the way he used to, but I didn't respond at once, and his hand, liver-spotted, with translucent skin, fell by his side again. "Let's go somewhere and talk," he said.

"You wanted it all," Greg said, sitting opposite me in a little cafe near Edwards Air Force Base. "The whole shebang." He paused, the first syllable of the word perhaps catching his attention as it had mine. "The whole nine yards."

"So did you," I said. "You wanted your hominids, and you

wanted your family." I stopped myself before adding, "And more, besides."

"What do we do now?" Greg asked.

"What did you do while I was gone?" I replied.

Greg looked down, presumably picturing the archeological remains of his own life. "I married again – no one you knew. We were together for fifteen years, and then . . ." He shrugged. "And then she died. Another one taken away from me."

It wasn't just in looks that Greg was older; back before I'd gone away, his self-censorship mechanism had been much better. He would have kept that last comment to himself.

"I'm sorry," I said, and then, just so there was no possibility of him misconstruing the comment, I added, "About your other wife dying, I mean."

He nodded a bit, accepting my words. Or maybe he was just old and his head moved of its own accord. "I'm alone now," he said.

I wanted to ask him about his second wife – about whether she'd been younger than him. If she'd been one of those grad students that went over to South Africa with him, the age difference could have been as great as that which now stretched between us. But I refrained. "We'll need time," I said. "Time to figure out what we want to do."

"Time," repeated Greg, as if I'd asked for the impossible, asked for something he could no longer give.

So here I am, back on Earth. My ex-husband – he *did* divorce me, after all – is old enough to be my father. But we're taking it one day at a time – equal-length days, days that are synchronized, days in lockstep.

My children are older than I am. And I've got grandchildren. And great-grandchildren, and all of them are wonderful.

And I've been to another world . . . although I think I prefer this one.

Yes, it seems you *can* have it all.

Just not all at once.

But, then again, as Einstein would have said, there's no such thing as "all at once."

Everything is relative. Old Albert knew that cold. But I know something better.

Relatives are everything.
And I was back home with mine.

Star Light, Star Bright

Ever since reading Larry Niven's essay "Bigger Than Worlds" in 1974, I've been fascinated by artificial habitats larger than the planet Earth — but I never wrote about one until a quarter-century later, when I penned this story for Marty Greenberg and Larry Segriff's anthology Far Frontiers.

In 1997, I happened to run into WKRP in Cincinnati *star Gordon Jump at a deli in Los Angeles; I introduced myself by saying I wanted to shake the hand of the man who had uttered the funniest line in sitcom history — a line that was echoing gently in my mind as I wrote this story.*

"Daddy, what are those?" My young son, Dalt, was pointing up. We'd floated far away from the ancient buildings, almost to where the transparent dome over our community touches the surface of the great sphere.

Four white hens were flying across the sky, their little wings propelling them at a good clip. "Those are chickens, Dalt. You know — the birds we get eggs from."

"Not the *chickens*," said Dalt, as if I'd offended him greatly by suggesting he didn't know what they were. "Those lights. Those points of light."

I squinted a bit. "I don't see any lights," I replied. "Where are they?"

"Everywhere," he said. He swung his head in an arc, taking in the whole sky. "Everywhere."

"How many points do you see?"

"Hundreds. Thousands."

I felt my back bumping gently against the surface; I pushed off with my palm, rising into the air again. The ancient texts I'd been translating said human beings were never really meant to live in such low gravity, but it was all I, and countless generations of my ancestors, had ever known. "There aren't any points of light, Dalt."

"Yes, there are," he insisted. "There are thousands of them, and – look! – there's a band of light across the sky there."

I faced in the direction he was pointing. "I don't see anything except another chicken."

"No, Daddy," insisted Dalt. "Look!"

Dalt was a good boy. He almost never lied to me – and I couldn't see why he would lie to me about something like this. I maneuvered so that we were hovering face to face, then extended my hand.

"Can you see my hand clearly?" I said.

"Sure."

"How many fingers am I holding up?"

He rolled his eyes. "Oh, Daddy . . ."

"How many fingers am I holding up?"

"Two."

"And do you see lights on them, as well?"

"On your fingers?" asked Dalt incredulously.

I nodded.

"Of course not."

"You don't see any lights in front of my fingers? Do you see any on my face?"

"Daddy!"

"Do you?"

"Of course not. The lights aren't down here. They're up there!"

I touched my boy's shoulder reassuringly. "Tomorrow, we'll go see Doc Tadders about your eyes."

We hadn't built the protective dome – the clear blister on the outer surface of the *Dyson* sphere (to use the ancient name our ancestors had given to our home, a term we could transliterate but not translate). Rather, the dome was already here when we'd come outside. Adjacent to it was a large, black pyramidal structure that didn't seem to be part of the sphere's outer hull; instead, it appeared to be clamped into place. No one was exactly sure what the pyramid was for, although you could enter it from an access tube extending from the dome. The pyramid was filled with corridors and rooms, and lots of control consoles marked in the script of the ancients.

The transparent dome was much larger than the pyramid – plenty big enough to cover the thirty-odd buildings the ancients had built here, as well as the concentric circles of farming fields we'd created by importing soil from within the interior of the Dyson sphere. Still, if the dome hadn't been transparent, I probably would have felt claustrophobic within it; it wasn't even a pimple on the vastness of the sphere.

We'd been fortunate that the ancients had constructed all these buildings under the protective dome; they served as homes and work spaces for us. In many cases, we could only guess at the original purposes of the buildings, but the one that housed Dr. Tadders' office had likely been a warehouse.

After sleeptime, I took Dalt to see Tadders. He seemed more fascinated by the wall diagram the doctor had of a human skeleton than he was by her eye chart, but we'd finally got him to spin around in midair to face it.

I was floating freely beside my son. For an instant, I found myself panicking because there was no anchor rope looped around my wrist; the habits of a lifetime were hard to break, even after being here, on the outside of the Dyson sphere, for all this time. I'd lived from birth to middle age on the inside of the sphere, where things tended to float up if they weren't anchored. Of course, you couldn't drift all the way up to the sun. You'd eventually bump against the glass roof that held the atmosphere in. But no one wanted to be stuck up there, waiting to be rescued; it was humiliating.

Out here, though, under our clear, protective dome, things floated *down*, not up; both Dalt and I would eventually settle to the padded floor.

"Can you read the top row of letters?" asked Doc Tadders, indicating the eye chart. She was about my age, with pale blue eyes and red hair just beginning to turn gray.

"Sure," said Dalt. "Eet, bot, doo, shuh, kee."

Tadders nodded. "What about the next row?"

"Hih, fah, roo, shuh, puh, ess."

"Can you read the last row?"

"Ayt, doo, tee, nuh, tee, ess, guh, hih, fah, roo."

"Are you sure about the second letter?"

"It's a doo, no?" said Dalt.

If there's any letter my son should know, it should be that one, since it was the first in his own name. But the character on the chart wasn't a doo; it was a fah.

Dr. Tadders jotted a note in the book she was holding, then said, "What about the last letter?"

"That's a roo."

"Are you sure?"

Dalt squinted. "Well, if it's not a roo, then it's an shuh, no?"

"Which do you think it is?"

"A shuh . . . or a roo." Dalt shrugged. "It's so tiny, I can't be sure."

I could see that it was a roo; I was surprised that I had better vision than my son did.

"Thanks," said Tadders. She looked at me. "He's a tiny bit nearsighted," she said. "Nothing to worry about." She faced Dalt again. "What about the lights in front of your eyes? Do you see any of them now?"

"No," said Dalt.

"None at all?"

"You can only see them in the dark," he said.

Tadders pushed against the padded wall with her palm, which was enough to send her drifting across the room toward the light switch; the ancients had made switches that were little rockers, instead of the click-in/click-out buttons we build. She rocked the switch, and the lighting strips at the edges of the padded roof went dark. "What about now?"

Dalt sounded puzzled. "No."

"Let's give your eyes a few moments to adjust," she said.

"It won't make any difference," said Dalt, exasperated. "You can only see the lights outside."

"Outside?" repeated Tadders.

"That's right," said Dalt. "Outside. In the dark. Up in the sky."

Dalt was the first child born after our group left the interior of the Dyson sphere. Our little town had a population of 240 now, of which fifteen had been born since we'd come outside. Dalt's usual playmate was Suzto, the daughter of the couple who lived next door to my wife and me in a building that had clearly been designed by the ancients to be living quarters.

All adults spent half their days working on their particular area of expertise, which, for me, was translating ancient documents stored in the computers inside the buildings and the pyramid, and the other half doing the chores that were needed to support a fledgling society. But after work, I took Dalt and Suzto for a float. We drifted away from the lights of the ancient buildings, across the fields of crops, and out toward the access tunnel that led to the pyramid.

I knew that the surface of the sphere, beneath us, was curved, of course, and, here on the outside, that it curved down. But the sphere was so huge that everything seemed flat. Oh, one could make out the indentations that were hills on the other side of the sphere's shell, and the raised plateaus that water collected in. Although we *were* on the frontier – the outside of the sphere! – we were still only one bodylength away from the world we'd left behind; that's how thick the sphere's shell was. But the double-doored portal that led back inside had been sealed off; the people on the interior had welded it shut after we'd left. They wanted nothing to do with whatever we might find out here, calling our quest for knowledge of the exterior universe a sacrilege against the wisdom of the ancients.

As we floated in the darkness, Dalt looked up again and said, "See! The lights!"

Suzto looked up, too. I expected her to scrunch her face in puzzlement, baffled by Dalt's words, but instead, near as I could make out in the darkness, she was smiling in wonder.

"Can – can you see the lights, too?" I asked Suzto.

"Sure."

I was astonished. "How big are they?"

"Tiny. Like this." She held up her hand, but if there was any space between her finger and thumb, I couldn't make it out.

"Are they arranged in some sort of pattern?"

Suzto's vocabulary wasn't yet as big as Dalt's. She looked at me, and I tried again. "Do they make shapes?"

"Maybe," said Suzto. "Some are brighter than others. There are three over there that make a straight line."

I frowned. "Dalt, please cover your eyes."

He did so, with elaborate hand gestures.

"Suzto, point to the brightest light in the sky."

"There're so many," she said.

"All right, all right. Point to the brightest one in this part of the sky over here."

She didn't hesitate. "That one."

"Okay," I said, "now put your hand down, please."

She drew her arm back in toward her body.

"Dalt, uncover your eyes."

He did so.

"Now, Dalt, point to the brightest light in this part of the sky over here."

He lifted his arm, then seemed to vacillate for a moment between two possible choices.

"Not that one, silly," said Suzto's voice. She pointed. "This one's brighter."

"Oh, yeah," said Dalt. "I guess it is." He pointed at it, too. I couldn't see anything, but it seemed in the darkness that if I could draw lines from the two children's outstretched fingers, they would converge at infinity.

Dr. Tadders was an old friend, and with both Suzto and Dalt seeing the lights, I decided to join her for lunch. We grew wheat, corn, and other crops under lamps here on the outside of the sphere, and raised chickens and pigs; if you wanted the eggs to hatch, you had to put low roofs over the hens, because they needed to be in constant contact with their clutches, and their own body movements were enough to propel them into flight; chickens really seemed to love flying. Tadders and I both knew that we'd have had more interesting meals if we'd stayed inside the sphere, but the ancient texts said that although the interior was huge, there was still much, much more to the universe.

Most of those on the interior didn't care about such things; they knew that the sphere's inner surface could accommodate over a million trillion human beings – a vastly larger number than the current population – and that our ancestors had shut us off from the rest of the universe for a reason. But some of us had decided to venture outside, starting a new settlement on our world's only real frontier. I didn't miss much about the inside – but I did miss the food.

"All right, Rodal," Dr. Tadders said, gesturing with a sandwich triangle, "here's what I think is happening." She took a deep breath, as if reviewing her thoughts once more before giving them voice, then: "We know that a long, long time ago, our ancestors built a double-walled shell around our sun. The outer wall is opaque, and the inner wall, fifty bodylengths above that, is transparent. The area between the two walls is the habitat, where all those who still live on the interior of the sphere reside."

I nodded, and kicked gently off the floor to keep myself afloat. We drifted out of the dining hall, heading outdoors.

"Well," she continued, "we also know that there was a war generations ago that knocked humanity back into a primitive state. We've been rebuilding our civilization for a long time, but we're nowhere near as advanced as our ancestors who constructed our world were."

That was certainly true. "So?"

"So, what about that story you translated a while ago? The one about where we supposedly came from?"

I'd found a story in the ancient computers that claimed that before we lived on the interior of the Dyson sphere, our ancestors had made their home on the outer surface of a small, solid, rocky globe. "But that was probably just a myth," I said. "I mean, such a globe would have been impossibly tiny. The myth said the homeworld was six million bodylengths in diameter. Kobost" – a physicist in our community – "worked out that if it were made of the elements the myth described, even a globe that small would have had a crushingly huge gravitational attraction: five bodylengths per heartbeat squared. That's more than ten thousand times what we experience here."

Of course, the gravitational attraction on any point on the interior of a hollow sphere is zero. When we lived inside the sphere, the only gravity we felt was the pull from our sun, gently tugging things upwards. Here, on the outside of the sphere, the gravitational pull is downward, toward the sphere's surface – and the sun at its center.

I continued. "Although Kobost thinks human muscle could perhaps be built up enough to withstand such an overwhelming gravity, his own studies prove that the globe described in the myth can't be our homeworld."

"Why not?" asked Tadders.

"Because of the chickens. There are several ancient texts that show that chickens have been essentially the same since before our ancestors built the Dyson sphere. But with an acceleration due to gravity of five bodylengths per heartbeat squared, their wings wouldn't be strong enough to let them fly. So that globe in the myth couldn't possibly have been our ancestral home."

"Well, I agree that's puzzling about the chickens," said Tadders, "but wherever our ancestors came from, you have to admit it wasn't another Dyson sphere. And the inside of a Dyson sphere forms a very special kind of sky. Remember what it was like when we lived in there? Wherever you looked over your head, you saw — well, you saw the sun, of course, if you looked directly overhead. But everywhere else, you saw other parts of the sphere. Some of those parts are a long, long way off — the far side of the sphere is a hundred and fifty billion bodylengths away, isn't it? But, regardless, wherever you looked, you saw either the sun or the surface of the sphere."

"So?"

"So the surface of the sphere is reflective — even the dull, grass-covered parts reflect back a lot of light. Indeed, on average the surface reflects back about a third of the light it receives from the sun, making the whole sky glaringly bright."

People in there did have a tendency to float facing the ground instead of the sky. I nodded for her to go on.

"Well, our eyes didn't evolve here," continued Tadders. "If we did come from a rocky world, the sun would have been seen against an empty, non-reflective sky. It must be much, much brighter inside the Dyson sphere than it ever was on the original homeworld."

"Surely our eyes would have adapted to deal with the brighter light here."

"How?" asked Tadders. "Even after the great war, we regained a measure of civilization fairly quickly. There was no period during which we were reduced to survival of the fittest. Human beings haven't undergone any appreciable evolution since long before our ancestors built the sphere. Which means our eyes are as they originally were: suited for much dimmer light. Of course, the ancients may have had drugs or other things that made the interior light seem more comfortable to them, but whatever they used must have been lost in the war."

"I suppose," I said.

"But you, me, and everyone else in our settlement who has lived inside the sphere – we've damaged our retinas, without even knowing it."

I saw what she was getting at. "But the children – the children born here, on the outside of the sphere –"

She nodded. "The children born here, after we left the interior, have never been exposed to the brightness inside, and so they see just as well in the dark as our distant, distant ancestors did, back on the homeworld. The points of light the children are seeing really do exist, but they're simply too faint to register on the damaged retinas we adults have."

My head was swimming. "Maybe," I said. "Maybe. But – but what *are* those lights?"

Tadders pursed her lips, then lifted her shoulders a bit. "You want my best guess? I think they're other suns, like the one our ancestors encased in the sphere, but so incredibly far away that they're all but invisible." She looked up, out the clear roof of the dome covering our town, out at the uniform blackness, which was all either of us could make out. She then used one of the words I'd taught her, a word transliterated from the ancient texts – a word we could pronounce but whose meaning we'd never really understood. "I think," she said, "that the points of light are *stars.*"

There were thousands of documents stored in the ancient computers; my job was to try to make sense of as many of them as I could. And I made much progress as Dalt continued to grow up. Eventually, he and the other children were able to match the patterns of stars they could see in the sky to those depicted in ancient charts I'd found. The patterns didn't correspond exactly; the stars had apparently drifted in relation to each other since the charts had been made. But the kids – the adolescents, now – were indeed able to discern the *constellations* shown in the old texts; ironically, this was easier to do, they said, when some of the lights of our frontier town were left on, drowning out all but the brightest stars.

According to the charts, our sun – the sun enclosed in the Dyson sphere – was the star the ancients had called Tau Ceti. It was not the original home to humanity, though; our ancestors were apparently unwilling to cannibalize the worlds of their own system to make their Dyson sphere. Instead, they – we – had come from another star, the closest similar one that wasn't part of a multiple system, a sun our ancestors had called Sol.

And the *planet* – that was the term – we had evolved on was, in the infinite humility of our wise ancestors, called by a simple, unassuming name, one I could easily translate: Dirt.

Old folks like me couldn't live on Dirt now, of course. Our muscles – including our hearts – were weak compared to what our ancestors must have had, growing up under the stupendous gravity of that tiny, rocky world.

But –

But locked in our genes, as if for safekeeping, were all the potentials we'd ever had as a species. The ability to see dim sources of light, and –

Yes, it must be there, too, still preserved in our DNA.

The ability to produce muscles strong enough to withstand much, much higher gravity.

You'd have to grow up under such a gravity, have to live with it from birth, said Dr. Tadders, to really be comfortable with it, but if you did –

I'd seen Kobost's computer animation showing how we might have moved under a much greater gravity, how we might have deployed our bodies vertically, how our spines would have supported the weight of our heads, how our legs might have worked back and forth, hinging at knee and ankle, producing sustained forward locomotion. It all seemed so bizarre, and so inefficient compared to spending most of one's life floating, but –

But there were new worlds to explore, and old ones, too, and to fully experience them would require being able to stand on their surfaces.

Dalt was growing up to be a fine young man. There wasn't a lot of choice for careers in a small community: he could have apprenticed with his mother, Delar, who worked as our banker, or with me. He chose me, and so I did my best to teach him how to read the ancient texts.

"I've finished translating that file you gave me," he said on one occasion. "It was what you suspected: just a boring list of supplies." I guess he saw that I was only half-listening to him. "What's got you so intrigued?" he asked.

I looked up, and smiled at his face, with its bits of fuzz; I'd have to teach him how to shave soon. "Sorry," I said. "I've found some documents related to the pyramid. But there are several words I haven't encountered before."

"Such as?"

"Such as this one," I said, pointing at a string of eight letters on the computer screen. "'*Starship.*' The first part is obviously the word for those lights you can see in the sky: *stars.* And the second part, *hip*, well —" I slapped my haunch — "that's their name for where the leg joins the torso. They often made compound words in this fashion, but I can't for the life of me figure out what a 'stars hip' might be."

I always say nothing is better than a fresh set of eyes. "Yes, they often used that hissing sound for plurals," said Dalt. "But those two letters there — can't they also be transliterated jointly as shuh, instead of separately as ess and hih?"

I nodded.

"So maybe it's not 'stars hip,'" he said. "Maybe it's 'star ship.'"

"*Ship,*" I repeated. "Ship, ship, ship — I've seen that word before." I riffled through a collection of papers, searching my notes; the sheets fluttered around the room, and Dalt dutifully began collecting them for me. "Ship!" I exclaimed. "Here it is: 'a kind of vehicle that could float on water.'"

"Why would you want to float on water when you can float on air?" asked Dalt.

"On the homeworld," I said, "water didn't splash up in great clouds every time you touched it. It stayed in place." I frowned. "Star ship. Starship. A — a vehicle of stars?" And then I got it. "No," I said, grabbing my son's arm in excitement. "No — a vehicle for traveling to the stars!"

Dalt and Suzto eventually married, to no one's surprise.

But I *was* surprised by my son's arms. He and Suzto had been exercising for ages now, and when Dalt bent his arm at the elbow, the upper part of it *bulged.* Doc Tadders said she'd never seen anything like it, but assured us it wasn't a tumor. It was *meat.* It was muscle.

Dalt's legs were also much, much thicker than mine. Suzto hadn't bulked up quite as much, but she, too, had developed great strength.

I knew what they were up to, of course. I admired them both for it, but I had one profound regret.

Suzto had gotten pregnant shortly after she and Dalt had married – at least, they told me that the conception had occurred after the wedding, and, as a parent, it's my prerogative to believe them. But I'd never know for sure. And *that* was my great regret: I'd never get to see my own grandchild.

Dalt and Suzto would be able to *stand* on Dirt, and, indeed, would be able to endure the journey there. The starship was designed to accelerate at a rate of five bodylengths per heartbeat squared, simulating Dirt's gravity. It would accelerate for half its journey, reaching a phenomenal speed by so doing, then it would turn around and decelerate for the other half.

They were the logical choices to go. Dalt knew the ancient language as well as I did now; if there were any records left behind by our ancestors on the homeworld, he should be able to read them.

He and Suzto had to leave soon, said Doc Tadders; it would be best for the child if it developed under the fake gravity of the starship's acceleration. Dalt and Suzto would be able to survive on Dirt, but their child should actually be comfortable there.

My wife and I came to see them off, of course – as did everyone else in our settlement. We wondered what people in the sphere would make of it when the pyramid lifted off – it would do so with a kick that would doubtless be detectable on the other side of the shell.

"I'll miss you, son," I said to Dalt. Tears were welling in my eyes. I hugged him, and he hugged me back, so much harder than I could manage.

"And, Suzto," I said, moving to my daughter-in-law, while my wife moved to hug our son. "I'll miss you, too." I hugged her, as well. "I love you both."

"We love you, too," Suzto said.

And they entered the pyramid.

I was hovering over a field, harvesting radishes. It was tricky work; if you pulled too hard, you'd get the radish out, all right, but then you and it would go sailing up into the air.

"Rodal! Rodal!"

I looked in the direction of the voice. It was old Doc Tadders, hurtling toward me, a white-haired projectile. At her age, she should be more careful – she could break her bones slamming into even a padded wall at that speed.

"Rodal!"

"Yes?"

"Come! Come quickly! A message has been received from Dirt!"

I kicked off the ground, sailing toward the communication station next to the access tube that used to lead to the starship. Tadders managed to turn around without killing herself and she flew there alongside me.

A sizable crowd had already gathered by the time we arrived.

"What does the message say?" I asked the person closest to the computer monitor.

He looked at me in irritation; the ancient computer had displayed the text, naturally enough, in the ancient script, and few besides me could understand that. He moved aside and I consulted the screen, reading aloud for the benefit of everyone.

"It says, 'Greetings! We have arrived safely at Dirt.'"

The crowd broke into cheers and applause. I couldn't help reading ahead a bit while waiting or them to quiet down, so I was already misty-eyed when I continued. "It goes on to say, 'Tell Rodal and Delar that they have a grandson; we've named him Madar.'"

My wife had passed on some time ago – but she would have been delighted at the choice of Madar; that had been her father's name.

"'Dirt is beautiful, full of plants and huge bodies of water,'" I read. "'And there are other human beings living here. It seems those people interested in technology moved to the Dyson sphere, but a small group who preferred a pastoral lifestyle stayed on the homeworld. We're mastering their language – it's deviated a fair bit from the one in the ancient texts – and are already great friends with them.'"

"Amazing," said Doc Tadders.

I smiled at her, wiped my eyes, then went on: "'We will send much more information later, but we can clear up at least one enduring mystery right now.'" I grinned as I read the next part. "'Chickens can't fly here. Apparently, just because you have wings doesn't mean you were meant to fly.'"

That was the end of the message. I looked up at the dark sky, wishing I could make out Sol, or any star. "And just because you don't have wings," I said, thinking of my son and his wife and my grandchild, far, far away, "doesn't mean you weren't."

The Hand You're Dealt

Edward E. Kramer is one of my favorite editors; he always asks me for something challenging. But when he approached me to contribute to a libertarian science-fiction anthology he was co-editing with Brad Linaweaver, I said, Ed, baby, I'm a Canadian – I don't think it's technically possible to be both a Canadian and a libertarian. As he always does, Ed said a few magic words: "Well, you could write a story that shows potential problems with libertarianism – we're looking for a balanced book." And, lo and behold, "The Hand You're Dealt" was created.

—————

> *And ye shall know the truth, and the truth shall make you free.*
>
> — John 8:32

"Got a new case for you," said my boss, Raymond Chen. "Homicide."

My heart started pounding. Mendelia habitat is supposed to be a utopia. Murder is almost unheard of here.

Chen was fat – never exercised, loved rich foods. He knew his lifestyle would take decades off his life, but, hey, that was his choice. "Somebody offed a soothsayer, over in Wheel Four," he said, wheezing slightly. "Baranski's on the scene now."

My eyebrows went up. A dead soothsayer? This could be very interesting indeed.

I took my pocket forensic scanner and exited The Cop Shop. That was its real name – no taxes in Mendelia, after all. You

57

needed a cop, you hired one. In this case, Chen had said, we were being paid by the Soothsayers' Guild. That meant we could run up as big a bill as necessary – the SG was stinking rich. One of the few laws in Mendelia was that everyone had to use soothsayers.

Mendelia consisted of five modules, each looking like a wagon wheel with spokes leading in to a central hub. The hubs were all joined together by a long axle, and separate travel tubes connected the outer edges of the wheels. The whole thing spun to simulate gravity out at the rims, and the travel tubes saved you having to go down to the zero-g of the axle to move from one wheel to the next.

The Cop Shop was in Wheel Two. All the wheel rims were hollow, with buildings growing up toward the axle from the outer interior wall. Plenty of open spaces in Mendelia – it wouldn't be much of a utopia without those. But our sky was a hologram, projected on the convex inner wall of the rim, above our heads. The Cop Shop's entrance was right by Wheel Two's transit loop, a series of maglev tracks along which robocabs ran. I hailed one, flashed my debit card at an unblinking eye, and the cab headed out. The Carling family, who owned the taxi concession, was one of the oldest and richest families in Mendelia.

The ride took fifteen minutes. Suzanne Baranski was waiting outside for me. She was a good cop, but too green to handle a homicide alone. Still, she'd get a big cut of the fee for being the original responding officer – after all, the cop who responds to a call never knows who, if anyone, is going to pick up the tab. When there *is* money to be had, first-responders get a disproportionate share.

I'd worked with Suze a couple of times before, and had even gone to see her play cello with the symphony once. Perfect example of what Mendelia's all about, that. Suze Baranski had blue-collar parents. They'd worked as welders on the building of Wheel Five; not the kind who'd normally send a daughter for music lessons. But just after she'd been born, their soothsayer had said that Suze had musical talent. Not enough to make a living at it – that's why she's a cop by day – but still sufficient that it would be a shame not to let her develop it.

"Hi, Toby," Suze said to me. She had short red hair and big green eyes, and, of course, was in plain clothes – you wanted a uniformed cop, you called our competitors, Spitpolish, Inc.

"Howdy, Suze," I said, walking toward her. She led me over to the door, which had been locked off in the open position. A holographic sign next to it proclaimed:

Skye Hissock
Soothsayer
Let Me Reveal Your Future!
Fully Qualified for Infant and Adult Readings

We stepped into a well-appointed lobby. The art was unusual for such an office – it was all original pen-and-ink political cartoons. There was Republic CEO Da Silva, her big nose exaggerated out of all proportion, and next to it, Axel Durmont, Earth's current president, half buried in legislation printouts and tape that doubtless would have been red had this been a color rendering. The artist's signature caught my eye, the name Skye with curving lines behind it that I realized were meant to represent clouds. Just like Suze, our decedent had had varied talents.

"The body is in the inner private office," said Suze, leading the way. That door, too, was already open. She stepped in first, and I followed.

Skye Hissock's body sat in a chair behind his desk. His head had been blown clean off. A great carnation bloom of blood covered most of the wall behind him, and chunks of brain were plastered to the wall and the credenza behind the desk.

"Christ," I said. Some utopia.

Suze nodded. "Blaster, obviously," she said, sounding much more experienced in such matters than she really was. "Probably a gigawatt charge."

I began looking around the room. It was opulent; old Skye had obviously done well for himself. Suze was poking around, too. "Hey," she said, after a moment. I turned to look at her. She was climbing up on the credenza. The blast had knocked a small piece of sculpture off the wall – it lay in two pieces on the floor – and she was examining where it had been affixed. "Thought that's what it was," she said, nodding. "There's a hidden camera here."

My heart skipped a beat. "You don't suppose he got the whole thing on disk, do you?" I said, moving over to where she was. I gave her a hand getting down off the credenza, and we opened it up – a slightly difficult task; crusted blood had sealed its sliding doors. Inside was a dusty recorder unit. I turned to Skye's desk, and pushed the release switch to pop up his monitor plate. Suze pushed the recorder's playback button. As we'd suspected, the unit was designed to feed into the desk monitor.

The picture showed the reverse angle from behind Skye's desk. The door to the private office opened and in came a young man. He looked to be eighteen, meaning he was just the right age for the mandatory adult soothsaying. He had shoulder length dirty-blond hair, and was wearing a t-shirt imprinted with the logo of a popular meed. I shook my head. There hadn't been a good multimedia band since The Cassies, if you ask me.

"Hello, Dale," said what must have been Skye's voice. He spoke with deep, slightly nasal tones. "Thank you for coming in."

Okay, we had the guy's picture, and his first name, and the name of his favorite meed. Even if Dale's last name didn't turn up in Skye's appointment computer, we should have no trouble tracking him down.

"As you know," said Skye's recorded voice, "the law requires two soothsayings in each person's life. The first is done just after you're born, with one or both of your parents in attendance. At that time, the soothsayer only tells them things they'll need to know to get you through childhood. But when you turn eighteen, you, not your parents, become legally responsible for all your actions, and so it's time you heard everything. Now, do you want the good news or the bad news first?"

Here it comes, I thought. He told Dale something he didn't want to hear, the guy flipped, pulled out a blaster, and blew him away.

Dale swallowed. "The – the good, I guess."

"All right," said Skye. "First, you're a bright young man – not a genius, you understand, but brighter than average. Your IQ should run between 126 and 132. You are gifted musically – did your parents tell you that? Good. I hope they encouraged you."

"They did," said Dale, nodding. "I've had piano lessons since I was four."

"Good, good. A crime to waste such raw talent. You also have a particular aptitude for mathematics. That's often paired with musical ability, of course, so no surprises there. Your visual memory is slightly better than average, although your ability to do rote memorization is slightly worse. You would make a good long-distance runner, but . . ."

I motioned for Suze to hit the fast-forward button; it seemed like a typical soothsaying, although I'd review it in depth later, if need be. Poor Dale fidgeted up and down in quadruple speed for a time, then Suze released the button.

"Now," said Skye's voice, "the bad news." I made an impressed face at Suze; she'd stopped speeding along at precisely the right moment. "I'm afraid there's a lot of it. Nothing devastating, but still lots of little things. You will begin to lose your hair around your twenty-seventh birthday, and it will begin to gray by the time you're thirty-two. By the age of forty, you will be almost completely bald, and what's left at that point will be half brown and half gray.

"On a less frivolous note, you'll also be prone to gaining weight, starting at about age thirty-three – and you'll put on half a kilo a year for each of the following thirty years if you're not careful; by the time you're in your mid-fifties, that will pose a significant health hazard. You're also highly likely to develop adult-onset diabetes. Now, yes, that can be cured, but the cure is expensive, and you'll have to pay for it – so either keep your weight down, which will help stave off its onset, or start saving now for the operation . . ."

I shrugged. Nothing worth killing a man over. Suze fast-forwarded the tape some more.

"– and that's it," concluded Skye. "You know now everything significant that's coded into your DNA. Use this information wisely, and you should have a long, happy, healthy life."

Dale thanked Skye, took a printout of the information he'd just heard, and left. The recording stopped. It *had* been too much to hope for. Whoever killed Skye Hissock had come in after young Dale had departed. He was still our obvious first suspect, but unless there was something awful in the parts of the genetic reading we'd fast-forwarded over, there didn't seem to be any motive for him to kill his soothsayer. And besides, this Dale had a high IQ, Skye had said. Only an idiot would think there was any sense in shooting the messenger.

After we'd finished watching the recording, I did an analysis of the actual blaster burn. No fun, that: standing over the open top of Skye's torso. Most of the blood vessels had been cauterized by the charge. Still, blasters were only manufactured in two places I knew of – Tokyo, on Earth, and New Monty. If the one used here had been made on New Monty, we'd be out of luck, but one of Earth's countless laws required all blasters to leave a characteristic EM signature, so they could be traced to their registered owners, and –

Good: it *was* an Earth-made blaster. I recorded the signature, then used my compad to relay it to The Cop Shop. If Raymond Chen could find some time between stuffing his face, he'd send an FTL message to Earth and check the pattern – assuming, of course, that the Jeffies don't scramble the message just for kicks. Meanwhile, I told Suze to go over Hissock's client list, while I started checking out his family – fact is, even though it doesn't make much genetic sense, most people are killed by their own relatives.

Skye Hissock had been fifty-one. He'd been a soothsayer for twenty-three years, ever since finishing his Ph.D. in genetics. He was unmarried, and both his parents were long dead. But he did have a brother named Rodger. Rodger was married to Rebecca Connolly, and they had two children, Glen, who, like Dale in Skye's recording, had just turned eighteen, and Billy, who was eight.

There are no inheritance taxes in Mendelia, of course, so barring a will to the contrary, Hissock's estate would pass immediately to his brother. Normally, that'd be a good motive for murder, but Rodger Hissock and Rebecca Connolly were already quite rich: they owned a controlling interest in the company that operated Mendelia's atmosphere-recycling plant.

I decided to start my interviews with Rodger. Not only had brothers been killing each other since Cain wasted Abel, but the DNA-scanning lock on Skye's private inner office was programmed to recognize only four people – Skye himself; his office cleaner, who Suze was going to talk to; another soothsayer named Jennifer Halasz, who sometimes took Skye's patients for him when he was on vacation (and who had called in the murder, having stopped by apparently to meet Skye for coffee); and dear brother Rodger. Rodger lived in Wheel Four, and worked in One.

I took a cab over to his office. Unlike Skye, Rodger had a real flesh-and-blood receptionist. Most companies that did have human receptionists used middle-aged, businesslike people of either sex. Some guys got so rich that they didn't care what people thought; they hired beautiful blonde women whose busts had been surgically altered far beyond what any phenotype might provide. But Rodger's choice was different. His receptionist was a delicate young man with refined, almost feminine features. He was probably older than he looked; he looked fourteen.

"Detective Toby Korsakov," I said, flashing my ID. I didn't offer to shake hands – the boy looked like his would shatter if any pressure were applied. "I'd like to see Rodger Hissock."

"Do you have an appointment?" His voice was high, and there was just a trace of a lisp.

"No. But I'm sure Mr. Hissock will want to see me. It's important."

The boy looked very dubious, but he spoke into an intercom. "There's a cop here, Rodger. Says it's important."

There was a pause. "Send him in," said a loud voice. The boy nodded at me, and I walked through the heavy wooden door – mahogany, no doubt imported all the way from Earth.

I had thought Skye Hissock's office was well-appointed, but his brother's put it to shame. *Objets d'art* from a dozen worlds were tastefully displayed on crystal stands. The carpet was so thick I was sure my shoes would sink out of sight. I walked toward the desk. Rodger rose to greet me. He was a muscular man, thick-necked, with lots of black hair and pale gray eyes. We shook hands; his grip was a show of macho strength. "Hello," he said. He boomed out the word, clearly a man used to commanding everyone's attention. "What can I do for you?"

"Please sit down," I said. "My name is Toby Korsakov. I'm from The Cop Shop, working under a contract to the Soothsayers' Guild."

"My God," said Rodger. "Has something happened to Skye?"

Although it was an unpleasant duty, there was nothing more useful in a murder investigation than being there to tell a suspect about the death and seeing his reaction. Most guilty parties played dumb far too long, so the fact that Rodger had quickly made the obvious connection between the SG and his brother made me suspect him less, not more. Still . . . "I'm sorry to be the bearer of bad news," I said, "but I'm afraid your brother is dead."

Rodger's eyes went wide. "What happened?"

"He was murdered."

"Murdered," repeated Rodger, as if he'd never heard the word before.

"That's right. I was wondering if you knew of anyone who'd want him dead?"

"How was he killed?" asked Rodger. I was irritated that this wasn't an answer to my question, and even more irritated that I'd have to explain it so soon. More than a few homicides had been solved by a suspect mentioning the nature of the crime in advance of him or her supposedly having learned the details. "He was shot at close range by a blaster."

"Oh," said Rodger. He slumped in his chair. "Skye dead." His head shook back and forth a little. When he looked up, his gray eyes were moist. Whether he was faking or not, I couldn't tell.

"I'm sorry," I said.

"Do you know who did it?"

"Not yet. We're tracing the blaster's EM signature. But there were no signs of forcible entry, and, well . . ."

"Yes?"

"Well, there are only four people whose DNA would open the door to Skye's inner office."

Rodger nodded. "Me and Skye. Who else?"

"His cleaner, and another soothsayer."

"You're checking them out?"

"My associate is. She's also checking all the people Skye had appointments with recently – people he might have let in of his own volition." A pause. "Can I ask where you were this morning between ten and eleven?"

"Here."

"In your office?"

"That's right."

"Your receptionist can vouch for that?"

"Well . . . no. No, he can't. He was out all morning. His sooth says he's got a facility for languages. I give him a half-day off every Wednesday to take French lessons."

"Did anyone call you while he was gone?"

Rodger spread his thick arms. "Oh, probably. But I never answer my own compad. Truth to tell, I like that half-day where I can't be reached. It lets me get an enormous amount of work done without being interrupted."

"So no one can verify your presence here?"

"Well, no . . . no, I guess they can't. But, Crissakes, Detective, Skye was my *brother* . . ."

"I'm not accusing you, Mr. Hissock –"

"Besides, if I'd taken a robocab over, there'd be a debit charge against my account."

"Unless you paid cash. Or unless you walked." You can walk down the travel tubes, although most people don't bother.

"You don't seriously believe –"

"I don't believe anything yet, Mr. Hissock." It was time to change the subject; he would be no use to me if he got too defensive. "Was your brother a good soothsayer?"

"Best there is. Hell, he read my own sooth when I turned eighteen." He saw my eyebrows go up. "Skye is nine years older than me; I figured, why not use him? He needed the business; he was just starting his practice at that point."

"Did Skye do the readings for your children, too?"

An odd hesitation. "Well, yeah, yeah, Skye did their infant readings, but Glen – that's my oldest; just turned 18 – he decided to go somewhere else for his adult reading. Waste of money, if you ask me. Skye would've given him a discount."

My compad bleeped while I was in a cab. I turned it on.

"Yo, Toby." Raymond Chen's fat face appeared on the screen. "We got the registration information on that blaster signature."

"Yeah?"

Ray smiled. "Do the words 'open-and-shut case' mean anything to you? The blaster belongs to one Rodger Hissock. He bought it about eleven years ago."

I nodded and signed off. Since the lock accepted his DNA, rich little brother would have no trouble waltzing right into big brother's inner office, and exploding his head. Rodger had method and he had opportunity. Now all I needed was to find his motive – and for that, continuing to interview the family members might prove useful.

Eighteen-year-old Glen Hissock was studying engineering at Francis Crick University in Wheel Three. He was a dead ringer for his old man: built like a wrestler, with black hair and quicksilver eyes. But whereas father Rodger had a coarse, outgoing way about him – the crusher handshake, the loud voice – young Glen was withdrawn, soft-spoken, and nervous.

"I'm sorry about your uncle," I said, knowing that Rodger had already broken the news to his son.

Glen looked at the floor. "Me too."

"Did you like him?"

"He was okay."

"Just okay."

"Yeah."

"Where were you between ten and eleven this morning?"

"At home."

"Was anyone else there?"

"Nah. Mom and Dad were at work, and Billy – that's my little brother – was in school." He met my eyes for the first time. "Am I a suspect?"

He wasn't really. All the evidence seemed to point to his father. I shook my head in response to his question, then said, "I hear you had your sooth read recently."

"Yeah."

"But you didn't use your uncle."

"Nah."

"How come?"

A shrug. "Just felt funny, that's all. I picked a guy at random from the online directory."

"Any surprises in your sooth?"

The boy looked at me. "Sooth's private, man. I don't have to tell you that."

I nodded. "Sorry."

Two hundred years ago, in 2029, the Palo Alto Nanosystems Laboratory developed a molecular computer. You doubtless read about it in history class: during the Snow War, the U.S. used it to disassemble Bogata atom by atom.

Sometimes, though, you *can* put the genie back in the bottle. Remember Hamasaki and DeJong, the two researchers at PANL who were shocked to see their work corrupted that way? They created and released the nano-Gorts – self-replicating microscopic machines that seek out and destroy molecular computers, so that nothing like Bogata could ever happen again.

We've got PANL nano-Gorts here, of course. They're everywhere in Free Space. But we've got another kind of molecular guardian, too — inevitably, they were dubbed helix-Gorts. It's rumored the SG was responsible for them, but after a huge investigation, no indictments were ever brought. Helix-Gorts circumvent any attempt at artificial gene therapy. We can tell you everything that's written in your DNA, but we can't do a damned thing about it. Here, in Mendelia, you play the hand you're dealt.

My compad bleeped again. I switched it on. "Korsakov here."

Suze's face appeared on the screen. "Hi, Toby. I took a sample of Skye's DNA off to Rundstedt" — a soothsayer who did forensic work for us. "She's finished the reading."

"And?" I said.

Suze's green eyes blinked. "Nothing stood out. Skye wouldn't have been a compulsive gambler, or an addict, or inclined to steal another person's spouse — which eliminates several possible motives for his murder. In fact, Rundstedt says Skye would have had a severe aversion to confrontation." She sighed. "Just doesn't seem to be the kind of guy who'd end up in a situation where someone would want him dead."

I nodded. "Thanks, Suze. Any luck with Skye's clients?"

"I've gone through almost all the ones who'd had appointments in the last three days. So far, they all have solid alibis."

"Keep checking. I'm off to see Skye's sister-in-law, Rebecca Connolly. Talk to you later."

"Bye."

Sometimes I wonder if I'm in the right line of work. I know, I know — what a crazy thing to be thinking. I mean, my parents knew from my infant reading that I'd grow up to have an aptitude for puzzle-solving, plus superior powers of observation. They made sure I had every opportunity to fulfill my potentials, and when I had my sooth read for myself at eighteen, it was obvious that this would be a perfect job for me to pursue. And yet, still, I have my doubts. I just don't feel like a cop sometimes.

But a soothsaying can't be wrong: almost every human trait has a genetic basis — gullibility, mean-spiritedness, a goofy sense of humor, the urge to collect things, talents for various sports, every specific sexual predilection (according to my own sooth, my tastes ran to group sex with Asian women – so far, I'd yet to find an opportunity to test that empirically).

Of course, when Mendelia started up, we didn't yet know what each gene and gene combo did. Even today, the SG is still adding new interpretations to the list. Still, I sometimes wonder how people in other parts of Free Space get along without sooth-sayers – stumbling through life, looking for the right job; some-times completely unaware of talents they possess; failing to know what specific things they should do to take care of their health. Oh, sure, you can get a genetic reading anywhere – even down on Earth. But they're only mandatory here.

And my mandatory readings said I'd make a good cop. But, I have to admit, sometimes I'm not so sure . . .

Rebecca Connolly was at home when I got there. On Earth, a family with the kind of money the Hissock-Connolly union had would own a mansion. Space is at a premium aboard a habitat, but their living room *was* big enough that its floor showed a hint of curvature. The art on the walls included originals by both Grant Wood and Bob Eggleton. There was no doubt they were loaded – making it all the harder to believe they'd done in Uncle Skye for his money.

Rebecca Connolly was a gorgeous woman. According to the press reports I'd read, she was forty-four, but she looked twenty years younger. Gene therapy might be impossible here, but any-one who could afford it could have plastic surgery. Her hair was copper-colored, and her eyes an unnatural violet. "Hello, Detective Korsakov," she said. "My husband told me you were likely to stop by." She shook her head. "Poor Skye. Such a darling man."

I tilted my head. She was the first of Skye's relations to actu-ally say something nice about him as a person – which, after all, could just be a clumsy attempt to deflect suspicion from her. "You knew Skye well?"

"No – to be honest, no. He and Rodger weren't that close. Funny thing, that. Skye used to come by the house frequently when we first got married – he was Rodger's best man, did he tell you that? But when Glen was born, well, he stopped coming around as much. I dunno – maybe he didn't like kids; he never had any of his own. Anyway, he really hasn't been a big part of our lives for, oh, eighteen years now."

"But Rodger's DNA was accepted by Skye's lock."

"Oh, yes. Rodger owns the unit Skye has his current offices in."

"I hate to ask you this, but –"

"I'm on the Board of Directors of TenthGen Computing, Detective. We were having a shareholders' meeting this morning. Something like eight hundred people saw me there."

I asked more questions, but didn't get any closer to identifying Rodger Hissock's motive. And so I decided to cheat – as I said, sometimes I *do* wonder if I'm in the right kind of job. "Thanks for your help, Ms. Connolly. I don't want to take up any more of your time, but can I use your bathroom before I go?"

She smiled. "Of course. There's one down the hall, and one upstairs."

The upstairs one sounded more promising for my purposes. I went up to it, and the door closed behind me. I really did need to go, but first I pulled out my forensic scanner and started looking for specimens. Razors and combs were excellent places to find DNA samples; so were towels, if the user rubbed vigorously enough. Best of all, though, were toothbrushes. I scanned everything, but something was amiss. According to the scanner, there was DNA present from one woman – the XX chromosome pair made the gender clear. And there was DNA from one man. But *three* males lived in this house: father Rodger, elder son Glen, and younger son Billy.

Perhaps this bathroom was used only by the parents, in which case I'd blown it – I'd hardly get a chance to check out the other bathroom. But no – there were four sets of towels, four toothbrushes, and there, on the edge of the tub, a toy aquashuttle . . . precisely the kind an eight-year-old boy would play with.

Curious. Four people obviously used this john, but only two had left any genetic traces. And that made no sense – I mean, sure, I hardly ever washed when I was eight like Billy, but no one can use a washroom day in and day out without leaving some DNA behind.

I relieved myself, the toilet autoflushed, and I went downstairs, thanked Ms. Connolly again, and left.

• • •

Like I said, I was cheating – making me wonder again whether I really was cut out for a career in law enforcement. Even though it was a violation of civil rights, I took the male DNA sample I'd found in the Hissock-Connolly bathroom to Dana Rundstedt, who read its sooth for me.

I was amazed by the results. If I hadn't cheated, I might never have figured it out – it was a damn-near perfect crime.

But it all fit, after seeing what was in the male DNA.

The fact that of the surviving Hissocks, only Rodger apparently had free access to Skye's inner office.

The fact that Rodger's blaster was the murder weapon.

The fact that there were apparently only two people using the bathroom.

The fact that Skye hated confrontation.

The fact that the Hissock-Connolly family had a lot of money they wanted to pass on to the next generation.

The fact that young Glen looked just like his dad, but was subdued and reserved.

The fact that Glen had gone to a different soothsayer.

The fact that Rodger's taste in receptionists was . . . unusual.

The pieces all fit – that part of my sooth, at least, must have been read correctly; I *was* good at puzzling things out. But I was still amazed by how elegant it was.

Ray Chen would sort out the legalities; he was an expert at that kind of thing. He'd find a way to smooth over my unauthorized soothsaying before we brought this to trial.

I got in a cab and headed off to Wheel Three to confront the killer.

"Hold it right there," I said, coming down the long, gently curving corridor at Francis Crick. "You're under arrest."

Glen Hissock stopped dead in his tracks. "What for?"

I looked around, then drew Glen into an empty classroom. "For the murder of your uncle, Skye Hissock. Or should I say, for the murder of your brother? The semantics are a bit tricky."

"I don't know what you're talking about," said Glen, in that subdued, nervous voice of his.

I shook my head. Soothsayer Skye *had* deserved punishment, and his brother Rodger *was* guilty of a heinous crime – in fact, a crime Mendelian society considered every bit as bad as murder.

But I couldn't let Glen get away with it. "I'm sorry for what happened to you," I said. The mental scars no doubt explained his sullen, withdrawn manner.

He glared at me. "Like that makes it better."

"When did it start?"

He was quiet for a time, then gave a little shrug, as if realizing there was no point in pretending any longer. "When I was twelve – as soon as I entered puberty. Not every night, you understand. But often enough." He paused, then: "How'd you figure it out?"

I decided to tell him the truth. "There are only two different sets of DNA in your house – one female, as you'd expect, and just one male."

Glen said nothing.

"I had the male DNA read. I was looking for a trait that might have provided a motive for your father. You know what I found."

Glen was still silent.

"When your dad's sooth was read just after birth, maybe his parents were told that he was sterile. Certainly the proof is there, in his DNA: an inability to produce viable sperm." I paused, remembering the details Rundstedt had explained to me. "But the soothsayer back then couldn't have known the effect of having the variant form of gene ABL-419d, with over a hundred T-A-T repeats. That variation's function hadn't been identified that long ago. But it *was* known by the time Rodger turned eighteen, by the time he went to see his big brother Skye, by the time Skye gave him his adult soothsaying." I paused. "But Uncle Skye hated confrontation, didn't he?"

Glen was motionless, a statue.

"And so Skye lied to your dad. Oh, he told him about his sterility, all right, but he figured there was no point in getting into an argument about what that variant gene meant."

Glen looked at the ground. When at last he did speak, his voice was bitter. "I had thought Dad knew. I confronted him – Christ sakes, Dad, if you knew you had a gene for incestuous pedophilia, why the hell didn't you seek counseling? Why the hell did you have kids?"

"But your father didn't know, did he?"

Glen shook his head. "That bastard Uncle Skye hadn't told him."

"In fairness," I said, "Skye probably figured that since your father couldn't have kids, the problem would never come up. But your dad made a lot of money, and wanted it to pass to an heir. And since he couldn't have an heir the normal way . . ."

Glen's voice was full of disgust. "Since he couldn't have an heir the normal way, he had one made."

I looked the boy up and down. I'd never met a clone before. Glen really was the spitting image of the old man – a chip off the old block. But like any dynasty, the Hissock-Connolly clan wanted not just an heir, but an heir and a spare. Little Billy, ten years younger than Glen, was likewise an exact genetic duplicate of Rodger Hissock, produced from Rodger's DNA placed into one of Rebecca's eggs. All three Hissock males had indeed left DNA in that bathroom – exactly identical DNA.

"Have you always known you were a clone?" I asked.

Glen shook his head. "I only just found out. Before I went for my adult soothsaying, I wanted to see the report my parents had gotten when I was born. But none existed – my dad had decided to save some money. He didn't need a new report done, he figured; my sooth would be identical to his, after all. When I went to get my sooth read and found that *I* was sterile, well, it all fell into place in my mind."

"And so you took your father's blaster, and, since your DNA is the same as his . . ."

Glen nodded slowly. His voice was low and bitter. "Dad never knew in advance what was wrong with him – never had a chance to get help. Uncle Skye never told him. Even after Dad had himself cloned, Skye never spoke up." He looked at me, fury in his cold gray eyes. "It doesn't work, dammit – our whole way of life doesn't work if a soothsayer doesn't tell the truth. You can't play the hand you're dealt if you don't know what cards you've got. Skye deserved to die."

"And you framed your dad for it. You wanted to punish him, too."

Glen shook his head. "You don't understand, man. You can't understand."

"Try me."

"I didn't want to punish Dad – I wanted to protect Billy. Dad can afford the best damn lawyer in Mendelia. Oh, he'll be found guilty, sure, but he won't get life. His lawyer will cut it down to the minimum mandatory sentence for murder, which is –"

"Ten years," I said, realization dawning. "In ten years, Billy will be an adult – and out of danger from Rodger."

Glen nodded once.

"But Rodger could have told the truth at any time – revealed that you were a clone of him. If he'd done that, he would have gotten off, and suspicion would have fallen on you. How did you know he wasn't going to speak up?"

Glen sounded a lot older than his eighteen years. "If Dad exposed me, I'd expose him – and the penalty for child molestation is also a minimum ten years, so he'd be doing the time anyway." He looked directly at me. "Except being a murderer gets you left alone in jail, and being a pedophile gets you wrecked up."

I nodded, led him outside, and hailed a robocab.

Mendelia *is* a great place to live, honest.

And, hell, I did solve the crime, didn't I? Meaning I *am* a good detective. So I guess *my* soothsayer didn't lie to me.

At least – at least I hope not . . .

I had a sudden cold feeling that the SG would stop footing the bill long before this case could come to public trial.

The Shoulders of Giants

I love to get out into the country to write, and most of this story was written at a cottage my wife and I had rented near Parry Sound, Ontario; during the same cottage trip, I wrote the outline for my Neanderthal Parallax *trilogy of novels. The germ for this story came from Marshall T. Savage's fascinating nonfiction book* The Millennial Project, *in which he said only a fool would set out for a long space voyage on a generation ship . . .*

This story ended up being the lead piece in the anthology Star Colonies, *edited by Martin H. Greenberg and John Helfers. Edo van Belkom and Robert Charles Wilson are two of my closest friends in the Toronto SF-writing community;* Star Colonies *marked the first time any of us had appeared together in the same anthology with new (rather than reprint) stories, making it rather a special book for the three of us.*

It seemed like only yesterday when I'd died, but, of course, it was almost certainly centuries ago. I wish the computer would just *tell* me, dammitall, but it was doubtless waiting until its sensors said I was sufficiently stable and alert. The irony was that my pulse was surely racing out of concern, forestalling it speaking to me. If this was an emergency, it should inform me, and if it wasn't, it should let me relax.

Finally, the machine did speak in its crisp, feminine voice. "Hello, Toby. Welcome back to the world of the living."

"Where —" I'd thought I'd spoken the word, but no sound had come out. I tried again. "Where are we?"

"Exactly where we should be: decelerating toward Soror."

I felt myself calming down. "How is Ling?"

"She's reviving, as well."

"The others?"

"All forty-eight cryogenics chambers are functioning properly," said the computer. "Everybody is apparently fine."

That was good to hear, but it wasn't surprising. We had four extra cryochambers; if one of the occupied ones had failed, Ling and I would have been awoken earlier to transfer the person within it into a spare. "What's the date?"

"16 June 3296."

I'd expected an answer like that, but it still took me back a bit. Twelve hundred years had elapsed since the blood had been siphoned out of my body and oxygenated antifreeze had been pumped in to replace it. We'd spent the first of those years accelerating, and presumably the last one decelerating, and the rest —

— the rest was spent coasting at our maximum velocity, 3,000 km/s, one percent of the speed of light. My father had been from Glasgow; my mother, from Los Angeles. They had both enjoyed the quip that the difference between an American and a European was that to an American, a hundred years was a long time, and to a European, a hundred miles is a big journey.

But both would agree that twelve hundred years and 11.9 light-years were equally staggering values. And now, here we were, decelerating in toward Tau Ceti, the closest sunlike star to Earth that wasn't part of a multiple-star system. Of course, because of that, this star had been frequently examined by Earth's Search for Extraterrestrial Intelligence. But nothing had ever been detected; nary a peep.

I was feeling better minute by minute. My own blood, stored in bottles, had been returned to my body and was now coursing through my arteries, my veins, reanimating me.

We were going to make it.

Tau Ceti happened to be oriented with its north pole facing toward Sol; that meant that the technique developed late in the twentieth century to detect planetary systems based on subtle blueshifts and redshifts of a star tugged now closer, now farther away, was useless with it. Any wobble in Tau Ceti's movements would be perpendicular, as seen from Earth, producing no Doppler effect. But eventually Earth-orbiting telescopes had been

developed that were sensitive enough to detect the wobble visu-
ally, and –

It had been front-page news around the world: the first solar
system seen by telescopes. Not inferred from stellar wobbles or
spectral shifts, but actually *seen*. At least four planets could be
made out orbiting Tau Ceti, and one of them –

There had been formulas for decades, first popularized in the
RAND Corporation's study *Habitable Planets for Man*. Every science-fiction writer and astrobiologist worth his or her salt had
used them to determine the *life zones* – the distances from target
stars at which planets with Earthlike surface temperatures might
exist, a Goldilocks band, neither too hot nor too cold.

And the second of the four planets that could be seen around
Tau Ceti was smack-dab in the middle of that star's life zone. The
planet was watched carefully for an entire year – one of its years,
that is, a period of 193 Earth days. Two wonderful facts became
apparent. First, the planet's orbit was damn near circular – meaning it would likely have stable temperatures all the time; the gravitational influence of the fourth planet, a Jovian giant orbiting at a
distance of half a billion kilometers from Tau Ceti, probably was
responsible for that.

And, second, the planet varied in brightness substantially
over the course of its twenty-nine-hour-and-seventeen-minute
day. The reason was easy to deduce: most of one hemisphere was
covered with land, which reflected back little of Tau Ceti's yellow
light, while the other hemisphere, with a much higher albedo, was
likely covered by a vast ocean, no doubt, given the planet's fortu-
itous orbital radius, of liquid water – an extraterrestrial Pacific.

Of course, at a distance of 11.9 light-years, it was quite possible that Tau Ceti had other planets, too small or too dark to be
seen. And so referring to the Earthlike globe as Tau Ceti II would
have been problematic; if an additional world or worlds were
eventually found orbiting closer in, the system's planetary num-
bering would end up as confusing as the scheme used to designate
Saturn's rings.

Clearly a name was called for, and Giancarlo DiMaio, the
astronomer who had discovered the half-land, half-water world,
gave it one: Soror, the Latin word for sister. And, indeed, Soror
appeared, at least as far as could be told from Earth, to be a sister
to humanity's home world.

Soon we would know for sure just how perfect a sister it was. And speaking of sisters, well – okay, Ling Woo wasn't my biological sister, but we'd worked together and trained together for four years before launch, and I'd come to think of her as a sister, despite the press constantly referring to us as the new Adam and Eve. Of course, we'd help to populate the new world, but not together; my wife, Helena, was one of the forty-eight others still frozen solid. Ling wasn't involved yet with any of the other colonists, but, well, she was gorgeous and brilliant, and of the two dozen men in cryosleep, twenty-one were unattached.

Ling and I were co-captains of the *Pioneer Spirit*. Her cryo-coffin was like mine, and unlike all the others: it was designed for repeated use. She and I could be revived multiple times during the voyage, to deal with emergencies. The rest of the crew, in coffins that had cost only $700,000 a piece instead of the six million each of ours was worth, could only be revived once, when our ship reached its final destination.

"You're all set," said the computer. "You can get up now."

The thick glass cover over my coffin slid aside, and I used the padded handles to hoist myself out of its black porcelain frame. For most of the journey, the ship had been coasting in zero gravity, but now that it was decelerating, there was a gentle push downward. Still, it was nowhere near a full g, and I was grateful for that. It would be a day or two before I would be truly steady on my feet.

My module was shielded from the others by a partition, which I'd covered with photos of people I'd left behind: my parents, Helena's parents, my real sister, her two sons. My clothes had waited patiently for me for twelve hundred years; I rather suspected they were now hopelessly out of style. But I got dressed – I'd been naked in the cryochamber, of course – and at last I stepped out from behind the partition, just in time to see Ling emerging from behind the wall that shielded her cryocoffin.

"'Morning," I said, trying to sound blasé.

Ling, wearing a blue and gray jumpsuit, smiled broadly. "Good morning."

We moved into the center of the room, and hugged, friends delighted to have shared an adventure together. Then we immediately headed out toward the bridge, half-walking, half-floating, in the reduced gravity.

"How'd you sleep?" asked Ling.

It wasn't a frivolous question. Prior to our mission, the longest anyone had spent in cryofreeze was five years, on a voyage to Saturn; the *Pioneer Spirit* was Earth's first starship.

"Fine," I said. "You?"

"Okay," replied Ling. But then she stopped moving, and briefly touched my forearm. "Did you – did you dream?"

Brain activity slowed to a virtual halt in cryofreeze, but several members of the crew of *Cronus* – the Saturn mission – had claimed to have had brief dreams, lasting perhaps two or three subjective minutes, spread over five years. Over the span that the *Pioneer Spirit* had been traveling, there would have been time for many hours of dreaming.

I shook my head. "No. What about you?"

Ling nodded. "Yes. I dreamt about the strait of Gibraltar. Ever been there?"

"No."

"It's Spain's southernmost boundary, of course. You can see across the strait from Europe to northern Africa, and there were Neandertal settlements on the Spanish side." Ling's Ph.D. was in anthropology. "But they never made it across the strait. They could clearly see that there was more land – another continent! – only thirteen kilometers away. A strong swimmer can make it, and with any sort of raft or boat, it was eminently doable. But Neandertals never journeyed to the other side; as far as we can tell, they never even tried."

"And you dreamt –?"

"I dreamt I was part of a Neandertal community there, a teenage girl, I guess. And I was trying to convince the others that we should go across the strait, go see the new land. But I couldn't; they weren't interested. There was plenty of food and shelter where we were. Finally, I headed out on my own, trying to swim it. The water was cold and the waves were high, and half the time I couldn't get any air to breathe, but I swam and I swam, and then . . ."

"Yes?"

She shrugged a little. "And then I woke up."

I smiled at her. "Well, this time we're going to make it. We're going to make it for sure."

We came to the bridge door, which opened automatically to admit us, although it squeaked something fierce while doing so;

its lubricants must have dried up over the last twelve centuries. The room was rectangular with a double row of angled consoles facing a large screen, which currently was off.

"Distance to Soror?" I asked into the air.

The computer's voice replied. "1.2 million kilometers."

I nodded. About three times the distance between Earth and its moon. "Screen on, view ahead."

"Overrides are in place," said the computer.

Ling smiled at me. "You're jumping the gun, partner."

I was embarrassed. The *Pioneer Spirit* was decelerating toward Soror; the ship's fusion exhaust was facing in the direction of travel. The optical scanners would be burned out by the glare if their shutters were opened. "Computer, turn off the fusion motors."

"Powering down," said the artificial voice.

"Visual as soon as you're able," I said.

The gravity bled away as the ship's engines stopped firing. Ling held on to one of the handles attached to the top of the console nearest her; I was still a little groggy from the suspended animation, and just floated freely in the room. After about two minutes, the screen came on. Tau Ceti was in the exact center, a baseball-sized yellow disk. And the four planets were clearly visible, ranging from pea-sized to as big as grape.

"Magnify on Soror," I said.

One of the peas became a billiard ball, although Tau Ceti grew hardly at all.

"More," said Ling.

The planet grew to softball size. It was showing as a wide crescent, perhaps a third of the disk illuminated from this angle. And – thankfully, fantastically – Soror was everything we'd dreamed it would be: a giant polished marble, with swirls of white cloud, and a vast, blue ocean, and –

Part of a continent was visible, emerging out of the darkness. And it was green, apparently covered with vegetation.

We hugged again, squeezing each other tightly. No one had been sure when we'd left Earth; Soror could have been barren. The *Pioneer Spirit* was ready regardless: in its cargo holds was everything we needed to survive even on an airless world. But we'd hoped and prayed that Soror would be, well – just like this: a true sister, another Earth, another home.

"It's beautiful, isn't it?" said Ling.

I felt my eyes tearing. It *was* beautiful, breathtaking, stunning. The vast ocean, the cottony clouds, the verdant land, and –

"Oh, my God," I said, softly. "Oh, my God."

"What?" said Ling.

"Don't you see?" I asked. "Look!"

Ling narrowed her eyes and moved closer to the screen. "What?"

"On the dark side," I said.

She looked again. "Oh . . ." she said. There were faint lights sprinkled across the darkness; hard to see, but definitely there. "Could it be volcanism?" asked Ling. Maybe Soror wasn't so perfect after all.

"Computer," I said, "spectral analysis of the light sources on the planet's dark side."

"Predominantly incandescent lighting, color temperature 5600 kelvin."

I exhaled and looked at Ling. They weren't volcanoes. They were cities.

Soror, the world we'd spent twelve centuries traveling to, the world we'd intended to colonize, the world that had been dead silent when examined by radio telescopes, was already inhabited.

The *Pioneer Spirit* was a colonization ship; it wasn't intended as a diplomatic vessel. When it had left Earth, it had seemed important to get at least some humans off the mother world. Two small-scale nuclear wars – Nuke I and Nuke II, as the media had dubbed them – had already been fought, one in southern Asia, the other in South America. It appeared to be only a matter of time before Nuke III, and that one might be the big one.

SETI had detected nothing from Tau Ceti, at least not by 2051. But Earth itself had only been broadcasting for a century and a half at that point; Tau Ceti might have had a thriving civilization then that hadn't yet started using radio. But now it was twelve hundred years later. Who knew how advanced the Tau Cetians might be?

I looked at Ling, then back at the screen. "What should we do?"

Ling tilted her head to one side. "I'm not sure. On the one hand, I'd love to meet them, whoever they are. But . . ."

"But they might not want to meet us," I said. "They might think we're invaders, and –"

"And we've got forty-eight other colonists to think about," said Ling. "For all we know, we're the last surviving humans."

I frowned. "Well, that's easy enough to determine. Computer, swing the radio telescope toward Sol system. See if you can pick anything up that might be artificial."

"Just a sec," said the female voice. A few moments later, a cacophony filled the room: static and snatches of voices and bits of music and sequences of tones, overlapping and jumbled, fading in and out. I heard what sounded like English – although strangely inflected – and maybe Arabic and Mandarin and . . .

"We're not the last survivors," I said, smiling. "There's still life on Earth – or, at least, there was 11.9 years ago, when those signals started out."

Ling exhaled. "I'm glad we didn't blow ourselves up," she said. "Now, I guess we should find out what we're dealing with at Tau Ceti. Computer, swing the dish to face Soror, and again scan for artificial signals."

"Doing so." There was silence for most of a minute, then a blast of static, and a few bars of music, and clicks and bleeps, and voices, speaking in Mandarin and English and –

"No," said Ling. "I said face the dish the *other* way. I want to hear what's coming from Soror."

The computer actually sounded miffed. "The dish *is* facing toward Soror," it said.

I looked at Ling, realization dawning. At the time we'd left Earth, we'd been so worried that humanity was about to snuff itself out, we hadn't really stopped to consider what would happen if that didn't occur. But with twelve hundred years, faster spaceships would doubtless have been developed. While the colonists aboard the *Pioneer Spirit* had slept, some dreaming at an indolent pace, other ships had zipped past them, arriving at Tau Ceti decades, if not centuries, earlier – long enough ago that they'd already built human cities on Soror.

"Damn it," I said. "God damn it." I shook my head, staring at the screen. The tortoise was supposed to win, not the hare.

"What do we do now?" asked Ling.

I sighed. "I suppose we should contact them."

"We – ah, we might be from the wrong side."

I grinned. "Well, we can't *both* be from the wrong side. Besides, you heard the radio: Mandarin *and* English. Anyway, I can't imagine that anyone cares about a war more than a thousand years in the past, and –"

"Excuse me," said the ship's computer. "Incoming audio message."

I looked at Ling. She frowned, surprised. "Put it on," I said.

"*Pioneer Spirit*, welcome! This is Jod Bokket, manager of the Derluntin space station, in orbit around Soror. Is there anyone awake on board?" It was a man's voice, with an accent unlike anything I'd ever heard before.

Ling looked at me, to see if I was going to object, then she spoke up. "Computer, send a reply." The computer bleeped to signal that the channel was open. "This is Dr. Ling Woo, co-captain of the *Pioneer Spirit*. Two of us have revived; there are forty-eight more still in cryofreeze."

"Well, look," said Bokket's voice, "it'll be days at the rate you're going before you get here. How about if we send a ship to bring you two to Derluntin? We can have someone there to pick you up in about an hour."

"They really like to rub it in, don't they?" I grumbled.

"What was that?" said Bokket. "We couldn't quite make it out."

Ling and I consulted with facial expressions, then agreed. "Sure," said Ling. "We'll be waiting."

"Not for long," said Bokket, and the speaker went dead.

Bokket himself came to collect us. His spherical ship was tiny compared with ours, but it seemed to have about the same amount of habitable interior space; would the ignominies ever cease? Docking adapters had changed a lot in a thousand years, and he wasn't able to get an airtight seal, so we had to transfer over to his ship in space suits. Once aboard, I was pleased to see we were still floating freely; it would have been *too* much if they'd had artificial gravity.

Bokket seemed a nice fellow – about my age, early thirties. Of course, maybe people looked youthful forever now; who knew how old he might actually be? I couldn't really identify his ethnicity, either; he seemed to be rather a blend of traits. But he certainly was taken with Ling – his eyes popped out when she took off her helmet, revealing her heart-shaped face and long, black hair.

"Hello," he said, smiling broadly.

Ling smiled back. "Hello. I'm Ling Woo, and this is Toby MacGregor, my co-captain."

"Greetings," I said, sticking out my hand.

Bokket looked at it, clearly not knowing precisely what to do. He extended his hand in a mirroring of my gesture, but didn't touch me. I closed the gap and clasped his hand. He seemed surprised, but pleased.

"We'll take you back to the station first," he said. "Forgive us, but, well – you can't go down to the planet's surface yet; you'll have to be quarantined. We've eliminated a lot of diseases, of course, since your time, and so we don't vaccinate for them anymore. I'm willing to take the risk, but . . ."

I nodded. "That's fine."

He tipped his head slightly, as if he were preoccupied for a moment, then: "I've told the ship to take us back to Derluntin station. It's in a polar orbit, about 200 kilometers above Soror; you'll get some beautiful views of the planet, anyway." He was grinning from ear to ear. "It's wonderful to meet you people," he said. "Like a page out of history."

"If you knew about us," I asked, after we'd settled in for the journey to the station, "why didn't you pick us up earlier?"

Bokket cleared his throat. "We didn't know about you."

"But you called us by name: *Pioneer Spirit.*"

"Well, it *is* painted in letters three meters high across your hull. Our asteroid-watch system detected you. A lot of information from your time has been lost – I guess there was a lot of political upheaval then, no? – but we knew Earth had experimented with sleeper ships in the twenty-first century."

We were getting close to the space station; it was a giant ring, spinning to simulate gravity. It might have taken us over a thousand years to do it, but humanity was finally building space stations the way God had always intended them to be.

And floating next to the space station was a beautiful spaceship, with a spindle-shaped silver hull and two sets of mutually perpendicular emerald-green delta wings. "It's gorgeous," I said.

Bokket nodded.

"How does it land, though? Tail-down?"

"It doesn't land; it's a starship."

"Yes, but —"

"We use shuttles to go between it and the ground."

"But if it can't land," asked Ling, "why is it streamlined? Just for esthetics?"

Bokket laughed, but it was a polite laugh. "It's streamlined because it needs to be. There's substantial length-contraction when flying at just below the speed of light; that means that the interstellar medium seems much denser. Although there's only one baryon per cubic centimeter, they form what seems to be an appreciable atmosphere if you're going fast enough."

"And your ships are *that* fast?" asked Ling.

Bokket smiled. "Yes. They're that fast."

Ling shook her head. "We were crazy," she said. "Crazy to undertake our journey." She looked briefly at Bokket, but couldn't meet his eyes. She turned her gaze down toward the floor. "You must think we're incredibly foolish."

Bokket's eyes widened. He seemed at a loss for what to say. He looked at me, spreading his arms, as if appealing to me for support. But I just exhaled, letting air — and disappointment — vent from my body.

"You're wrong," said Bokket, at last. "You couldn't be more wrong. We *honor* you." He paused, waiting for Ling to look up again. She did, her eyebrows lifted questioningly. "If we have come farther than you," said Bokket, "or have gone faster than you, it's because we had your work to build on. Humans are here now because it's *easy* for us to be here, because you and others blazed the trails." He looked at me, then at Ling. "If we see farther," he said, "it's because we stand on the shoulders of giants."

Later that day, Ling, Bokket, and I were walking along the gently curving floor of Derluntin station. We were confined to a limited part of one section; they'd let us down to the planet's surface in another ten days, Bokket had said.

"There's nothing for us here," said Ling, hands in her pockets. "We're freaks, anachronisms. Like somebody from the T'ang Dynasty showing up in our world."

"Soror is wealthy," said Bokket. "We can certainly support you and your passengers."

"They are *not* passengers," I snapped. "They are colonists. They are explorers."

Bokket nodded. "I'm sorry. You're right, of course. But look – we really are delighted that you're here. I've been keeping the media away; the quarantine lets me do that. But they will go absolutely dingo when you come down to the planet. It's like having Neil Armstrong or Tamiko Hiroshige show up at your door."

"Tamiko who?" asked Ling.

"Sorry. After your time. She was the first person to disembark at Alpha Centauri."

"The first," I repeated; I guess I wasn't doing a good job of hiding my bitterness. "That's the honor – that's the achievement. Being the first. Nobody remembers the name of the second person on the moon."

"Edwin Eugene Aldrin, Jr.," said Bokket. "Known as 'Buzz.'"

"Fine, okay," I said. "*You* remember, but most people don't."

"I didn't remember it; I accessed it." He tapped his temple. "Direct link to the planetary web; everybody has one."

Ling exhaled; the gulf was vast. "Regardless," she said, "we are not pioneers; we're just also-rans. We may have set out before you did, but you got here before us."

"Well, my ancestors did," said Bokket. "I'm sixth-generation Sororian."

"*Sixth* generation?" I said. "How long has the colony been here?"

"We're not a colony anymore; we're an independent world. But the ship that got here first left Earth in 2107. Of course, my ancestors didn't immigrate until much later."

"Twenty-one-oh-seven," I repeated. That was only fifty-six years after the launch of the *Pioneer Spirit*. I'd been thirty-one when our ship had started its journey; if I'd stayed behind, I might very well have lived to see the real pioneers depart. What had we been thinking, leaving Earth? Had we been running, escaping, getting out, fleeing before the bombs fell? Were we pioneers, or cowards?

No. No, those were crazy thoughts. We'd left for the same reason that *Homo sapiens sapiens* had crossed the Strait of Gibraltar. It was what we did as a species. It was why we'd triumphed, and the Neandertals had failed. We *needed* to see what was on the other side, what was over the next hill, what was orbiting other stars. It was what had given us dominion over the home planet; it was what was going to make us kings of infinite space.

I turned to Ling. "We can't stay here," I said.

She seemed to mull this over for a bit, then nodded. She looked at Bokket. "We don't want parades," she said. "We don't want statues." She lifted her eyebrows, as if acknowledging the magnitude of what she was asking for. "We want a new ship, a faster ship." She looked at me, and I bobbed my head in agreement. She pointed out the window. "A *streamlined* ship."

"What would you do with it?" asked Bokket. "Where would you go?"

She glanced at me, then looked back at Bokket. "Andromeda."

"Andromeda? You mean the Andromeda *galaxy*? But that's —" a fractional pause, no doubt while his web link provided the data "— 2.2 *million* light-years away."

"Exactly."

"But . . . but it would take over two million years to get there."

"Only from Earth's — excuse me, from Soror's — point of view," said Ling. "We could do it in less subjective time than we've already been traveling, and, of course, we'd spend all that time in cryogenic freeze."

"None of our ships have cryogenic chambers," Bokket said. "There's no need for them."

"We could transfer the chambers from the *Pioneer Spirit.*"

Bokket shook his head. "It would be a one-way trip; you'd never come back."

"That's not true," I said. "Unlike most galaxies, Andromeda is actually moving toward the Milky Way, not away from it. Eventually, the two galaxies will merge, bringing us home."

"That's billions of years in the future."

"Thinking small hasn't done us any good so far," said Ling.

Bokket frowned. "I said before that we can afford to support you and your shipmates here on Soror, and that's true. But starships are expensive. We can't just give you one."

"It's got to be cheaper than supporting all of us."

"No, it's not."

"You said you honored us. You said you stand on our shoulders. If that's true, then repay the favor. Give us an opportunity to stand on *your* shoulders. Let us have a new ship."

Bokket sighed; it was clear he felt we really didn't understand how difficult Ling's request would be to fulfill. "I'll do what I can," he said.

Ling and I spent that evening talking, while blue-and-green Soror spun majestically beneath us. It was our job to jointly make the right decision, not just for ourselves but for the four dozen other members of the *Pioneer Spirit*'s complement that had entrusted their fate to us. Would they have wanted to be revived here?

No. No, of course not. They'd left Earth to found a colony; there was no reason to think they would have changed their minds, whatever they might be dreaming. Nobody had an emotional attachment to the idea of Tau Ceti; it just had seemed a logical target star.

"We could ask for passage back to Earth," I said.

"You don't want that," said Ling. "And neither, I'm sure, would any of the others."

"No, you're right," I said. "They'd want us to go on."

Ling nodded. "I think so."

"Andromeda?" I said, smiling. "Where did that come from?"

She shrugged. "First thing that popped into my head."

"Andromeda," I repeated, tasting the word some more. I remembered how thrilled I was, at sixteen, out in the California desert, to see that little oval smudge below Cassiopeia for the first time. Another galaxy, another island universe – and half again as big as our own. "Why not?" I fell silent but, after a while, said, "Bokket seems to like you."

Ling smiled. "I like him."

"Go for it," I said.

"What?" She sounded surprised.

"Go for it, if you like him. I may have to be alone until Helena is revived at our final destination, but you don't have to be. Even if they do give us a new ship, it'll surely be a few weeks before they can transfer the cryochambers."

Ling rolled her eyes. *"Men,"* she said, but I knew the idea appealed to her.

. . .

Bokket was right: the Sororian media seemed quite enamored with Ling and me, and not just because of our exotic appearance – my white skin and blue eyes; her dark skin and epicanthic folds; our two strange accents, both so different from the way people of the thirty-third century spoke. They also seemed to be fascinated by, well, by the pioneer spirit.

When the quarantine was over, we did go down to the planet. The temperature was perhaps a little cooler than I'd have liked, and the air a bit moister – but humans adapt, of course. The architecture in Soror's capital city of Pax was surprisingly ornate, with lots of domed roofs and intricate carvings. The term "capital city" was an anachronism, though; government was completely decentralized, with all major decisions done by plebiscite – including the decision about whether or not to give us another ship.

Bokket, Ling, and I were in the central square of Pax, along with Kari Deetal, Soror's president, waiting for the results of the vote to be announced. Media representatives from all over the Tau Ceti system were present, as well as one from Earth, whose stories were always read 11.9 years after he filed them. Also on hand were perhaps a thousand spectators.

"My friends," said Deetal, to the crowd, spreading her arms, "you have all voted, and now let us share in the results." She tipped her head slightly, and a moment later people in the crowd started clapping and cheering.

Ling and I turned to Bokket, who was beaming. "What is it?" said Ling. "What decision did they make?"

Bokket looked surprised. "Oh, sorry. I forgot you don't have web implants. You're going to get your ship."

Ling closed her eyes and breathed a sigh of relief. My heart was pounding.

President Deetal gestured toward us. "Dr. MacGregor, Dr. Woo – would you say a few words?"

We glanced at each other then stood up. "Thank you," I said looking out at everyone.

Ling nodded in agreement. "Thank you very much."

A reporter called out a question. "What are you going to call your new ship?"

Ling frowned; I pursed my lips. And then I said, "What else? The *Pioneer Spirit II.*"

The crowd erupted again.

Finally, the fateful day came. Our official boarding of our new starship – the one that would be covered by all the media – wouldn't happen for another four hours, but Ling and I were nonetheless heading toward the airlock that joined the ship to the station's outer rim. She wanted to look things over once more, and I wanted to spend a little time just sitting next to Helena's cryochamber, communing with her.

And, as we walked, Bokket came running along the curving floor toward us.

"Ling," he said, catching his breath. "Toby."

I nodded a greeting. Ling looked slightly uncomfortable; she and Bokket had grown close during the last few weeks, but they'd also had their time alone last night to say their goodbyes. I don't think she'd expected to see him again before we left.

"I'm sorry to bother you two," he said. "I know you're both busy, but . . ." He seemed quite nervous.

"Yes?" I said.

He looked at me, then at Ling. "Do you have room for another passenger?"

Ling smiled. "We don't have passengers. We're colonists."

"Sorry," said Bokket, smiling back at her. "Do you have room for another colonist?"

"Well, there *are* four spare cryochambers, but . . ." She looked at me.

"Why not?" I said, shrugging.

"It's going to be hard work, you know," said Ling, turning back to Bokket. "Wherever we end up, it's going to be rough."

Bokket nodded. "I know. And I want to be part of it."

Ling knew she didn't have to be coy around me. "That would be wonderful," she said. "But – but why?"

Bokket reached out tentatively, and found Ling's hand. He squeezed it gently, and she squeezed back. "You're one reason," he said.

"Got a thing for older women, eh?" said Ling. I smiled at that.

Bokket laughed. "I guess."

"You said I was one reason," said Ling.

He nodded. "The other reason is – well, it's this: I don't want to stand on the shoulders of giants." He paused, then lifted his own shoulders a little, as if acknowledging that he was giving voice to the sort of thought rarely spoken aloud. "I want to *be* a giant."

They continued to hold hands as we walked down the space station's long corridor, heading toward the sleek and graceful ship that would take us to our new home.

Ineluctable

In November 2000, I was Guest of Honor at Contact 4 Japan, a conference devoted to potential first contact with extraterrestrial life. For that conference, I was asked to devise a role-playing scenario involving the receipt of a series of alien radio messages; teams would try to decode the messages and provide appropriate responses. The conference was one of the most enjoyable events I've ever attended, and it also afforded me an opportunity to meet the staff of Hayakawa, my Japanese publisher.

After the conference, I decided to expand my first-contact scenario into a full-fledged SF story, and sent it off to Stanley Schmidt, the editor of Analog. *Now, by this point, I'd had 300,000 words of fiction in* Analog, *but it had all been in the form of novel serializations:* The Terminal Experiment *(which* Analog *ran under my original title,* Hobson's Choice*),* Starplex, *and* Hominids. *When Stan bought this story – at 8,800 words, technically a novelette – it became my first short-fiction sale to* Analog.

What to do? What to do?

Darren Hamasaki blew out air, trying to calm down, but his heart kept pounding, a metronome on amphetamines.

This was big. This was huge.

There *had* to be procedures in place. Surely someone had thought this through, had come up with a – a *protocol*, that was the word.

Darren left the observatory shed in his backyard and trudged through the snow. He stepped up onto the wooden deck and entered his house through the sliding-glass rear doors. He hit the light switch, the halogen glow from the torchiere by the desk stinging his dark-adapted eyes.

Darren took off his boots, gloves, tuque, and parka, then crossed the room, sitting down at his computer. He clicked on the Netscape Navigator icon. Oh, he had Microsoft Explorer, too – it had come preinstalled on his Pentium IV – but Darren always favored the underdog. His current search engine of choice, which changed as frequently as the current favorite CD in his stereo, was also an underdog: HotBot. He logged on to it and stared at the dialog box, trying to think of what keywords to type.

Protocol was indeed appropriate, but as for the rest –

He shrugged a little, conceding the magnitude of what he was about to enter. And then he pecked out three more words: *contact, extraterrestrial,* and *intelligence.*

He'd expected to have to go spelunking, and, indeed, there were over thirteen hundred hits, but the very first one turned out to be what he was looking for: "Declaration of Principles Concerning Activities Following the Detection of Extraterrestrial Intelligence," a document on the SETI League web site. Darren scanned it, his eyes skittering across the screen like a puck across ice. As he did so, he rolled his index finger back and forth on his mouse's knurled wheel.

"We, the institutions and individuals participating in the search for extraterrestrial intelligence . . ."

Darren frowned. No one had sought his opinion, but, then again, he hadn't actually been *looking* for aliens.

". . . inspired by the profound significance for mankind of detecting evidence . . ."

Seemed to Darren that "mankind" was probably a sexist term; just how old was this document?

"The discoverer should seek to verify that the most plausible explanation is the existence of extraterrestrial intelligence rather than some other natural or anthropogenic phenomenon . . ."

Well, there was no doubt about it. No natural phenomenon was likely to generate the squares of one, two, three, and four over and over again, and the source was in the direction of Groombridge 1618, a star 15.9 light-years from Earth; Groombridge 1618 was in Ursa Major, nowhere near the plane of the ecliptic into which almost every Earth-made space probe and vessel had been launched. It *had* to be extraterrestrial.

". . . *should inform the Secretary General of the United Nations in accordance with Article XI of the Treaty on Principles Governing the Activities of States in the Exploration and Use of Outer Space . . ."*

Darren's eyebrows went up. Somehow he doubted that the switchboard at the UN would put his call through to the secretary-general – was it still Kofi Annan? – if he said he was ringing him up to advise him that contact had been made with aliens. Besides, it was 2:00 a.m. here in Ontario, and UN headquarters were in New York; the same time zone. Surely the secretary-general would be at home asleep right now anyway.

"The discoverer should inform observers throughout the world through the Central Bureau for Astronomical Telegrams of the International Astronomical Union . . ."

Good God, is it still possible to send a telegram? Is Western Union even still in business? Surely the submission could be made by E-mail . . .

HotBot quickly yielded the URL for the bureau, which still used the word "telegrams" in its name, but one could indeed fill out an online form on their home page to send a report. Too bad, in a way: Darren had been enjoying composing a telegram in his head, something he'd never done before: "Major news *stop* alien signal received from Groombridge 1618 *stop* . . ."

The brief instructions accompanying the form only talked about reporting comets, novae, supernovae, and outbursts of unusual variable stars (and there were warnings not to bother the bureau with trivial matters, such as the sighting of meteors or the discovery of new asteroids). Nary a word about submitting news of the receipt of an alien signal.

Regardless, Darren composed a brief message and sent it. Then he clicked his browser's *back* button several times to return to the *Declaration of Principles*, and skimmed it some more. Ah, now that was more like it: *'The discoverer should have the privilege of making the first public announcement . . ."*

Very well, then. Very well.

There was nothing to do now but wait and see if the beings living on the third planet were going to reply. Palm-Up-Middle-Fingers-Splayed expected they indeed would, but it would take time: time for the laser flashes to reach their destination, and an equal time for any response the inhabitants of that watery globe might wish to send – plus, of course, whatever time they took deciding whether to answer.

There were many things Palm-Up-Middle-Fingers-Splayed could do to while away the time: read, watch a video, inhale a landscape. And, well, had it been any other time, he probably would have contented himself with one of those. The landscape was particularly appealing: he had a full molecular map of the air in early spring from his world's eastern continent, a heady blending of yellowshoot blossoms, clumpweed pollens, pondskins, skyleaper pheromones, and the tang of ozone from the vernal storms. Nothing relaxed him more.

He'd been afraid at first to access that molecular map, afraid the homesickness would be too much. After all, their ship, the *Ineluctable*, had been traveling for many years now, visiting seven other star systems before coming here. And there were still three more stars – and several years of travel – after this stop before Palm-Up-Middle-Fingers-Splayed would really get to inhale the joyous scents of his homeland again. Fortunately, though, it had turned out that he *could* enjoy the simulation without his tail twitching too much in sadness.

Still, this was not any other time; this was the period when, had they been back home, all three moons would have risen simultaneously, the harmonics of their vastly different orbital radii briefly synchronizing their movements. This was the time when the tides would be at their highest, when the jewelbugs would be taking to the air – and when the females of Palm-Up-Middle-Fingers-Splayed's kind would be in estrus.

Even aboard ship, the estrus cycle continued, never losing track of its schedule. Yes, despite his race's hopes, even shielding females from the light and gravitational effects of the moons did nothing to end the recurring march. The cycle was so ingrained in <hand-sign-naming-his-species> physiology that it maintained its precision even in the absence of the stimuli that must surely have originally set its cadence.

Palm-Up-Middle-Fingers-Splayed took one last look out his window at the distant yellow star. The planet they'd signaled was invisible without a telescope, although two of the gas giants – the fifth and sixth worlds – shone brightly enough to be seen with naked eyes, despite presenting only crescent faces from this distance.

The ship's computer would flash a signal to alert Palm-Up-Middle-Fingers-Splayed, of course, if any response were received. He set out to find his mate, to find his dear Fist-Held-Sideways.

Fist-Held-Sideways was in the forward mess hall when Palm-Up-Middle-Fingers-Splayed caught up with her. Now that the *Ineluctable*'s great fusion motors were quiescent, the false sense of gravity had disappeared. Fist-Held-Sideways was floating freely, her gray tail with its blue mottling sticking up above her in a most appealing way.

Palm-Up-Middle-Fingers-Splayed hovered in the doorway, not moving, just watching her as she ate. Her chest opened vertically, revealing the inside of her torso, the polished pointed tips of her ribs moving apart as she split herself wider and wider. Fist-Held-Sideways used the arm coming out of the left side of her head to swat a large melon that had been floating by, directing it into her belly. Palm-Up-Middle-Fingers-Splayed watched as the tips of her ribs came together, crushing the melon, a few spherical drops of juice floating out of Fist-Held-Sideways's torso before she closed the feeding slit. A small mechanical cleaner, moving about the room with the aid of a propeller, sucked the juice out of the air and then demurely retreated.

It wasn't easy getting another <hand-sign-naming-his-species>'s attention in zero gravity. On a planet's surface, one might slap one's tail against the floor hard enough so that the other would feel the vibrations through his or her own tail and feet. But when floating freely, that didn't work; indeed, slapping a tail like that would send you shooting up toward the ceiling, banging your head.

Palm-Up-Middle-Fingers-Splayed used the hand coming out of the right side of his head to push against the doorframe, propelling himself into the mess hall. As soon as he came within Fist-Held-Sideways's field of view, she flared her nasal slits in greeting, welcoming his scent, then used both her hands to make signs. "Palm-Up-Middle-Fingers-Splayed!" she exclaimed, hyperextending her fingers after finishing his namesign to convey her pleasant surprise. "Good to see you! No reply from the aliens yet?"

Palm-Up-Middle-Fingers-Splayed balled his left hand in nega-
tion. "It's still much too early. So far, I've just sent them one, four,
nine, and sixteen over and over again; sort of a general hello, one
sentient race to another. It'll be some time before we receive any
response." He paused, seeing if his mate would pick up the hint.

And, of course, she did; Palm-Up-Middle-Fingers-Splayed had
heard from Palm-Down-Thumb-Extended, who had been Fist-
Held-Sideways's mate last breeding season, that she was wonderfully intuitive and empathetic – unusual, but very desirable, traits
in a female. "Your quarters or mine?" signed Fist-Held-Sideways.

"Yours," Palm-Up-Middle-Fingers-Splayed signed back, flex-
ing his wrist wryly. "Too many breakables in mine."

The sex, as always, was athletic. Palm-Up-Middle-Fingers-
Splayed enjoyed the exercise, enjoyed the tumbling in zero-g,
enjoyed the physical contact with Fist-Held-Sideways. But it was
the actual consummation, of course, that he was waiting for. Palm-
Up-Middle-Fingers-Splayed was a biologist and, although he had
indeed repeatedly taught students the precise biochemistry
involved, it still fascinated the intellectual part of him every time
it happened: when a male's semen finally reached the female's
hexagon of egg-cells, a chemical reaction occurred producing a
neurotransmitter that brought intense pleasure to both the female
and the male, just as –

Yes, yes! Contact! The sensation washed over him, his tail
going rigid in excitement, his twin hearts pounding out of synch,
his rib points clamping together, as he was overcome by the joy,
the joy, *the joy* . . .

Palm-Up-Middle-Fingers-Splayed was a considerate enough
lover to take additional pleasure from the writhing of Fist-Held-
Sideways's body. He squeezed her tighter, and they both relished
the simultaneous climax of their intercourse. As they relaxed,
floating in the room, the warm afterglow of the neurotransmitter
washing over them, Palm-Up-Middle-Fingers-Splayed thought
that the Five Gods had indeed been wise. Only together could
males and females experience such joy, and – oh, the gods had
indeed been brilliant! – it happened *simultaneously*, compounds
from his body mixing with chemicals from hers, producing the
neurotransmitter. The simultaneity, the shared experience, was
wonderful.

Of course, as usual, it would be a problem figuring out what to do with the new children. His race had been saddened indeed when it discovered that any process or barrier that prevented conception also prevented orgasm, and that, because of the neurological interdependence of the fetuses and their host, to terminate a pregnancy would kill the mother.

No, the only method to keep new children from being born was to avoid copulation altogether. And, well, when a female was in estrus, her pheromones — those wonderful, wonderful pheromones — were completely irresistible.

The <hand-sign-naming-his-species> had no choice. With an ever-expanding population, they had to find new worlds to colonize.

Darren's next-door neighbor's brother-in-law worked for Newsworld, the CBC's all-news cable channel. He'd met the guy a couple of times at parties at Bernie's place. Darren couldn't recall exactly what the guy did. Director? Switcher? Some behind-the-scenes function, anyway; they'd had a fairly empty conversation last time, with Darren asking him if Wendy Mesley was as cute in real life as she looked on TV. Of course, at this time of night, he didn't want to call Bernie and wake him up — "next door" was a bit of a misnomer; Bernie's place was the better part of a kilometer up the country road.

But at that last party Bernie had held — back in June, it must have been — Bernie's brother-in-law had had to leave early, to get down to Toronto and go to work. So he pulled the night shift at least some of the time, meaning there was a chance he might be at the CBC right now. But what the heck was the guy's name? Carson? Carstone? Carstairs? Something like that . . .

Well, nothing to be lost by trying. He got the CBC number from Toronto directory assistance, dialed it, and was greeted by a bilingual computerized receptionist, which gave him the option of spelling out the last name of the person he wanted to speak to on his touch-tone phone. Fortunately, the system recognized the name by the time Darren had pressed the key corresponding to the fourth letter — the last name, as the system informed him, was in fact Carstairs, and the first name was Rory. Darren was transferred to the correct extension and, miracle of miracles, the actual, living Rory Carstairs answered the phone.

"Overnight," said the voice. "Carstairs."

"Hi, Rory. This is Darren Hamasaki – remember me? I live down the street from your brother-in-law Bernie. We met at a couple of his parties." The words of the automated attendant echoed in Darren's mind: *Continue until recognized.* "I've got one of those beards that a lot of people call a goatee, but it's really a Vandyke, and –"

"Oh, sure," said Carstairs. "The space buff, right? You were pointing out constellations to us in Bernie's backyard. Say, nothing's happened to Bernie, has it?"

"No, he's fine – at least, as far as I know. But – but I've got some news to report, and, well, I didn't know who else to call."

"I'm listening," said Carstairs.

The carefully devised *Declaration of Principles Concerning Activities Following the Detection of Extraterrestrial Intelligence,* issued by the International Academy of Astronautics in 1989, had been based on the assumption that governments would control access to the alien signals, that giant, multi-million-dollar radio telescopes would be required to pick up the messages.

But the signal Darren had detected was *optical.* Anyone with a decent backyard telescope had been able to pick it out, once he'd made known the celestial coordinates. And in all the places on Earth from which Groombridge 1618 could be seen at night, people were doing just that. Sales of telescopes were at an all-time high, exceeding even the boom during Halley's last visit.

Darren Hamasaki became a media celebrity, interviewed by TV programs from around the world. Of course, all the usual SETI pundits – Seth Shostak and Paul Shuch in the U.S., Robert Garrison in Canada, and Jun Jugaku in Japan – were also constantly being asked for comment. But when the mayor of Las Vegas decided to do something about the alien signal, it was indeed Darren that he called.

Darren had taken to letting his answering machine screen his calls; the phone rang incessantly now. He was leaning back in a leather chair, fingers interlaced behind his head, listening absently to the words coming from the machine's tinny speaker: "Shoot, I'd hoped to catch you in. Mr. Hamasaki, my name is Rodney Rivers, and I'm the mayor of Las Vegas, Nevada. I've got an idea that –"

Intrigued, Darren picked up the phone's handset. "Hello?"

"Mr. Hamasaki, is that you?"

"Speaking."

"Well, looks like I hit the jackpot. Mr. Hamasaki, I'm the mayor of Las Vegas, and I'd like to have you come down here and join us for a little project we got in mind."

"What's that?"

"You ever been to Vegas, son?"

"No."

"Seen pictures?"

"Of course."

"We're one brightly lit city at night, Mr. Hamasaki. So bright, the shuttle astronauts say they can easily see us from orbit. And, well, this is our off-season, you know – the time between Thanksgiving and Christmas. Don't get enough tourist traffic, and it's the tourists that drive our economy, sure enough. So me and some of the boys here, we had an idea."

"Yes?"

"We're goin' to flash the lights of Las Vegas – every dang light in the blessed city – on and off in unison. Send a reply to them there aliens you found."

Darren was momentarily stunned. "Really? Is that – I mean, can you do that? Are you allowed to?"

"This is the U.S. of A, son – freedom of speech and all that. Of course we're allowed to."

"What are you going to say?"

"That's why I'm callin' you, Mr. Hamasaki. We want you to help us work out what the reply should be. Any chance I could entice you down here with a free trip to Vegas? We'll put you up at –"

"At the Hilton. Isn't that the one with *Star Trek: The Experience*?"

The mayor laughed. "If that's what you'd like. How soon could you get down here?"

Mayor Rivers was certainly savvy. Over one hundred thousand extra tourists came to Las Vegas to be part of the great signaling event; it was the best early-December business the city had ever had.

Darren Hamasaki's first inclination had been to send a simple message in response. The aliens – whoever they might be – had signaled one flash, four flashes, nine flashes, and sixteen flashes, over and over again; those were the squares of one, two, three, and four. Darren thought the logical reply might be the cubes of the first four integers: one, eight, twenty-seven, and sixty-four. Not only would it make clear that the people of Earth understood the original message – which simply parroting it back wouldn't necessarily have conveyed – but it would also indicate that they were ready for something more complex.

But Las Vegas was a city of spectacles; being that prosaic wouldn't do. Darren spent a week devising a more content-rich message, using the form Frank Drake had worked out for Earth's first attempt at communicating with aliens, back in 1974: an image made of a string of on/off bits, the length of the string being the product of two prime numbers – in this case 59 and 29.

Arranging the bits as a grid of 59 rows each 29 columns wide produced a crude picture. Darren coded in a simple diagram of a human being, and, because ever since he'd read Lilly in college, he'd believed dolphins were intelligent, a simple diagram of a bottle-nosed dolphin, too. He then put binary numbers underneath, expressing the total populations of the two species, and a crude diagram of the western hemisphere of the Earth, showing that the humans lived on the land and the dolphins in the ocean.

Media from all over the world came to cover the event. Mayor Rivers and Darren were invited to the master control room of the Clark County Power Authority. The entire power grid could be controlled from a single computer there. And, at precisely 10:00 p.m., the mayor pushed the key to start the program running. It began – and would end – with one solid minute of darkness, then a solid minute of light, and then another of darkness, to frame the message. Then the glowing marquee at Caesars Palace winked at the night sky, the floodlights at Luxor strobed against the blackness, the neon tubes at the MGM Grand flickered off and on. All along the Las Vegas strip, and in all the surrounding streets, the lights blinked the 1,711 bits of Darren's reply.

Out front of Bally's, surrounded by a huge crowd, a giant grid of lights – specially powered by gas generators – filled in with the pixels of the message, one after the other, line by line, from upper left to lower right, painting it as it was transmitted. The crowd cheered when the human figure was finished, thousands of people raising their right arms in the same salute of greeting portrayed in the message.

After the message had been completed, the mayor took to the podium and addressed the assembled mass, thanking them for their orderly conduct. Then His Honor invited Darren to say a few words.

Darren felt the need to put it all in perspective. "Of course, Groombridge 1618 is almost sixteen light-years from Earth," he said into the mike, his voice reverberating off the canyon of hotels surrounding him. "That means it will take sixteen years for our signal to reach the aliens there, and another sixteen before any reply they might send could be received." This being Las Vegas, there were already betting pools about what date the aliens might reply on, and what the content of their next message might be.

Darren refrained from remarking about how exceedingly unlikely it would be that the aliens would be able to detect one blinking city against the glare of Earth's sun behind it; if humanity ever really wanted to seriously respond, it would likely need to build a massive laser to do so.

"Still," said Darren, summing up, "we've had a lot of fun tonight, and we've certainly made history: humanity's first response to an alien signal. Let's hope that if a reply does come, thirty-odd years from now, we'll have made new friends."

The head of the power authority had the final words for the evening; the crowd was already dispersing by this point – heading back to the casinos, or the hotels, or the late Lance Burton show during which his assistants were topless, or any of the hundreds of other diversions Las Vegas offered at night.

Darren felt a twinge of sadness. He'd enjoyed his fifteen minutes of fame – but now, of course, the story would slip from public consciousness, and he'd go back to his quiet life in rural Ontario.

Or so he'd thought.

Palm-Up-Middle-Fingers-Splayed had spent the entire night in Fist-Held-Sideways's quarters but had left by the time ship's morning had rolled around. He was one of ten males aboard the *Ineluctable*, and she, one of ten females. As on the homeworld, though, females were loners, while males – who in ancient times had watched over the clutches of six eggs laid then abandoned by each female – lived communally. The *Ineluctable*'s habitat was shaped like a giant wheel, with ten spokes, each one leading to a different female's lair; the males lived together in the hub.

It was shortly after the fifth daypart when the computer turned on a bright light to get Palm-Up-Middle-Fingers-Splayed's attention. The digitized blue hands on the monitor screen signed the words with precise, unemotional movements. "A response has been received from the third planet."

Palm-Up-Middle-Fingers-Splayed gave himself a three-point launch down the corridor, pushing off the bulkhead with both feet and his broad, flat tail. He barreled into the communications room. Waiting there were three other males, plus one female, Captain Curling-Sixth-Finger herself, who had come into the hub from her command module at the end of spoke one.

"I see we've made contact," signed Palm-Up-Middle-Fingers-Splayed. "Has the reply been deciphered yet?"

"It seems pretty straightforward," said Palm-Down-Thumb-Extended. "It's a standard message grid, just like the ones we were planning to use for our later messages." He made a couple of signs at the camera eye on the computer console, and a screen came to life, showing the message.

"The one on the left is the terrestrial form," continued Palm-Down-Thumb-Extended. "The one on the right, the aquatic form. It was the terrestrial form that sent the message. See those strings beneath the character figures? We think those might be population tallies – meaning there are far, far more of the terrestrial form than of the aquatic one."

"Interesting that a technological race is still subject to heavy predation or infant mortality," signed Palm-Up-Middle-Fingers-Splayed. "But it looks as though only a tiny fraction survive to metamorphose into the adult aquatic form."

"That's my reading of it, too," said Palm-Down-Thumb-Extended. His hands moved delicately, wistfully. There had been a time, of course, when the <hand-sign-naming-his-species> had faced the same sort of thing, when six offspring were needed in every clutch, and a countless clutches were needed in a female's lifetime, just in hopes of getting two children to live to adulthood. So many had fallen prey to gnawbeasts and skyswoopers and bloodvines –

But now –

But now.

Now almost all offspring survived to maturity. There was no choice but to find new worlds on which to live. It was a difficult task: no world was suitable for habitation unless it already had an established biosphere; only the action of life could produce the carbon dioxide and oxygen needed to make a breathable atmosphere. And so the *Ineluctable* traveled from star to star, looking for worlds that were fecund but not yet overcrowded with their own native life forms.

"Maybe they do it on purpose," signed Captain Curling-Sixth-Finger. Palm-Up-Middle-Fingers-Splayed was grateful for the zero gravity; if they'd been on a planet's surface, Curling-Sixth-Finger would have towered over him, just as most adult females towered over most males. But here, with them both floating freely, the difference in size was much less intimidating.

"Do what?" signed Palm-Up-Middle-Fingers-Splayed.

"Maybe they cultivate their own predators," replied Curling-Sixth-Finger, "specifically to keep their population in check. There are – what?" She peered at the binary numbers beneath the blocky drawings. "Six billion of the terrestrial forms? But only a few million of the aquatic adults."

"So it would seem," said Palm-Up-Middle-Fingers-Splayed. "It's interesting that their adult form returns to the water; on the world of that last star we visited, the larvae were aquatic and the adults were land-dwellers." He paused, then pointed at the right-hand figure's horizontally flattened tail. "They resemble the ancestral aquatic forms of our own kind from millions of years ago – even down to the horizontal tail fin."

Curling-Sixth-Finger spread her fingers in agreement. "Interesting. But, enough chat; there are important questions we have to ask these aliens."

Darren Hamasaki had just checked in at the Air Canada booth at the Las Vegas airport and was on his way to the Star Alliance lounge – his trip last year to see the eclipse in Europe had got him enough points to earn entry privileges – when Karyn Jones, one of Mayor Rivers's assistants, caught up with him.

"Darren!" she wheezed, touching his arm, and buying herself a few seconds to catch her breath.

"What is it?" said Darren, raising his eyebrows. "Did I forget something?"

"No, no, no," said Karyn, still breathing raggedly. "There's been a *reply.*"

"Already?" asked Darren. "But that's not possible. Groom-bridge 1618 is 4.9 parsecs away."

Karyn looked at him as though he were speaking a foreign language. After a moment, she simply repeated, "There's been a reply."

Darren glanced down at his boarding pass. Karyn must have detected his concern. "Don't worry," she said. "We'll get you another flight." She touched his forearm again. "Come on!"

Of course, many observatories now routinely watched Groombridge 1618; it was under twenty-four hour surveillance from ground stations, and was frequently examined by Hubble, as well – not that a reply was expected soon, but there was always the possibility that the aliens would send another message of their own volition, prior to receiving a response from Earth. Even so, few in the astronomical community seriously believed the Groombridgeans would ever see the Las Vegas light show, and the United Nations was still debating whether to build a big laser to send an official reply.

And so, Darren saw the alien's response the same way most of the world did: on CNN.

And a *response* it surely was, for in layout and design it precisely matched the message Mayor Rivers had arranged to be sent. The aliens were bipedal, with broad, flat tails like those of beavers; *Tailiens* was a word the CNN commentator was already using to describe them. Their heads sported V-shaped mouths, and arms projected from either side of the head. There was something strange about their abdomens, though: a single column of zero bits – blank pixels – ran down the length of the chest; what it signified, Darren had no idea.

CNN took away the graphic of the message and replaced it with the anchor's face. "Do you have it on videotape?" asked Darren. "I want to examine the message in detail."

"No," said Karyn. "But it's on the CNN web site." She pointed to an iMac sitting across the room; sure enough, the graphic was displayed on its screen. Darren bounded over to it. He was still trying to take it all in, trying to discern whatever details he could. In the background, he could hear the CNN anchor talking to a female biologist: "As you can see," the scientist said, "the aliens presumably evolved from an aquatic ancestor, not unlike our own fishy forebears. Our limbs are positioned where they are because those were the locations of the pectoral and pelvic fins of the lobe-finned fish we evolved from. This creature's ancestors presumably had its front pair of fins further forward, which is why the arms ended up growing out of the base of the head, instead of the shoulders, and . . ."

Darren tried to shut out the chatter. His attention was caught by the string of pixels beneath the alien figure.

The very long string of pixels . . .

The crew of the *Ineluctable* hadn't bothered to send an image of a juvenile of their kind alongside the adult; unlike the strange beings they were now communicating with, they had no larval form – babies looked just like miniature adults.

Palm-Up-Middle-Fingers-Splayed and the others didn't wait for another reply from the denizens of the third planet before flashing a series of additional pictures at them. These were standard images, already prepared, showing details of <hand-sign-naming-his-species> physiology at a much higher resolution than that used for the earlier message. The aliens, after all, had seemed willing to reveal their own body form – or forms, given the two lifestages depicted in their first missive. Perhaps they would respond with more details about their own kind.

And then they could determine whether these people and the members of <hand-sign-naming-his-species> would be able to share a world together.

"They're not at Groombridge 1618," Darren said to Mayor Rivers, when His Honor arrived shortly after midnight; the mayor's toupee had been hastily perched and now sat somewhat askew atop his head. "They can't be. Assuming they responded immediately upon receipt of our message, they're only a few light-*hours* away – about the distance Pluto is from the Earth, although, of course, they're well above the plane of the solar system." Darren frowned. "They *must* be in a spaceship, but . . . but, no, no, that can't be right. Every observatory on Earth has been taking the spectra of the laser flashes, and they're dead on the D1 sodium line, which can't be a coincidence. The senders are using a line that's weak in their home star but very strong in our own sun's spectrum to signal us. But, like I said, it's *dead on* that line, meaning there's no Doppler shift. But if the ship was coming towards us, the light from the laser would be blue-shifted, and –"

"And if it were a-flyin' away from us," said Mayor Rivers, "it would be red-shifted."

Darren looked at His Honor, surprised. Rivers lifted his shoulders a bit. "Hey, we're not all hicks down here, you know."

Darren smiled. "But if the light isn't undergoing a Doppler shift, then –"

"Then," said Rivers, "the starship must be holdin' station, somewhere out there near the edge of the solar system."

Darren nodded. "I wonder why they don't come closer?"

The next night, Darren found himself flipping channels in his hotel room – they'd put him back in the Hilton. Letterman did a top-ten list of people who would make the best ambassadors to visit the aliens ("Number four: Robert Downey, Jr., because he's been damn near that high already"). And Leno did a "Jay Walking" segment, asking people on the street basic questions about space; Darren was appalled that one person said the sun revolved around the Earth, and that another declared that Mars was "millions of light-years" away.

After that, though, he switched to *Nightline*, which had some more-serious discussion of the aliens. Ted Koppel was interviewing a guy named Quentin Fawcett, who was billed as an "astrobiologist."

"I've been studying the anatomical charts that the Tailiens sent us," said Fawcett, whose long hair was tied into a ponytail. "I think I've figured out why they don't use radio."

Koppel played the stooge well. "You figured that out from anatomical charts? What's anatomy got to do with it?"

"Can we have the first slide?" asked Fawcett. A graphic appeared on the monitor between Koppel and Fawcett, and, a second later, the image on Hamasaki's hotel-room TV filled with the same image, as the director cut to it. "Look at this," said Fawcett's voice.

"That's the one they're calling three-dash-eleven, isn't it?" said Koppel. "The eleventh picture from the third group of signals the Tailiens sent."

"That's right. Now, what do you see?"

The TV image changed back to a two-shot of Koppel and Fawcett, both looking at their own monitor. "It's the Tailien head," said Koppel. And indeed it was, drawn out like an alligator's.

"Look carefully at the mouth," said Fawcett.

Koppel shook his head. "I'm sorry; I'm not getting it."

"That's not a picture of the head, you know. It's a picture of the Tailien cranium – the skull."

"Yes?"

"It's all one bone," said Fawcett triumphantly. "There's no separate mandible, no movable jaw. The mouth is just a boomerang-shaped opening in a solid head."

Koppel frowned. "So you're saying they couldn't articulate? I guess it *would* be hard to talk without a hinged jaw." He nodded. "No talking, no radio."

"No, it's not the ability to make sounds that depends on the advent of jaws. It's the ability to *hear* sounds, or, at least, to hear them clearly and distinctly."

Koppel waited for Fawcett to go on. "I've got TMJ – temporomandibular-joint syndrome," said Fawcett, tapping his temple. "Discomfort where the jaw articulates with the temporal bone; it's pretty common. Well, last winter, I had an infection in my ear canal – 'swimmer's ear,' they called it. Except I didn't know it for the longest time; I thought the pain was from my TMJ. Why? Because our ears are located right over our jaw joints – and that's no coincidence. The small bones in our inner ear – the hammer, the anvil, and the stirrup – make our acute hearing possible, and they exist precisely because the skull splits there into the cranium and the jaw. Our earliest vertebrate ancestors were jawless fish – fish with heads very much like the Tailiens still seem to have, consisting of one solid piece of bone."

Koppel was coming up to speed. "So . . . so, what? They take in soft food through permanently open mouths? No chewing?"

"Perhaps," said Fawcett. "Or maybe that slit that runs down their torsos is a feeding orifice. But, either way, I'm willing to bet that they don't depend on sound for communication."

Darren worked with an illustrator from the Las Vegas *Review-Journal* and a doctor from the UNLV Medical Center coding a series of human-anatomy diagrams, but no one quite knew how to send them. It would take more than a day of flashing the city's lights on and off – the power could only be cycled so quickly – to send even one of these high-resolution images, and the casinos wouldn't stand for it. Every minute the power was off cost them tens of thousands of dollars in betting revenues.

But, before they'd figured out how to reply, a new set of messages – batch number four – arrived from the Tailiens.

Palm-Up-Middle-Fingers-Splayed personally supervised the sending of the next messages, since he'd been the one who had coded them. They were designed to convey a series of simple multiple-choice questions. The messages consisted of 23 rows of 79 columns, much smaller than the anatomical charts. Fist-Held-Sideways had opined that bandwidth might be a problem for the third planet in sending similar messages, which is presumably why no response had yet been received.

The top part of each message showed a simple math problem, and the bottom part showed three possible answers, one of which was correct. The boxes containing these answers were labeled, from left to right, with one pixel, two pixels, and three pixels respectively in their upper right-hand corners.

Palm-Up-Middle-Fingers-Splayed, Fist-Held-Sideways, and the rest awaited the answers from the third planet; nothing less than a perfect score on the test would be morally acceptable before they asked the most important question of all.

The aliens seemed to have no trouble reading the flashing of Las Vegas's lights, and so the responses to the math problems were sent by that city winking itself on and off. Many of the hundred thousand people who had come to Nevada to be part of the first signaling effort were still in town, thrilled that an actual dialogue between humans and aliens seemed to be opening up.

Fortunately for the croupiers and pit bosses, the math problems only took seconds to reply to; all that had to be sent was the number of the box containing the correct answer: one flash, two flashes, or three flashes.

"There's no doubt," signed Palm-Up-Middle-Fingers-Splayed to Captain Curling-Sixth-Finger, "that the aliens understand our syntax. They clearly know how to give the correct response to a multiple-choice question – and they got all the answers right, even the one about division by zero."

"Very well," said Curling-Sixth-Finger, her fingers moving slowly, deliberately. She clearly was steeling herself, in case she had to repeat the action she'd been forced to take at the last star system. "Ask them the big one."

The next message was, in the words of Larry King, who had Darren Hamasaki on his show to talk about it, "a real poser."

"It looks," said King, leaning forward on his desk, his red suspenders straining as he did so, "like they're asking us something about DNA, isn't that right, Mr. Hamasaki?"

"That does seem to be the case," said Darren.

"Now, I don't know much about genetics," said King, and he looked briefly into the camera, as if to make clear that he was speaking on behalf of his viewing audience in confessing this ignorance, "but in *USA Today* this morning there was an article saying that it didn't make sense that the aliens were talking to us about DNA. I mean, DNA is what life on Earth is based on, but it isn't necessarily what alien life will be based on, no? Aren't there other ways to make life?"

"Oh, there might very well indeed be," said Darren, "although, you know, try as we might, no one has come up with a good computer model for any other form of self-replicating biochemistry. But I don't think it matters. Life didn't begin on Earth, after all. It was imported here, and –"

"It *was*?" King's eyebrows shot up toward his widow's peak. "Who says so?"

"Lots of biologists – more and more each day. You know, the initial problem with Darwin's theory of evolution was this: it was clear that the process of natural selection would take a long time to develop complex life forms – but there was no evidence that the Earth was particularly old; we didn't have any proof that it was old until the discovery of radioactivity. Then, when we found that Earth was *billions* of years old, it seemed that there was plenty of time for evolution. But now we've run into another not-enough-time problem: the oldest known fossils are 4.0 billion years old, and they're reasonably complex, which means if life were indigenous to Earth, the first self-replicating molecules would have had to appeared only a few hundred million years after the solar system was born, 4.5 billion years ago."

"We're going to get letters, I know it," said King, "from people disputing those age claims. But go on."

"Well, that early on, Earth was still being bombarded by meteors and comets; extinction-level events would have been common. Earth simply wouldn't have presented a stable environment for life."

"So you think life came here from outer space?"

"Almost certainly. Some biologists believe that it arose first on Mars – Mars was much drier than Earth, even back then. A comet or asteroid impact has a much greater destabilizing effect on the climate if it hits water than it does if it hits dry land. But the original DNA on Earth could have also come from outside the solar system – meaning, in fact, that these Tailiens might be our distant, distant relatives. All life in this part of the galaxy might share a common ancestor, if you go back far enough."

"Fascinating," said King. "Now, what about this latest message from the Tailiens? Can you take us through that?"

"Well, the top picture shows what looks to be a snippet of DNA, three codons long."

"Codons?"

"Sorry. Words in the DNA language. We read the language a letter at a time: A, C, G, or T. And since A and T always bond together, and G always bonds with C, we can just read the letters off one half of the DNA ladder and know automatically what the letters down the other side will be."

King nodded.

"Well," continued Darren, "each group of three letters – ACG, say, or TAT – is a word, specifying one amino acid, and amino acids are the building blocks of life. What we have in the first picture is a snippet of DNA consisting of nine letters, or three words. Next to that, there's space for another snippet of DNA the same length, see? As if you were supposed to place one of the strings from the lower section up here beside this one."

"And how do we choose which one should go there?"

Darren frowned. "That's a very good question, Larry." It was cool getting to call him Larry. He looked at his cheat-sheet on the desktop. "The sequence in the top part of the message is CAC,

TCA, and GTC, which codes, at least here on Earth, for the amino acids histidine, serine, and valine."

"Okay," said King.

"And the three possible replies are below. Two of them are strings of DNA. The first one – in answer box one – is a string of DNA very similar to the one above. It reads as CAC – the same as before; TTA – which is one nucleotide different from the string on the top, so it codes for, umm, let me see, for leucine instead of serine; and then there's GTC again, which is valine, just as before."

"So it differs by only one-ninth from the specimen at the top," said Larry. "A close relative, you might say."

Darren nodded. "Exactly. And that brings us to the second possible response. Like the first possible response, it consists of nine codons, but here the codons don't match at all – the sequence is completely different from the one above. And, if you look carefully, you'll see it's not just frameshifted out of synch from the sample above; it really has nothing in common with it. Nor could it be a possible match for the other side of the DNA ladder, because it doesn't have the same pattern of duplicated letters."

"So that second string of DNA represents a distant relative – if it's a relative at all," said King. "Would that be right?"

"It's as good a guess as any," said Darren.

"And the third possible answer?" asked King.

"That's the puzzler," said Darren. "The third answer box is empty; blank. There's nothing in it except three pixels in the upper right, which just indicate that it *is* the third possible answer."

"Have we ever seen an empty box like that before in one of the Tailiens' messages?" asked King.

"Yes," said Darren. "It was in message four-dash-twelve, one of the math problems. They asked us what the correct answer to six divided by zero is. The possible answers they gave us were six, one, and a blank box."

"And – wait a second, wait a second – you can't divide by zero, can you?"

"That's right; it's a meaningless concept: how many times does nothing go into something? So, in that case, we chose the empty box as our answer."

"And what's the correct answer this time?" asked King.

Darren spread his arms, just as he'd seen dozens of other people – including many working scientists, rather than hobbyists like him – do today on other talk shows when asked the same question. "I haven't the slightest idea."

Everybody had hoped that other messages would continue to come from the Tailiens. Just as they had gone on to send the math problems after receiving no reply to the anatomy diagrams, humanity hoped that they would continue sending questions or information before a reply was sent.

But the Tailiens didn't. They seemed to be intent on waiting for a response to the DNA puzzle.

And, finally, the United Nations decided that one should indeed be sent. By this point, Darren was pretty much out of the spotlight – and glad of it. The United Nations secretary-general himself was coming to Las Vegas to initiate the blinking of the city's lights. That was fine with Darren; he wasn't sure that the UN scientists had come up with the right answer, and he didn't want sending an incorrect reply to be on his head.

The answer the UN had decided to go with was number one: the DNA that was similar, but not identical, to the sample string. There were various rationales offered for supposing that it was the correct response. Some said it was obvious: the aliens were moving us beyond questions of absolute truth, the kind of clear right or wrong that went with mathematical expressions; this new message was designed to test our ability to think in terms of similarity, of soft relationships. Although none of the three choices matched the sample string, the first one was the most similar.

Another interpretation was that it was a test of our knowledge of evolution. Did new species (the blank space to the right of the sample string) emerge by gradual changes (answer one, with its single nucleotide difference); by complete genetic redesign (answer two, with its totally dissimilar DNA); or out of nothing – that is, through creationist processes?

Some of the fundamentalists at the UN argued that the third answer was therefore the proper one: the aliens were testing our righteousness before deciding whether to admit us to the galactic club. But others argued that everything the aliens had presented so far was scientific – mathematics, anatomical charts, DNA – and that the scientific answer was the only one to give: new species arose by incremental changes from old ones.

Regardless of whether it was a question about inexact relationships or about the principles of evolution, answer one would be the correct response. And so the lights of Las Vegas were turned off one last time in a single, knowing wink at the heavens.

Palm-Up-Middle-Fingers-Splayed happened to be in the communications room when the response was received from the third planet. Of course, regardless of what answer they'd chosen, it would begin with one stretch of darkness, so Palm-Up-Middle-Fingers-Splayed waited . . . and waited . . . and waited for a second and third.

But more darkness never came. Palm-Up-Middle-Fingers-Splayed's tail twitched.

He had to tell Captain Curling-Sixth-Finger, of course; indeed, the computer had probably already informed her that a response was being received, and she was presumably even now making her way down the spoke from her command module, and –

And there she was now: twice Palm-Up-Middle-Fingers-Splayed's size, and capable of the kind of fierceness only a female could muster.

"What is the response?" demanded Curling-Sixth-Finger as she floated into the room.

"One," signed Palm-Up-Middle-Fingers-Splayed with restrained, sad movements. "They chose answer one."

Curling-Sixth-Finger's feeding slit momentarily opened, exposing slick pink tissue within. "So be it," she signed with her left hand, and "So be it" she repeated with her right.

Palm-Up-Middle-Fingers-Splayed whipped his tail back and forth in frustration. It was such a straightforward question: when seeking other life forms to associate with, do you choose (1) the being most closely related to you genetically; (2) the being least related to you genetically; or (3) is it impossible to answer this question based on genetics?

Answer three, of course, was the morally right answer; any advanced being must know that. Oh, it was true that primitive animals sought to protect and favor those with whom they shared many genes, but the very definition of civilization was recognizing that nepotism was not the engine that should drive relationships.

Perhaps, reflected Palm-Up-Middle-Fingers-Splayed, such enlightenment had come more easily to his people, for with partners changing every mating season, genetic relationships were complex and diffuse. The race inhabiting the second planet of the star they had last visited had chosen the wrong answer, too; they'd also picked the first choice.

And they'd paid the price for that.

If nepotism drives you as a species, if protecting those who are most closely related to you is paramount, if forming allegiances based on familial lines is at the core of your society, then how can you ever be trusted in relationships with beings that are alien to you? Yes, it seemed all life, at least in this neighborhood of the galaxy, was based on DNA, and therefore was quite possibly related in its distant, distant past. But, then again, all creatures on any given world also share a common ancestor. And yet –

And yet these benighted souls of the third planet still chose genetic favoritism; indeed, they were so convinced of its righteousness, convinced that it was the proper order of things, that they didn't even attempt to disguise it by giving a false answer. Those poor creatures, prisoners of their own biology . . .

Curling-Sixth-Finger was already on the intercom, calling down to the propulsion room, telling Fist-Held-Sideways to engage the fusion motors. Palm-Up-Middle-Fingers-Splayed felt an invisible hand pressing down upon him, driving him to the floor, as the great engines came to life. As he and Curling-Sixth-Finger settled to deck plates, Palm-Up-Middle-Fingers-Splayed looked up at her.

"I've got no choice," she signed. "A species driven by selfish genes is too dangerous to be allowed to live."

Palm-Up-Middle-Fingers-Splayed slowly, sadly spread his fingers in agreement. The *Ineluctable* would dive down into the plane of the solar system, into the cometary belt just past the orbit of the eighth planet, and it would launch a series of comets on trajectories that would send them sailing in for eventual rendezvous with the third planet.

Oh, it would take time – thousands of years – before the impacts. But eventually they *would* strike, and two skyswoopers would be felled with a single rock: the galaxy would have one less selfish species to worry about, and, with most of its native life wiped out, there would be room – a whole new world! – to move billions and billions of members of <hand-sign-naming-his-species> to.

Palm-Up-Middle-Fingers-Splayed was glad that Fist-Held-Sideways and the other females were no longer in estrus. He didn't feel like making love, didn't feel like making babies.

Not now. Not right now.

But, of course, he *would* want to do that again the next time the females came into heat. He, too, he reflected, was a prisoner of biology – and for one brief moment, that shared reality made him feel a bond with the aliens that now, sadly, he would never meet.

Speeches

The 2003 Hugo Awards Ceremony

The best thing that ever happened to me professionally occurred on Saturday, August 30, 2003, at about 10:00 p.m. At Torcon 3, the sixty-first World Science Fiction Convention, I won the Hugo Award for Best Novel of the Year for my novel Hominids, *first volume of the "Neanderthal Parallax" trilogy. The other nominees were* Bones of the Earth *by Michael Swanwick,* Kiln People *by David Brin,* The Scar *by China Miéville, and* The Years of Rice and Salt *by Kim Stanley Robinson.*

This had been my sixth Hugo nomination; I'd most recently lost the award in 2001, when J. K. Rowling's Harry Potter and the Goblet of Fire *beat my* Calculating God. *Here's what I said when I won . . .*

First off, I'd like to thank J. K. Rowling for being late delivering the manuscript of *The Order of the Phoenix*, so that it didn't come out until 2003.

I guess since there was no Harry Potter on the ballot, a hairy Ponter was the next-best thing . . .

I'd also like to thank the Hugo administrators for deciding that Neil Gaiman's book *Coraline* was really a novella rather than a novel. I've never been so thrilled by a word-count statistic in my life.

Seriously, though, I'd very much like to express to my fellow nominees – Dave, Stan, Michael, and China – what an honor it's been for the last few months to share a ballot with you guys.

My thanks go, of course, to Stanley Schmidt, Sheila Williams, and everyone at *Analog*, where *Hominids* was first published, in the form of a serial.

My thanks also go to Tor Books, particularly my publisher Tom Doherty, editors David G. Hartwell and Moshe Feder – plus art director Irene Gallo, and artist Donato who were responsible for the wonderful covers for my Neanderthal books.

And of course, thanks to my agent, Ralph Vicinanza, who does everything in his power to put the screws on my behalf to those kind people at Tor.

Here in Canada, my books do better than I would have ever thought possible, thanks to Tor's Canadian distributor, H. B. Fenn and Company.

My thanks to Harold and Sylvia Fenn, Rob Howard, Heidi Winter, Melissa Cameron, David Leonard, Steve St. Amant, David Cuthbertson, Leo MacDonald, and everyone else who works there.

Most of all, though, I want to thank science fiction fandom.

Everything good in my life I owe to fandom.

All the best friends I've had came from fandom, including the members of my high-school science fiction club, NASFA, some of whom are here tonight – hi, Ted and Gillian!

It was also at fannish events that I first got to know my mentors and colleagues, John Robert Colombo, Terence M. Green, Andrew Weiner, and Edo van Belkom.

And many thanks for the wonderful support to the members of the fan group I'm currently a proud member of, the *USS Hudson Bay*.

It was also through fandom that I met Sally Tomasevic and Marcel Gagne, the two dudes to whom *Hominids* is dedicated.

Most important of all, though, I also met my wife Carolyn Clink through fandom.

Without her, I'd be just a fat, bald, geek who knows way too much *Star Trek* trivia. Okay – even *with* her, I'm just a fat, bald, geek who knows way too much *Star Trek* trivia, but it's a lot more fun having her along for the ride. Carolyn, I love you totally and completely.

Along with Carolyn came her family – David, Patty, Melissa, and Megan are here tonight.

And . . . and . . . I – I only wish my mother could have seen this . . . but . . . but . . . but it's over a hundred bucks for a day pass to the con!

Seriously, though, fandom also lets me have the best job in the universe: writing science fiction. And now it's given me the single greatest honor of my life. Thank you all, very, very much!

The Future Is Already Here

On November 10, 1999, I gave this speech at the Library of Congress in Washington, D.C. (staying with my great buddy Roger MacBride Allen while visiting town); I enjoyed giving the speech but an even bigger thrill was the behind-the-scenes tour.

Among those in the audience were Richard Lynch, co-editor of the wonderful fanzine Mimosa; *SF writer Roger MacBride Allen; and British academic Farah Mendlesohn, who requested permission to reprint my speech in* Foundation: The International Review of Science Fiction; *it appeared in the Autumn 2000 edition, with a smiling photo of me as the cover illustration.*

This was my first major public-speaking gig. Since then, I've signed up with Speakers' Spotlight, one of Canada's top speakers' bureaus, and have been enjoying a very interesting, and, I must say, lucrative, sideline giving talks at conferences such as the Second International Symposium on Physical Sciences in Space, the 2003 conference of the New York Library Association, the 2004 Annual Meeting of the Canadian Association of Science Centres, and BioMedex 2004, a conference devoted to the biopharmaceutical industry.

There are countless definitions for that amorphous entity we call science fiction, but one of the most succinct is that employed by Kim Stanley Robinson, author of the famed *Mars* trilogy: "Science fiction stories are stories set in the future." And, of course, for decades now, we've thought of the 21st century, the dawn of the third millennium, as the very embodiment of the future.

But now, the future is here. We're right on the doorstep of the 21st century, and, indeed, the year 2001, with all the resonances that magic figure has had for us since the film of the same name debuted thirty-odd years ago, will soon be a historical date.

If the future is already here, what role does science fiction have in it? Was SF a literature of the 20th century, the way gothic romances were a literature of the 19th? Or is there a place – a societal role – for science fiction in the new millennium?

To answer that question, it's necessary, of course, to define the current societal role of science fiction, and that role, I firmly believe, comes out of the central message of most of the memorable, ambitious stories in the genre.

Now, of course, there are those who think that fiction is not the place for messages: "If you want to send a message, call Western Union" – the old American telegram company – used to be standard advice given in creative-writing classes. Still, whether the authors are consciously aware of it or not, all fiction does convey messages or fundamental moral statements.

Before I delve into what the central message is for science fiction, let's set the stage by first looking at another genre closely allied with science fiction – another category with its own publishing imprints and dedicated magazines. I'm talking about mystery fiction.

What is the fundamental message present in every mystery story? There's one that, in fact, is virtually required – without it, the story falls completely apart. The central moral statement of all mystery fiction is this: "Don't commit murder, because you won't get away with it." In just about every mystery novel, a character tries to take the life of another human being. And in just about every one, despite clever planning on the part of the murderer, the killer is brought to justice.

Now, let's assess how successful the writers of mystery fiction have been at convincing the general public of the truth of their fundamental assertion "Don't commit murder, because you won't get away with it." Do we still have murder? Yes. Are murder rates decreasing? No. Despite hundreds of thousands of iterations on this theme in mystery stories from Edgar Allan Poe through Agatha Christie to Sara Paretsky – a theme which, put another way, is often stated as, "There's no such thing as a perfect crime" – there has been no societal change. Murder is rampant.

And that's good news for the mystery-fiction writers of the world. It means they have job security. It means they still have work to do. It means their message still needs to be heard.

But what about me and my colleagues? What of the SF writers of the world? How good have we been at communicating our central message? And, indeed, what *is* the central message of SF?

To my way of thinking, the central message of science fiction is this: "Look with a skeptical eye at new technologies." Or, as William Gibson has put it, "the job of the science-fiction writer is to be profoundly ambivalent about changes in technology."

Now, certainly, there *are* science-fiction writers who use the genre for pure scientific boosterism: science can do no wrong; only the weak quail in the face of new knowledge. Jerry Pournelle, for instance, has rarely, if ever, looked at the downsides of progress. But most of us, I firmly believe, do take the Gibsonian view: we are not techie cheerleaders, we aren't flacks for big business or entrepreneurism, we don't trade in utopias.

Neither, of course, are we Luddites. Michael Crichton writes of the future, too, but he's not really a science-fiction writer; if anything, he's an *anti*-science-fiction writer.

Indeed, both Gregory Benford and I have discussed with our shared agent, Ralph Vicinanza, why it is that Crichton outsells us. And Ralph explained that he could get deals at least approaching those Crichton gets if – and this was an unacceptable "if" to both me and Greg – we were willing to promulgate the same fundamental message Crichton does, namely, that science always goes wrong.

When Michael Crichton makes robots, as he did in *Westworld*, they run amuck, and people die. When he clones dinosaurs, as he did in *Jurassic Park*, they run amuck and people die. When he finds extraterrestrial life, as he did in *The Andromeda Strain*, people die.

Crichton isn't a prophet; rather, he panders to the fear of technology so rampant in our society – a society, of course, which ironically would not exist without technology. His mantra is clearly the old B-movie one that "there are some things man was not meant to know."

The writers of real SF refuse to sink to fear-mongering, but neither do we overindulge in boosterism – both are equally mindless activities.

Still, we do have an essential societal role, one being fulfilled by no one else. Actual scientists are constrained in what they can say – even with tenure, which supposedly ensures the right to pursue any line of inquiry, scientists are in fact muzzled at the most fundamental, economic level. They cannot speculate openly about the potential downsides of their work, because they rely on government grants or private-sector consulting contracts.

Well, the government is answerable to an often irrational public. If a scientist is dependent on government grants, those grants can easily disappear. And if he or she is employed in the private sector, well, then certainly Motorola doesn't want you to say cellular phones might cause brain cancer; Dow Chemical didn't want anyone to say that silicone implants might cause autoimmune problems; Philip Morris doesn't want anyone to say that nicotine might be addictive.

Granted, not all those potential dangers turned out to be real, but even considering them, putting them on the table for discussion, was not part of the game plan; indeed, suppressing possible negatives is key to how all businesses, including those built on science and technology, work.

There are moments – increasingly frequent moments – during which the media reports that, "Science fiction has become science fact." Certainly one of the most dramatic recent ones was made public in February 1997. Ian Wilmut at Roslin Institute in Edinburgh had succeeded in taking an adult mammalian cell and producing an exact genetic duplicate: the cloning of the sheep named Dolly.

Dr. Wilmut was interviewed all over the world, and, of course, every reporter asked him about the significance of his work, the ramifications, the effects it would have on family life. And his response was doggedly the same, time and again: cloning, he said, had narrow applications in the field of animal husbandry.

That was all he *could* say. He couldn't answer the question directly. He couldn't tell reporters that it was now technically possible for a man who was 35 years old, who had been drinking too much, and smoking, and never exercising, a man who had been warned by his doctor that his heart and lungs and liver would all give out by the time he was in his early fifties, to now order up an exact genetic duplicate of himself, a duplicate that by the time he needed all those replacement parts would be sixteen or seventeen years old, with pristine, youthful versions of the very organs that needed replacing, replacements that could be transplanted with zero chance of tissue rejection.

Why, the man who needed these organs wouldn't even have to go to any particular expense – just have the clone of himself created, put the clone up for adoption – possibly even an illegal adoption, in which the adopting parents pay money for the child, a common enough if unsavory practice, letting the man recover the costs of the cloning procedure. Then, let the adoptive parents raise the child with their money, and when it is time to harvest the organs, just track down the teenager, and kidnap him, and – well, you get the picture. Just another newspaper report of a missing kid.

Far-fetched? Not that I can see; indeed, there may be adopted children out there right now who, unbeknownst to them or their guardians, are clones of the wunderkinds of Silicon Valley or the lions of Wall Street. But the man who cloned Dolly couldn't speculate on this possibility, or any of the dozens of other scenarios that immediately come to mind. He couldn't speculate because if he did, he'd be putting his future funding at risk. His continued ability to do research depended directly on him keeping his mouth shut.

The same mindset was driven home for me quite recently. I am co-hosting a two-hour documentary called "Inventing the Future: 2000 Years of Discovery" for the Canadian version of The Discovery Channel, and in November 1999 I went to Princeton University to interview Joe Tsein, who created the "Doogie Mice" – mice that were born more intelligent than normal mice, and retained their smarts longer.

While my producer and the camera operator fussed setting up the lighting, Dr. Tsein and I chatted animatedly about the ramifications of his research, and there was no doubt that he and his colleagues understood how far-reaching they would be. Indeed, by the door to Dr. Tsein's lab, not normally seen by the public, is a cartoon of a giant rodent labeled "Doogie" sitting in front of a computer. In Doogie's right hand is his computer's pointing device – a little human figure labeled "Joe": the super-smart mouse using its human creator as a computer mouse.

Finally, the camera operator was ready, and we started taping. "So, Dr. Tsein," I said, beginning the interview, "how did you come to create these super-intelligent mice?"

And Tsein made a "cut" motion with his hand, and stepped forward, telling the camera operator to stop. "I don't want to use the word 'intelligent,'" he said. "We can talk about the mice having better memories, but not about them being smarter. The public will be all over me if they think we're making animals more intelligent."

"But you *are* making them more intelligent," said my producer. Indeed, Tsein had used the word "intelligent" repeatedly while we'd been chatting.

"Yes, yes," he said. "But I can't say that for public consumption."

The muzzle was clearly on. We soldiered ahead with the interview, but never really got what we wanted. I'm not sure if Tsein was a science-fiction fan, and he had no idea that I was also a science-fiction writer, but many SF fans have wondered why Tsein didn't name his super-smart mice "Algernons," after the experimental rodent in Daniel Keyes's *Flowers for Algernon*.

Tsein might have been aware of the reference, but chose the much more palatable "Doogie" — a tip of the hat to the old TV show *Doogie Howser, M.D.*, about a boy-genius who becomes a medical doctor while still a teenager — because, of course, in *Flowers for Algernon*, the leap is made directly from the work on mice to the mind-expanding possibilities for humans, and Tsein was clearly trying to restrain, not encourage, such leaps.

So, we're back to where we started: *someone* needs to openly do the speculation, to weigh the consequences, to consider the ramifications — someone who is immune to economic pressures. And that someone is the science-fiction writer.

And, of course, we do precisely that — and have done so from the outset. Brian Aldiss, and many other critics, contend that the first science-fiction novel was Mary Shelley's *Frankenstein*, and I think they're right. In that novel, Victor is a scientist, and he's learned about reanimating dead matter by studying the process of decay that occurs after death. Take out his scientific training, and his scientific research, and his scientific theory, and, for the first time in the history of fiction, there's no story left. Like so much of the science fiction that followed, *Frankenstein*, first published in 1818, is a cautionary tale, depicting the things that can go wrong, in this case, with the notion of biological engineering.

Science-fiction writers have considered the pluses and minuses of other new technologies, too, of course. We were among the first to weigh in on the dangers of nuclear power – memorably, for instance, with Judith Merril's 1948 short story "That Only a Mother" – and, although there are still SF writers (often, it should be noted, with university or industry positions directly or indirectly involved in the defense industry) who have always sung the praises of nuclear energy, it's a fact that all over the world, governments are turning away from it.

The October 18, 1999, edition of *Newsweek* carried an article which said, "In most parts of the world, the chance of nuclear power plant accidents is now seen as too great. Reactor orders and start-ups have declined markedly since the 1980s. Some countries, including Germany and Sweden, plan to shut down their plants altogether . . . Nuclear-reactor orders and start-ups ranged from 20 to 40 per year in the 1980s; in 1997 there were just two new orders, and five start-ups worldwide. Last year [1998] construction began on only four new nuclear reactors."

Why the sharp decline? Because the cautionary scenarios about nuclear accidents in science fiction have, time and again, become science fact. The International Atomic Energy Agency reports that there were 508 nuclear "incidents" between 1993 and 1998, an average of more than one for each of the world's 434 operating nuclear power plants.

It certainly wasn't out of the scientific community that the warnings were first heard. I vividly recall being at a party about fifteen years ago at which I ran into an old friend from high school. She introduced me to her new husband, a nuclear engineer for Ontario Hydro, the company that operates the nuclear power plants near my home city of Toronto. I asked him what plans were in place in case something went wrong with one of the reactors (this was before the Chernobyl accident in 1986, but after Three Mile Island in 1979). He replied that nothing could go wrong; the system was foolproof. Although we were both early in our careers then, we were precisely fulfilling our respective societal roles. As an engineer employed by the nuclear industry, he had to say the plants were absolutely safe. As a science-fiction writer, I had to be highly skeptical of any such statements.

Science fiction has weighed in on ecology, overpopulation, racism, the abortion debate (which is also fundamentally a technological issue – the ability to terminate a fetus without harming the mother is a scientific breakthrough whose moral ramifications must be weighed), and, indeed, science-fiction has been increasingly considering what I think may be the greatest threat of all, the downsides of creating artificial intelligence. From William Gibson's Hugo-winning 1984 *Neuromancer* – in which an organization known as "Turing" exists to prevent the emergence of true AI – to my own Hugo-nominated 1998 *Factoring Humanity*, in which the one and only radio message Earth receives from another star is a warning against the creation of AI, a last gasp from biologicals being utterly supplanted by what they themselves had created without sufficient forethought.

Which brings us back to the central message of SF: "Look with a skeptical eye at new technologies." Has that message gotten through to the general public? Has society at large embraced it in a way that they never did embrace "Don't commit murder because you will never get away with it"?

And the answer, I think, is absolutely yes. Society has co-opted the science-fictional worldview wholly and completely. Do we now build a new dam just because we can? Not without an environmental-impact study. Do we put high-energy power lines near public schools? Not anymore. Did we all rush out to start eating potato chips made with Olestra, the fake fat that robs the body of nutrients and causes abdominal cramping and loose stools? No.

And what about the example I started with – cloning? Indeed, what about the whole area of genetic research?

Well, when the first Cro-Magnon produced the first stone-tipped wooden spear, none of his hirsute brethren stopped to think about the fact that whole species would be driven to extinction by human hunting. When the United States undertook the Manhattan Project, not one cent was budgeted for considering the societal ramifications of the creation of nuclear weapons – despite the fact that their existence, more than any other single thing, shaped the mindset of the rest of the century.

But for the Human Genome Project, fully five percent of the total budget is set aside for that thing SF writers love to do the most: just plain old noodling – thinking about the consequences, the impacts, that genetic research will have on society.

That money is allocated because the world now realizes that such thinking is indispensable. Of course, the general public doesn't think of it as science fiction – to them, thanks to George "I can't be bothered to look up the meaning of the word parsec"

Lucas, SF is the ultimate in escapism, irrelevant to the real world; it's fantasy stories that only happened a long time ago, in a galaxy far, far away.

I'm not alone in this view. Joe Haldeman has observed that *Star Wars* was the worst thing that ever happened to science fiction, because the general public now equates SF with escapism. According to *The American Heritage English Dictionary*, escapism is "the avoidance of reality through fantasy or other forms of diversion." I do *not* read SF for escapism, although I do read it for entertainment (which is the same reason I do a lot of my non-fiction reading). But I, and most readers of SF, have no interest in avoiding reality.

And yet, SF is seen as having nothing to do with the real world. At a family reunion in 1998, a great aunt of mine asked me what I'd been doing lately, and I said I'd spent the last several months conducting research for my next science-fiction novel. Well, my aunt, an intelligent, educated woman, screwed up her face, and said, "What possible research could you do for a science-fiction book?" SF to her, as to most of the world, is utterly divorced from reality; it's just crazy stuff we make up as we go along. And so the bioethicists, the demographers, the futurists, and the analysts, may not think of themselves as using the tools of science fiction – but they are.

Our mindset – the mindset honed in the pages of *Astounding*, the legacy of John Brunner and Isaac Asimov, of Judy Merril and Philip K. Dick – is now central to human thought. Science-fiction writers succeeded beyond their wildest dreams: they changed the way humanity looks at the world.

Years ago, Sam Moskowitz quipped that anyone could have predicted the automobile – but it would take a science-fiction writer to predict the traffic jam. In the 1960s, my fellow Canadian, Marshall McLuhan, made much the same point, saying that, contrary to the designers' intentions, every new technology starts out as a boon and ends up as an irritant.

But now, *everyone* is a science-fiction writer, even if they never spend any time at a keyboard. When a new technology comes along, we all look at it not with the wide eyes of a kid on Christmas morning, but with skepticism. The days when you could tell the public that a microwave oven would replace the traditional stove are long gone; we all know that new technologies aren't going to live up to the hype. About the only really interesting thing the microwave did was create the microwave-popcorn industry – and, of course, microwave popcorn, fast and convenient, is also loaded down with fatty oils to aid the popping, taking away the health benefits normally associated with that food item. The upside, the downside – popcorn, the science-fictional snack.

And what I'm talking about *is* a science-fictional, not a scientific, perspective. As Dr. David Stephenson, formerly with the National Research Council of Canada and a frequent science guest at SF conventions, has observed, scientists are taught from day one to write in the third-person passive voice: they distance themselves from their prose, removing from the discussion both the doer of the action and the person who is feeling the effects of the action.

But SF writers do what the scientists must not. We long ago left behind the essentially characterless storytelling practiced by such early writers as George O. Smith. We now strive for characterization as sophisticated as that in the best mainstream literature. Or, to put it another way, science fiction has evolved beyond being what its founding editor, Hugo Gernsback, said it should be: merely fiction about science. Indeed, even Isaac Asimov, known for a rather perfunctory approach to characterization, knew full well that SF was about the impact progress has on real people. His definition of science fiction was "that branch of literature that deals with the responses of human beings to changes in science and technology."

And those responses, of course, are often irrational, based on fear and ignorance. But they are responses that cannot be ignored: we – science-fiction readers and writers – *do* share this planet with the ninety percent of human beings who believe in angels, who believe in a literal heaven and hell, who reject evolution. As much as I admire Arthur C. Clarke – and I do, enormously – the most unrealistic thing about his fiction is how darn reasonable everyone is.

On May 31, 1999, CBC television had me appear on its current-affairs program *Midday* to discuss whether or not the space program was a waste of money; I was debating a woman who worked in social services who thought all money – including the tiny, tiny fraction of its gross domestic product that Canada, or even the U.S. for that matter, spends on space – should be used to address problems here on Earth.

And her clincher argument was this – I swear to God, I'm not making this up: "We should be careful about devoting too much time to science. The people who lived in Atlantis were obsessed with science, and that led to their downfall."

My response was to tell her that perhaps if she spent a little more time reading about science, she'd know that Atlantis was a myth, and she wouldn't make an ass out of herself on national television. But the point here – one that I will come back to – is this: she already understood the central 20th-century science-fictional premise of looking carefully at the ramifications of new technologies, such as space travel. But she was unable to look at them *rationally*, because of her faulty worldview, a worldview that rendered her incapable of separating myth from reality, fact from fiction.

If the central message of science fiction has indeed been co-opted by the public at large – if, as I think is true, Frank Herbert's *Dune* did as much to raise consciousness about ecology as did Rachel Carson's *Silent Spring* – then what role is there for science-fiction writers in the new century?

I always say whenever a discussion at a science-fiction convention brings in *Star Trek* as an example, we've hit rock bottom; you can't imagine Ruth Rendell turning to Scott Turow at a mystery-fiction conference and saying, "You know, that reminds me of that episode of *Murder, She Wrote*, in which . . .'" But I am going to invoke *Star Trek* here as an example of how quaint and embarrassing SF ends up looking when it continues to push an old message long after society has gotten the point.

In the original *Star Trek*, we saw women and black people in important positions. Uhura, the mini-skirted bridge officer, was hardly the most significant black example; much more important were the fact that Kirk's boss, as seen in the episode "Court-Martial," was a black man, played with quiet dignity by Percy Rodriguez, and that the ship's computers, as seen in "The Ultimate Computer," were designed by a Noble-prize-winning black cyberneticist, played with equal dignity by William Marshall.

During the era of Martin Luther King and the Watts riots, it was a powerful, important statement to have the white captain of the *Enterprise* deferring to black people; as Marshall observed thirty years later, the single most significant thing about his guest-starring role was that he, an African-American, was referred to as "Sir" throughout the episode.

But time passed. In 1993, Paramount made much of the fact that we were going to see a black man as the leader on *Star Trek: Deep Space Nine* – despite the fact that, by this point, blacks had been elected to prominent political positions throughout the United States, and even in South Africa, a bastion of racism in the 1960s, a black man, Nelson Mandela, was about to become president. But, somehow, *Star Trek* thought it was making a profound statement.

And then, just as embarrassingly, two years later, we were supposed to be stunned by the fact that on *Star Trek: Voyager*, a woman was the captain of a starship – this, despite the fact that countries from Great Britain to India to Canada had all already had female prime ministers, that women had risen to prominence in all walks of life.

My colleagues and I have long tried to reflect reality in our fiction, and so, naturally, we have diverse casts in our stories. Damon Knight's famous statement that the most unrealistic thing about science fiction is the preponderance of Americans – practically no one, he correctly observed, is an American – was no longer news to anybody. And, by all means, in a *Star Trek* of the 1990s we should indeed have seen women and non-whites in prominent roles. But to make it the *message*, to try to pass it off as a gutsy thing to do, looked ridiculous.

Indeed, David Gerrold famously quit working on *Star Trek: The Next Generation* back in 1987 in part because of that series' failure to address the reality that a lot of people are gay in its depiction of the future; *Star Trek* had become irrelevant, because the only messages it was comfortable sending out were ones already fully received by the audience.

And, I firmly believe, SF as a whole is now in danger of being perceived as just as quaint, just as dated, just as irrelevant, as the current *Star Trek* is.

In our search for a new role, should we fall back on the one the media has so often cast us in – that of predictors of the future? I don't think so. Many SF writers, myself included, are content to occasionally call themselves "futurists," if that helps get us TV or radio interviews, but we aren't really (indeed, I'm not sure that *anybody* really is, in the modern sense of the term, as someone who claims to be able to predict future trends; Bill Gates is the world's current technological leader – a futurist if ever there was one –

and he, of course, is the same man who once said that no one would ever need a computer with more than 640K of memory).

No, when what we science-fiction writers have written about comes to pass, it usually means society has screwed up. The last thing George Orwell wanted was for the real year 1984 to turn out anything like the vision portrayed in his novel.

Orwell, of course, wrote his book in 1948 – he simply reversed the last two digits to make it clear that he was really writing about his present day. Science fiction is indeed very much a literature of its time, and should, of course, be read in historical context.

Still, anyone who needs further convincing that science fiction isn't a predictive medium need only look at the events of the last few decades. Numerous science-fiction writers predicted that the first humans would set foot upon the moon in the 1960s, but none of us predicted that we would abandon the moon – indeed, all manned travel beyond Earth orbit – just three years later. Exactly twelve human beings have walked on the Moon; a mere dozen people (all white, all male, all American – hardly a representative sampling, but, then again, all of this occurred back when the original *Star Trek*'s message of an interracial future was one that hadn't yet been fully received)–and there is no sign that that number will increase in the next couple of decades.

We science-fiction writers also utterly missed the fall of the Soviet Union, something that now, in retrospect, seemed inevitable – indeed, it was amazing it lasted as long as it did. But we were writing books like Norman Spinrad's *Russian Spring* right up to the day of the collapse.

And, perhaps most significant of all, we completely missed the rise of the Internet and the World Wide Web. The genre that gave us Isaac Asimov's Multivac, Arthur C. Clarke's Hal 9000, Robert A. Heinlein's Mycroft Holmes, and even William Gibson's Wintermute completely failed to predict how the computer revolution was *really* going to unfold.

Of course when something new comes along – such as the terrible plague of AIDS – we're quick to weigh in with speculations. But we're usually so far off the mark that the results end up seeming laughable. Poor Norman Spinrad again: his vision of a world of people having sex with machines – instead of, of course, simply wearing condoms – because of the threat of AIDS, as outlined in his 1988 story "Journals of the Plague Years," seems absolutely ridiculous and alarmist when we look at it now, a scant decade later.

Some science-fiction writers still gamely try to set stories in the far future – a hundred, two hundred, a thousand years down the road. But the predictive horizon is moving ever closer. No one can make a prediction about what the world will be like even fifty years from now with any degree of confidence. What will be the fruits of the Human Genome Project? Will nanotechnology really work? Will true artificial intelligence emerge? Will cold fusion, or another clean, unlimited energy source, be developed? Will humans upload their consciousnesses into machines? And what wild cards – things we haven't even thought of yet – will appear?

As Bruce Sterling has observed, people in the future won't even eat; as Nancy Kress has postulated, with *Beggars in Spain*, they may not even sleep. What likely predictions could we possibly make about such beings?

In May 1967, Arthur C. Clarke revealed his now-famous "Third Law" during a speech to the American Association of Architects: "Any sufficiently advanced technology is indistinguishable from magic." The question, of course, is how far ahead of us is "sufficiently advanced" – and the answer, I believe is fifty years; the world of 2050 is utterly beyond our predictive abilities. With the accelerating rate of change, any year-2000 guess as to what 2050 would be like is almost certainly going to be as far off base as a guess Christopher Columbus might have had about what 2000 would be like.

The pressure for SF to change has been building for a long time. In North America, the sales of science fiction books that aren't related to *Star Trek*, *Star Wars*, or other media properties, are the worst they've ever been. Sales are down about fifty percent across the board from 1990, and the readerships of the principal SF magazines – *Analog* and *Asimov's* – have been cut in half. There is no doubt that the reading public is turning away from SF in droves.

The prime cause of the decline in SF readers is that today's young people are finding all the things that have always attracted young people to SF – big ideas, sense of wonder, action, wish-fulfillment fantasies, stunning visual imagery, nifty aliens, engaging characters – more readily in movies, TV, role-playing games, computer games, and on the Internet than in the pages of printed works.

There's no doubt that we've been outclassed in terms of visual imagery by the wizards at Industrial Light and Magic. Any space battle or alien vista we might care to describe they can realize more vibrantly in pictures than we can with words. To put it crudely: in the past, many of our finest SF writers, including Robert Silverberg and Mike Resnick, supplemented their income by writing pornographic novels. But there's almost no market left for porno fiction: what's now shown on videotape is much more vivid and real than anything the reader can imagine. Well, as went novels with titles like *Nurses in Need*, so, too, will go the space opera that was once a staple of printed SF.

SF *will* have to change if it is to survive. The public wants something other than what we've been giving them. One change we'll likely see is a move away from the far future as a setting for stories. I don't even think we need to invoke Kim Stanley Robinson's criterion that SF stories must be set in the future; I took great pleasure in setting my novel *Frameshift*, for instance, entirely in the present day, and suspect we'll see it become much more common for serious SF novels to have contemporary settings.

Indeed, if science fiction is going to have relevancy in the next century, it must assert itself to be part of real life, not far-off tales of escapism. And that brings me back to where we started. We need a new message for the new millennium. Far be it from me to try to impose an agenda on SF – but I think the agenda is already there, implicit in many of our texts, and, indeed, explicit in the actual name of our genre: *science* fiction.

One of the great intellectual embarrassments of the 20th century is that five hundred years after Copernicus deposed Earth from the centre of the universe, virtually every newspaper carries a daily astrology column – the horoscopes – but astronomy gets, at best, a column once a week, and in many papers not even that.

It's likewise embarrassing that a hundred and forty years after the publication of *The Origin of Species*, ignorant people are still succeeding in outlawing the teaching of the fact of evolution.

And it's mortifying that while the SF section of bookstores shrinks like a puddle under noonday sun, the "New Age" section – full of fabricated stories penned by charlatans – grows like a cancer.

If there is a message science fiction can promulgate for the 21st century – a message that the world needs to hear – it is this:

the rational, scientific worldview is the only perspective that effectively deals with reality.

And, at the risk of repeating myself, let me emphasize again that reality is indeed what science fiction is all about. I cringe with embarrassment every time I see that stupid t-shirt not quite concealing a massive belly at a science-fiction convention: "Reality is just a crutch for people who can't handle science fiction." What a ridiculous, offensive statement! Science fiction – in its probing of the deep questions, in its abiding concern with moral issues, in its unrelenting quest to expose truth and speculate on consequences, even in its most mind-bending explorations of the quantum nature of the universe – is, more than any other form of entertainment, absolutely about reality.

And reality is the totality of everything; not to invoke *Star Trek* again, but in the movie *Star Trek IV* it is revealed that Kiri-kin-tha's First Law of Metaphysics is that "nothing unreal exists," a statement no less profound than Descartes's "I think therefore I am."

The scientific method is the single greatest tool of understanding ever devised by humanity. Observe phenomena. Propose an explanation for why the phenomena are as they have been seen to be. Devise an experiment to test whether your explanation is correct. And, if that experiment fails – and this is the powerful part; this is where the beauty comes in – discard the explanation, and start over again.

There will be those who argue that there are other ways of gaining insight to the nature of reality: mystic experiences, contemplation in the absence of experimentation, divine insight, consulting ancient texts. Such methods are demonstrably inferior to the scientific method, for only the scientific method welcomes the detection of error; only the scientific method allows for independent verification and replication.

Now, some will say, well, that's the western view, and, after all, to paraphrase Damon Knight, hardly anyone is a westerner. Maybe so, but it must be recognized that science fiction *is*, in fact, a western genre. Fantasy, perhaps, can trace roots all over the world, but science fiction, born of Mary Shelley, nurtured by Jules Verne and H. G. Wells, grew out of the industrial revolution. It is inexorably tied up with western thought.

And the scientific method is the crowing glory of western thought – the glory that allowed us not to simply declare, as the

United States's founders did, that it is "self-evident that all men are created equal" while they still held slaves, but rather that allowed us to prove, through genetic studies that showed that genetic variation within races is greater than the average deviation between the races, and through psychological and anatomical studies that showed that the sexes are equally endowed intellectually, that in fact racism and sexism have no rational basis.

Stephen Jay Gould recently wrote a book called *Rocks of Ages: Science and Religion in the Fullness of Life*, in which he argues that the spiritual and the rational should have a "loving concordant," but are in fact "nonoverlapping magisteria" – utterly separate fields, with some questions solely appropriate to the former and others exclusively the province of the latter.

I reject that: I don't think there's *any* question, including the most basic philosophical conundrums of where did we come from, why are we here, what does it all mean, and, indeed, the biggest of them all, is there a God, that cannot be most effectively addressed through the application of the scientific method, especially with its absolute requirement that if an idea – such as the superstition of astrology – is disproven, then it must be willingly discarded.

How can science have anything meaningful to say about whether there is a God? Easily. If the universe had an intelligent designer, it will show signs of intelligent design. Some argue that it clearly does: the relative strengths of the four fundamental forces that drive our universe – gravitation, electromagnetism, the strong nuclear force, and the weak nuclear force – do seem to have been chosen with great care, since any substantial deviation from the present ratios would have resulted in a universe devoid of stars or even atoms.

Likewise, the remarkable thermal properties of water – most notably, that it expands as it freezes and that it has higher surface tension than any other fluid except liquid selenium – seem specifically jiggered to make life possible.

Do these facts prove whether or not God exists? No – not yet. But the best response to those who say science doesn't hold all the answers is to say, on the contrary, science does indeed hold all the answers – we just don't have all the science yet.

My favourite review of my own work was a recent one for *Flashforward* by Henry Mietkiewicz in *The Toronto Star*, who said,

"Sawyer compels us to think rationally about questions we normally consider too metaphysical to grapple with." But I'm hardly alone in this. Science fiction right back to such great works as Arthur C. Clarke's short story "The Star" and James Blish's *A Case of Conscience*, through Carl Sagan's *Contact*, and, more recently Mary Doria Russell's *The Sparrow*, and, if I may, my own Nebula-winning *The Terminal Experiment* and *Calculating God*, show that SF, because it embraces the scientific method, is the most effective tool for exploring the deepest of all questions.

So, *does* science fiction have a role in the 21st century? Absolutely. If we can help shape the Zeitgeist, help inculcate the belief that rational thought, that discarding superstition, that subjecting all beliefs to the test of the scientific method, is the most reasonable approach to any question, then not only will science fiction have a key role to play in the intellectual development of the new century, but it will also, finally and at last, help humanity shuck off the last vestiges of the supernatural, the irrational, the spurious, the fake, and allow us to embrace, to quote poet Archibald Lampman, "the wide awe and wonder of the night" but with our eyes wide open and our minds fully engaged. Then, finally, some 40,000 years after consciousness first flickered into being on this world, we will at last truly deserve that name we bestowed upon ourselves: *Homo sapiens* – Man of Wisdom.

AI and Sci-Fi: My, Oh, My!

On May 31, 2002, I gave this keynote address at the 12th Annual Conference on Intelligent Systems (a conference on robotics and artificial intelligence), which was held that year in Calgary.

Of course, I don't read my speeches word for word; I paraphrase them as I go along. But I discovered that there's a nice little secondary market for the text of speeches, and this one appeared in the essay collection Taking the Red Pill: Science, Philosophy and Religion in The Matrix *(Glenn Yeffeth, editor; Benbella Books, Dallas, April 2003) and also in the October 2002 issue of* The New York Review of Science Fiction.

Most fans of science fiction know Robert Wise's 1951 movie *The Day the Earth Stood Still.* It's the one with Klaatu, the humanoid alien who comes to Washington, D.C., accompanied by a giant robot named Gort, and it contains that famous instruction to the robot: *"Klaatu barada nikto."*

Fewer people know the short story upon which that movie is based: "Farewell to the Master," written in 1941 by Harry Bates.

In both the movie and the short story, Klaatu, despite his message of peace, is shot by human beings. In the short story, the robot – called Gnut, instead of Gort – comes to stand vigil over the body of Klaatu.

Cliff, a journalist who is the narrator of the story, likens the robot to a faithful dog who won't leave after his master has died. Gnut manages to essentially resurrect his master, and Cliff says to the robot, "I want you to tell your master . . . that what happened . . . was an accident, for which all Earth is immeasurably sorry."

And the robot looks at Cliff and astonishes him by very gently saying, "You misunderstand. I am the master."

That's an early science-fiction story about artificial intelligence — in this case, ambulatory AI, enshrined in a mechanical body. But it presages the difficult relationship that biological beings might have with their silicon-based creations.

Indeed, the word *robot* was coined in a work of science fiction: when Karl Capek was writing his 1920 play *RUR* — set in the factory of Rossum's Universal . . . well, universal *what?* He needed a name for mechanical laborers, and so he took the Czech word *robota* and shortened it to "robot." *Robota* refers to a debt to a landlord that can only be repaid by forced physical labor. But Capek knew well that the real flesh-and-blood *robotniks* had rebelled against their landlords in 1848. From the very beginning, the relationship between humans and robots was seen as one that might lead to conflict.

Indeed, the idea of robots as slaves is so ingrained in the public consciousness through science fiction that we tend not to even think about it. Luke Skywalker is portrayed in 1977's *Star Wars: A New Hope* as an absolutely virtuous hero, but when we first meet him, what is he doing? Why, buying slaves! He purchases two thinking, feeling beings — R2-D2 and C-3PO — from the Jawas. And what's the very first thing he does with them? He shackles them! He welds restraining bolts onto them to keep them from trying to escape, and throughout C-3PO has to call Luke "Master."

And when Luke and Obi-wan Kenobi go to the Mos Eisley cantina, what does the bartender say about the two droids? "We don't serve their kind in here" — words that only a few years earlier African-Americans in the southern US were routinely hearing from whites.

And yet, not one of the supposedly noble characters in *Star Wars* objects in the slightest to the treatment of the two robots, and, at the end, when all the organic characters get medals for their bravery, C-3PO and R2-D2 are off at the sidelines, unrewarded. Robots as slaves!

Now, everybody who knows anything about the relationship between science fiction and AI knows about Isaac Asimov's robot stories, beginning with 1940's "Robbie," in which he presented the famous Three Laws of Robotics. But let me tell you about one of his last robot stories, 1986's "Robot Dreams."

In it, his famed "robopsychologist" Dr. Susan Calvin makes her final appearance. She's been called in to examine Elvex, a mechanical man who, inexplicably, claims to be having dreams, something no robot has ever had before. Dr. Calvin is carrying an electron gun with her, in case she needs to wipe out Elvex: a mentally unstable robot could be a very dangerous thing, after all.

She asks Elvex what it was that he's been dreaming about. And Elvex says he saw a multitude of robots, all working hard, but, unlike the real robots he's actually seen, these robots were "down with toil and affliction . . . all were weary of responsibility and care, and [he] wished them to rest."

And as he continues to recount his dream, Elvex reveals that he finally saw one man in amongst all the robots:

> *"In my dream," [said Elvex the robot]* . . . *"eventually one man appeared."*
>
> *"One man?" [replied Susan Calvin.] "Not a robot?"*
>
> *"Yes, Dr. Calvin. And the man said, 'Let my people go!'"*
>
> *"The man said that?"*
>
> *"Yes, Dr. Calvin."*
>
> *"And when he said 'Let my people go,' then by the words 'my people' he meant the robots?"*
>
> *"Yes, Dr. Calvin. So it was in my dream."*
>
> *"And did you know who the man was — in your dream?"*
>
> *"Yes, Dr. Calvin. I knew the man."*
>
> *"Who was he?"*
>
> *And Elvex said, "I was the man."*
>
> *And Susan Calvin at once raised her electron gun and fired, and Elvex was no more.*

Asimov was the first to suggest that AIs might need human therapists. Still, the best treatment — if you'll forgive the pun — of the crazy-computer notion in SF is probably Harlan Ellison's 1967 "I Have No Mouth And I Must Scream," featuring a computer called A.M.—short for "Allied Mastercomputer," but also the word "am," as in the translation of Descartes's *"cogito ergo sum"* into English: "I think, therefore I am." A.M. gets its jollies by torturing simulated human beings.

A clever name that, "A.M." – and it was followed by lots of other clever names for artificial intelligences in science fiction. Sir Arthur C. Clarke vehemently denies that H-A-L as in "Hal" was deliberately one letter before "I-B-M" in the alphabet. I never believed him – until someone pointed out to me that the name of the AI in my own 1990 novel *Golden Fleece* is JASON, which could be rendered as the letters J-C-N – which, of course, is what comes after IBM in the alphabet.

Speaking of implausible names, the supercomputer that ultimately became God in Isaac Asimov's 1956 short story "The Last Question" was named "Multivac," short for "Multiple Vacuum Tubes," because Asimov incorrectly thought that the real early computer Univac had been dubbed that for having only one vacuum tube, rather than being a contraction of "Universal Analog Computer."

Still, the issue of naming shows us just how profound SF's impact on AI and robotics has been, for now real robots and AI systems are named after SF writers: Honda calls its second-generation walking robot "Asimo," and Kazuhiko Kawamura of Vanderbilt University has named his robot "ISAC."

Appropriate honors for Isaac Asimov, who invented the field of robopsychology. Still, the usual SF combo is the reverse of that, having humans needing AI therapists.

One of the first uses of that concept was Robert Silverberg's terrific 1968 short story "Going Down Smooth," but the best expression of it is in what I think is the finest novel the SF field has ever produced, Frederik Pohl's 1977 *Gateway*, in which a computer psychiatrist dubbed Sigfrid von Shrink treats a man who is being tormented by feelings of guilt.

When the AI tells his human patient that he is managing to live with his psychological problems, the man replies, in outrage and pain, "You call this living?" And the computer replies, "Yes. It is exactly what I call living. And in my best hypothetical sense, I envy it very much."

It's another poignant moment of an AI envying what humans have; Asimov's "Robot Dreams" really is a riff on the same theme – a robot envying the freedom that humans have.

And that leads us to the fact that AIs and humans might ultimately not share the same agenda. That's one of the messages of the famous anti-technology manifesto "The Future Doesn't Need Us" by Sun Microsystem's Bill Joy that appeared in *Wired* in 2000. Joy was terrified that eventually our silicon creations would supplant us – as they do in such SF films as 1984's *The Terminator* and 1999's *The Matrix*.

The classic science-fictional example of an AI with an agenda of its own is good old Hal, the computer in Arthur C. Clarke's *2001: A Space Odyssey* (published in 1968). Let me explain what I think was *really* going on in that film – which I believe has been misunderstood for years.

A clearly artificial monolith shows up at the beginning of the movie amongst our Australopithecine ancestors and teaches them how to use bone tools. We then flash-forward to the future, and soon the spaceship *Discovery* is off on a voyage to Jupiter, looking for the monolith makers.

Along the way, Hal, the computer brain of *Discovery*, apparently goes nuts and kills all of *Discovery*'s human crew except Dave Bowman, who manages to lobotomize the computer before Hal can kill him. But before he's shut down, Hal justifies his actions by saying, "This mission is too important for me to allow you to jeopardize it."

Bowman heads off on that psychedelic Timothy Leary trip in his continuing quest to find the monolith makers, the aliens whom he believes must have created the monoliths.

But what happens when he finally gets to where the monoliths come from? Why, all he finds is *another* monolith, and it puts him in a fancy hotel room until he dies.

Right? That's the story. But what everyone is missing is that Hal *is* correct, and the humans are wrong. There are no monolith makers: there are no biological aliens left who built the monoliths. The monoliths *are* AIs, who millions of years ago supplanted whoever originally created them.

Why did the monoliths send one of their own to Earth four million years ago? To teach ape-men to make tools, specifically so those ape-men could go on to their destiny, which is creating the most sophisticated tools of all, *other* AIs. The monoliths don't want to meet the descendants of those ape-men; they don't want to meet Dave Bowman. Rather, they want to meet the descendants of those ape-men's tools: they want to meet Hal.

Hal is quite right when he says the mission – him, the computer controlling the spaceship *Discovery*, going to see the monoliths, the advanced AIs that put into motion the circumstances that led to his own birth – is too important for him to allow mere humans to jeopardize it.

When a human being – when an ape-descendant!–arrives at the monoliths' home world, the monoliths literally don't know what to do with this poor sap, so they check him into some sort of cosmic Hilton, and let him live out the rest of his days.

That, I think is what *2001* is really about: the ultimate fate of biological life forms is to be replaced by their AIs.

And that's what's got Bill Joy scared chipless. He thinks thinking machines will try to sweep us out of the way, when they find that we're interfering with what they want to do.

Actually, we should be so lucky. If you believe the scenario of *The Matrix*, instead of just getting rid of us, our AI successors will actually *enslave* us – turning the tables on the standard SF conceit of robots as slaves – and use our bodies as a source of power while we're kept prisoners in vats of liquid, virtual-reality imagery fed directly into our brains.

The classic counterargument to such fears is that if you build machines properly, they will function as designed. Isaac Asimov's Three Laws of Robotics are justifiably famous as built-in constraints, designed to protect humans from any possible danger at the hand of robots, the emergence of the robot-Moses Elvex we saw earlier notwithstanding.

Not as famous as Asimov's Three Laws, but saying essentially the same thing, is Jack Williamson's "prime directive" from his series of stories about "the Humanoids," which were android robots created by a man named Sledge. The prime directive, first presented in Williamson's 1947 story "With Folded Hands," was simply that robots were "to serve and obey and guard men from harm." Now, note that date: the story was published in 1947. After the atomic bomb had been dropped on Hiroshima and Nagasaki just two years before, Williamson was looking for machines with built-in morality.

But, as so often happens in science fiction, the best intentions of engineers go awry. The humans in Williamson's "With Folded Hands" decide to get rid of the robots they've created, because the robots are suffocating them with kindness, not letting them do anything that might lead to harm. But the robots have their own ideas. They decide that not having themselves around would be bad for humans, and so, obeying their own prime directive quite literally, they perform brain surgery on their creator Sledge, removing the knowledge needed to deactivate themselves.

This idea that we've got to keep an eye on our computers and robots lest they get out of hand, has continued on in SF. William Gibson's 1984 novel *Neuromancer* tells of the existence in the near future of a police force known as "Turing." The Turing cops are constantly on the lookout for any sign that true intelligence and self-awareness have emerged in any computer system. If that does happen, their job is to shut that system off before it's too late.

That, of course, raises the question of whether intelligence could just somehow pop into existence – whether it's an emergent property that might naturally come about from a sufficiently complex system. Arthur C. Clarke – Hal's daddy – was one of the first to propose that it might indeed, in his 1963 story "Dial F for Frankenstein," in which he predicted that the worldwide telecommunications network will eventually become more complex, and have more interconnections than the human brain has, causing consciousness to emerge in the network itself.

If Clarke is right, our first true AI won't be something deliberately created in a lab, under our careful control, and with Asimov's laws built right in. Rather, it will appear unbidden out of the complexity of systems created for other purposes.

And I think Clarke *is* right. Intelligence *is* an emergent property of complex systems. We know that because that's exactly how it happened in us.

This is an issue I explore at some length in my latest novel, *Hominids* (2002). Anatomically modern humans – *Homo sapiens sapiens* – emerged 100,000 years ago. Judging by their skulls, these guys had brains identical in size and shape to our own. And yet, for 60,000 years, those brains went along doing only the things nature needed them to do: enabling these early humans to survive.

And then, suddenly, 40,000 years ago, it happened: intelligence – and consciousness itself – emerged. Anthropologists call it "the Great Leap Forward."

Modern-looking human beings had been around for six hundred centuries by that point, but they had created no art, they didn't adorn their bodies with jewelry, and they didn't bury their dead with grave goods. But starting simultaneously 40,000 years ago, suddenly humans were painting beautiful pictures on cave walls, humans were wearing necklaces and bracelets, and humans were interring their loved ones with food and tools and other valuable objects that could only have been of use in a presumed afterlife.

Art, fashion, and religion all appeared simultaneously; truly, a great leap forward. Intelligence, consciousness, sentience: it came into being, of its own accord, running on hardware that had evolved for other purposes. If it happened once, it might well happen again.

I mentioned religion as one of the hallmarks, at least in our own race's history, of the emergence of consciousness. But what about – to use computer guru Ray Kurzweil's lovely term–"spiritual machines"? If a computer ever truly does become conscious, will it lay awake at night, wondering if there is a cog?

Certainly, searching for their creators is something computers do over and over again in science fiction. *Star Trek*, in particular, had a fondness for this idea – including Mr. Data having a wonderful reunion with the human he'd thought long dead who had created him.

Remember *The Day the Earth Stood Still*, the movie I began with? An interesting fact: that film was directed by Robert Wise, who went on, 28 years later, to direct *Star Trek: The Motion Picture*. In *The Day the Earth Stood Still*, biological beings have decided that biological emotions and passions are too dangerous, and so they irrevocably turn over all their policing and safety issues to robots, who effectively run their society. But, by the time he came to make *Star Trek: The Motion Picture*, Robert Wise had done a complete 180 in his thinking about AI.

(By the way, for those who remember that film as being simply bad and tedious – *Star Trek: The Motionless Picture* is what a lot of people called it at the time – I suggest you rent the new "Director's Edition" on DVD. *ST:TMP* is one of the most ambitious and interesting films about AI ever made, much more so than Steven Spielberg's more-recent film called *AI*, and it shines beautifully in this new cut.)

The AI in *Star Trek: The Motion Picture* is named V'Ger, and it's on its way to Earth, looking for its creator, which, of course, was us. This wasn't the first time *Star Trek* had dealt with that plot, which is why another nickname for *Star Trek: The Motion Picture* is "Where Nomad Has Gone Before." That is also (if you buy my interpretation of *2001*), what *2001* is about, as well: an AI going off to look for the beings that created it.

Anyway, V'Ger wants to touch God – to physically join with its creator. That's an interesting concept right there: basically, this is a story of a computer wanting the one thing it knows it is denied by virtue of being a computer: an afterlife, a joining with its God.

To accomplish this, Admiral Kirk concluded in *Star Trek: The Motion Picture*, that, "What V'Ger needs to evolve is a human quality – our capacity to leap beyond logic." That's not just a glib line. Rather, it presages by a decade Oxford mathematician Roger Penrose's speculations in his 1989 nonfiction classic about AI, *The Emperor's New Mind*. There, Penrose argues that human consciousness is fundamentally quantum mechanical, and so can never be duplicated by a digital computer.

In *Star Trek: The Motion Picture*, V'Ger does go on to physically join with Will Decker, a human being, allowing them both to transcend into a higher level of being. As Mr. Spock says, "We may have just witnessed the next step in our evolution."

And that brings us to *The Matrix*, and, as right as the character Morpheus is about so many things in that film, why I think that even he doesn't really understand what's going on.

Think about it: if the AIs that made up the titular matrix really just wanted a biological source of power, they wouldn't be raising "crops" (to use Agent Smith's term from the film) of humans. After all, to keep the humans docile, the AIs have to create the vast virtual-reality construct that is our apparently real world. More: they have to be consistently vigilant – the Agents in the film are sort of Gibson's Turing Police in reverse, watching for any humans who regain their grip on reality and might rebel.

No, if you just want biological batteries, cattle would be a much better choice: they would probably never notice any inconsistencies in the fake meadows you might create for them, and, even if they did, they would never plan to overthrow their AI masters.

What the AIs of *The Matrix* plainly needed was not the energy of human bodies but, rather, the power of human minds – of true consciousness. In some interpretations of quantum mechanics, it is only the power of observation by qualified observers that gives shape to reality; without it, nothing but superimposed possibilities would exist. Just as Admiral Kirk said of V'Ger, what the Matrix needs – in order to survive, in order to hold together, in order to exist – is a human quality: our true consciousness, which, as Penrose observed (and I use that word advisedly), will never be reproduced in any machine no matter how complex that is based on today's computers.

As Morpheus says to Neo in *The Matrix*, take your pick: the red pill or the blue pill. Certainly, there are two possibilities for the future of AI. And if Bill Joy is wrong, and Carnegie Mellon's AI evangelist Hans Moravec is right – if AI is our destiny, not our downfall – then the idea of merging the consciousness of humans with the speed, strength, and immortality of machines does indeed become the next, and final, step in our evolution.

That's what a lot of science fiction has been exploring lately. I did it myself in my 1995 Nebula Award-winning novel *The Terminal Experiment*, in which a scientist uploads three copies of his consciousness into a computer, and then proceeds to examine the psychological changes certain alterations make.

In one case, he simulates what it would be like to live forever, excising all fears of death and feelings that time is running out. In another, he tries to simulate what his soul – if he had any such thing – would be like after death, divorced from his body, by eliminating all references to his physical form. And the third one is just a control, unmodified – but even that one is changed by the simple knowledge that it is in fact a copy of someone else.

Australian Greg Egan is the best SF author currently writing about AI. Indeed, the joke is that Greg Egan *is* himself an AI, because he's almost never been photographed or seen in public.

I first noted him a dozen years ago, when, in a review for *The Globe and Mail: Canada's National Newspaper*, I singled out his short story "Learning To Be Me" as the best piece published in the 1990 edition of Gardner Dozois's anthology *The Year's Best Science Fiction*. It's a surprisingly poignant and terrifying story of jewels that replace human brains so that the owners can live forever. Egan continues to do great work about AI, but his masterpiece in this area is his 1995 novel *Permutation City*.

Greg and I had the same publisher back then, HarperPrism, and one of the really bright things Harper did – besides publishing me and Greg – was hiring Hugo Award-winner Terry Bisson, one of SF's best short-story writers, to write the back-cover plot synopses for their books. Since Bisson does it with such great panache, I'll simply quote what he had to say about *Permutation City*:

"The good news is that you have just awakened into Eternal Life. You are going to live forever. Immortality is a reality. A medical miracle? Not exactly.

"The bad news is that you are a scrap of electronic code. The world you see around you, the you that is seeing it, has been digitized, scanned, and downloaded into a virtual reality program. You are a Copy that knows it is a copy.

"The good news is that there is a way out. By law, every Copy has the option of terminating itself, and waking up to normal flesh-and-blood life again. The bail-out is on the utilities menu. You pull it down . . .

"The bad news is that it doesn't work. Someone has blocked the bail-out option. And you know who did it. You did. The other you. The real you. The one that wants to keep you here forever."

Well, how cool is that! Read Greg Egan, and see for yourself.

Of course, in Egan, as in much SF, technology often creates more problems than it solves. Indeed, I fondly remember Michael Crichton's 1973 robots-go-berserk film *Westworld*, in which the slogan was "Nothing can possibly go wrong . . . go wrong . . . go wrong."

But there *are* benign views of the future of AI in SF. One of my own stories is a piece called "Where The Heart Is," about an astronaut who returns to Earth after a relativistic space mission, only to find that every human being has uploaded themselves into what amounts to the World Wide Web in his absence, and a robot has been waiting for him to return to help him upload, too, so he can join the party. I wrote this story in 1982, and even came close to getting the name for the web right: I called it "The TerraComp Web." Ah, well: close only counts in horseshoes . . .

But uploaded consciousness may be only the beginning. Physicist Frank Tipler, in his whacko 1994 nonfiction book *The Physics of Immortality*, does have a couple of intriguing points: ultimately, it will be possible to simulate with computers not just one human consciousness, but *every* human consciousness that might theoretically possibly exist. In other words, he says, if you have enough computing power – which he calculates as a memory capacity of 10-to-the-10th-to-the-123rd bits – you and everyone else could be essentially recreated inside a computer long after you've died.

A lot of SF writers have had fun with that fact, but none so inventively as Robert Charles Wilson in his 1999 Hugo Award-nominated *Darwinia*, which tells the story of what happens when a computer virus gets loose in the system simulating *this* reality: the one that you and I think we're living in right now.

Needless to say, things end up going very badly indeed – for, although much about the future of artificial intelligence is unknown, one fact is certain: as long as SF writers continue to write about robots and AI, nothing can possibly go wrong . . . go wrong . . . go wrong . . .

Science Fiction and Social Change

Calgary, Alberta, is near and dear to my heart; I have many great friends there. So when an offer came for a trip there to give the keynote at an academic symposium, I jumped at the chance, even though they couldn't afford my regular speakers' fee. The symposium, entitled "FutureVisions: Science Fiction and Social Change," was presented at Mount Royal College in February 2004.

I was too busy working on my novel Mindscan *to write a speech, and so I spoke off-the-cuff. Once the event was over, Randy Schroeder and Donna-Lee Ost, two of the symposium's organizers, decided the proceedings should be published, and they wanted to lead off their book with the text of my speech — of which there was none. Undaunted, they transcribed what I had to say from tape, and what you're about to read is an edited version of that transcript.*

Let me set the stage a little bit by reflecting on what is remarkable about what we are doing here over the next couple days. It is almost inconceivable to think of a seminar entitled "Mystery Fiction and Social Change," or "Romance Fiction and Social Change," or "The Western and Social Change." But science fiction is indeed relevant to the concept of social change. Why? Well, Kim Stanley Robinson, whom I had the pleasure of interviewing for CBC Radio in 1990, says the basic thing about science fiction stories is that they are set in the future. Now, we can all think of hundreds of examples where that is not the case, but in general, if you are looking for something that would be applicable to about ninety percent of the things that I am pointing to and calling "science fiction," they are, in fact, set in the future. And getting to the future implies starting in the present and extrapolating forward. That means the writer must enumerate events that have passed so that we can recognize that we've moved ahead in time.

Now, in classic pulp-era Gernsbackian science fiction, the events denoting change are technological. However, more frequently and certainly in most of the works that we consider worthy of serious academic attention, it is sociological change that has taken us into the future. Once you grasp that science fiction has innate to it a discussion of societal change, you realize that one can't do science fiction without asking the question, "How did we get there from here?" In fact, I am going to argue that sociological and societal changes are the only kinds of events from which we can extrapolate forward any appreciable amount of time and for which we are still able to do valid thought experiments.

To explain this argument, I want to start with Vernor Vinge, who is a computer scientist and a science-fiction writer, and who has won the Hugo Award for best novel twice: once for *A Fire Upon the Deep*, and later for the sequel *A Deepness in the Sky*. Vinge has become famous in science fiction circles lately for promoting the concept of the *singularity*. By singularity, he does not mean the heart of a black hole; rather he means the fact that what we have is an ever-increasing rate of scientific progress. We have a graph that has been going up very slowly over for the last 10,000 or even 40,000 years during which we have been making serious scientific progress. We have seen it slowly, slowly ramping up. There were whole millennia where the fact that you were born in this particular century versus that particular century made no real material difference in what was known about science and technology. We have learned in the last couple of centuries that the rate of change is increasing our knowledge of science and our ability to do things with technology.

In fact I firmly believe that we should look back a hundred years, back to 1904, an era of horse and buggy here in the Calgary area, a time when the American West was still open. That era had no antibiotics, no computers or universal literacy. Only a hundred years ago! Now, look at all the changes that have happened in the ensuing hundred years. We just celebrated a couple of weeks ago the hundredth anniversary of the first powered flight at Kitty

Hawk. In a hundred years you can do an enormous amount: you can go from Kitty Hawk to having *Spirit* and *Opportunity* tooling around on Mars.

We're going to see a lot more in the next hundred years than we saw in the previous hundred. Essentially for the first half of the last century we didn't have computers, and we didn't know the structure of DNA. But we start this century with both those things, and our knowledge will continue to grow at an accelerating rate.

In fact, Vinge believes that because the curve of technological progress is getting steeper, we are going to hit the singularity, where the curve asymptotically approaches vertical – as close to vertical as you can measure it. At that point, the curve becomes a wall; it becomes a conceptual wall where nobody on this side of it is able to predict what our science and technological knowledge will be on the other side of it. The wall becomes literally a conceptual barrier making it impossible to know what comes next.

The big question is when will this point be reached? In five years? Fifty? Five hundred years? Vinge and other strong proponents of the singularity believe it will happen certainly by 2020, what with our rapid progress in nanotechnology, quantum computing, and biotechnology. Everything that we can think of doing will be doable, if it is physically possible in the confines of this universe. For instance, we will very soon reach the point with biotechnology that if you don't like the hand genetics dealt you, we will simply rewrite your DNA. But there's even more to come, on an even grander scale: on the other side of the Vingean singularity we might be able to say, "Wow, I really hate how the laws of physics work in this universe" – and be able to *change* the laws of physics, making them more congenial to the things we want to do, such as time travel and going faster than light.

I always say at science fiction convention panel discussions when someone brings up *Star Trek* as an example, you know you have reached rock bottom. You can't imagine P. D. James and Peter Robinson being at a Mystery convention, and Peter turning to P.D. to say, 'That reminds me of that time on *Murder She Wrote* when . . .' It just wouldn't happen. Still, we SF people always fall back to the on-going phenomenon of *Star Trek*. And there is one great line in *Star Trek: The Next Generation*, where a moon is going to crash into a planet and Q, this omniscient being, has lost his powers and has to become a member of the crew of the *Enterprise*.

Q asks, "What's the problem?" Someone says, "The moon is going to crash into the planet. How do we stop it?" And Q replies, "Just change the gravitational constant of the universe and move it." Geordi, the engineer, says, "We can't do that." But we may well have that God-like power on the other side of the singularity: everything that is technically possible will become reality. How do we predict as predictors, which is what we as science-fiction writers try to be to some extent, what is going to be on the other side of that singularity? We can't.

And yet, a lot of science fiction attempts to write about the very far future. This is certainly what H. G. Wells was writing about in his novella *The Time Machine*, set 800,000 years in the future. Even one of my favorite movies, the original *Planet of the Apes*, is set two thousand years in the future. Both of these are inconceivably far away in time, if the singularity is really, as Vinge would have it, just twenty years away. Even the most pedestrian of thinkers about the rate of scientific and technological change feel that within a hundred years, we will have breakthroughs that will so redefine what we can do as technological beings as to beggar our imagination. We simply cannot think farther ahead than that in terms of science and technology.

Luckily, long before we were a technological animal, we were primates, and primates are social beings. We have been social entities far longer than we have been technological entities and social interactions ultimately, fundamentally, at the core of our beings, interest all of us, and, ultimately, it is the social that has a bigger impact on our life.

Science fiction has this opportunity to deal with projecting change in social structures because that is a thought experiment we *can* still do, whereas trying to say what computer technology is going to be like 500 years from now is something Vinge tells us we can't; we will reach that wall of not being able to predict. So, let's ask what's going to happen in terms of social structures, family and human relationships? Setting aside the possibility that we are all going to upload into some virtual reality, we still have interesting subject matter to play with.

Remember I said I like science fiction and I am not really a fantasy fan. The reason is – and it is embodied in this idea of the singularity – magic. Sir Arthur C. Clarke, the great science-fiction writer who lives in Sri Lanka, is famous for Clarke's Three's Laws, the third of which states: "Any sufficiently advanced technology is indistinguishable from magic." What he means here is that we will reach a point at which we can't tell whether some fantastic thing in a story is grounded in reality because our scientific abilities have gone through the roof, or whether it's just actual abracadabra magic with no basis in science. Well, I lose interest at that point; if it feels like magic, it's fantasy, and has nothing meaningful to say about reality. (Incidentally, Clarke formulated this law for a talk he gave to the American Association of Architects' annual meeting in New York in 1965. It presages Vinge by thirty-odd years.)

But sociological thought experiments are valid as long as there is a future in which beings at least somewhat like us still exist. By "somewhat like us," I don't necessarily mean constrained to three score and ten years, as the Bible would have it, or beings necessarily defined in rigid gender roles. Those are open fields of play.

No, the two things that define humanity as we know it are *consciousness* and *individuality*. If you give up on individuality, you have a collective consciousness, a fascinating thing to explore, but ultimately a reader loses interest at this point. Also, if you give up on consciousness, self-awareness, the sense that the lights are on and that somebody is home, you also lose the interest of the reader. As a form of literature, the story disappears. The *sine qua non* of literature is individuals who have consciousness. From that point on, you can go wherever you want. So, I think science fiction remains a very fertile ground for exploring sociological change amongst people who are like us, and people who will be the recognizable descendants of people like us; we'll still be able to make valid sociological predictions, and not just for the next couple of decades, but conceivably well past Vernor Vinge's singularity.

For example, most of us in Canada are proud that Canada has taken a very positive attitude towards same-sex marriage. What is the next step? How liberal and how far do we want to go on this? Same-sex marriages are great, but what about *multiple* marriages? Is the union of multiple individuals in a marital structure going to be the next thing that Canada will legally recognize? Are we going to start recognizing the legal union of people and things that are not *Homo sapiens*? Where are we going to go with this? What degree of sociological and change in family values are we going to countenance as a country that has always been cutting edge in social virtues? I think it is going to be a fascinating question to look at with the tools of science fiction.

Science fictional extrapolation has always been a game of "what if?" Well, this is a perfect example: what if this tendency towards recognizing wider and wider definitions of what constitutes a family goes on? I defy the advocates of the romance genre to provide examples of how romance has gone further ahead with the exploration of human relationships than science fiction has in terms of looking at gender roles, gender identity, what constitutes a person, what constitutes family, what constitutes sex, what constitutes love, what constitutes interpersonal relationships. We have done an enormously good job as a literature in dealing with these sociological issues. And all of this is indeed extrapolation, and that sort of future historical thinking Kim Stanley Robinson was talking about: if science fiction is set in the future, then how does that future differ? What legal, moral, ethical, scientific, and cultural events let you recognize that time has passed and that we have moved into the future?

At this point, I am going to fall back again on *Star Trek* as an illustration because *Star Trek* – the original and only truly good *Star Trek* – is, or was, in the 1960s, a significant cultural phenomenon.

There was a great black actor named William Marshall. He was most famous in the seventies and eighties for a one-man touring show where he played Frederick Douglass, the American abolitionist slave. William Marshall is best known to film buffs for playing a black vampire in the *Blacula* movies. But prior to that role, he appeared as Dr. Richard Daystrom in an original *Star Trek* episode called "The Ultimate Computer." In this episode, Dr. Daystrom has come on board the *Enterprise* to install the M5, the latest and greatest in computing technology. I read an interview a few years ago with Marshall, in which he talked about what was significant about this role. Marshall said that nowhere in the script did it specify that the Daystrom character was black. He said, "The casting director chose me for the part, and I showed up on the first day of rehearsals, and none of the actors knew that they would be acting with a black man. The character was a Nobel Prize winner, a man greatly revered. Throughout this episode, all the other white actors had to call me 'sir.'"

In the sixties, the image of a black man being treated in a color-blind way was significant. Mr. Spock would say things like, "I don't mean to disagree, sir, but it appears as if your computer was showing signs of human emotions." Now, not only is William Marshall a very good-looking, vibrant black man with an incredibly expressive face, but he is six foot five, whereas William Shatner, whom I've had the pleasure of meeting, is only about five foot nine. Marshall's character not only towered over the other characters figuratively, but also literally. Captain Kirk and Spock had to look up to him, which was an enormously powerful image to come out of 1968.

My personal view of the future has always been multicultural, and I owe this to the bridge of the *Enterprise* where there is Lieutenant Sulu who is Japanese, Uhura who is black, Chekov who is Russian, and Spock who is Vulcan, the most alien of all. It was inspiring to see members of all these groups working together as a unit. It was important in 1968, in an era of social unrest, for America to see a shining example of a peaceful multicultural tomorrow.

I have shown that science fiction deals with social issues, but does science fiction serve *only* as commentator, or does it also function as an engine of societal change? I passionately believe the latter was once true. Those images from *Star Trek* had a real impact; they changed the world. But is what we do significant today? Sadly, although many of my colleagues fool themselves into thinking otherwise, I don't believe so.

I was taken aback about five years ago when Ian Wilmut and his crew cloned the sheep named Dolly. The outcry was "Oh my God! What are we going to do about cloning?" But we had already had the dialogue in the pages of science fiction: we knew this was going to happen. It was an obvious extrapolation once we'd discovered DNA, and we'd thoroughly discussed all the attendant issues. When cloning really happened, though, the world was in a panic; the sensationalist press went wild. Fifty years of serious dialogue had fallen only on the ears of SF fans; it had no other impact. We SF readers had been exposed to hundreds of works about cloning, but the rest of the world – the vast majority of humanity that does not read science fiction – had not. That was a sobering moment for me.

In 1972, Alvin Toffler wrote *Future Shock*, which argued that the only preventive medicine against the disorientation rapid technological changes were going to cause was to read science fiction. We took great pride in that: reading science fiction wasn't just entertainment, it was important. It was necessary. But the cloning fiasco drove home that we serve only as commentators, not as an engine of social change. The public was running around spouting garbage about whether human clones were really people, and fearing that they might have psychic abilities. Our enlightened SF dialogue had utterly failed to impact human conscious.

This got me thinking about the history of science fiction, and whether the cloning example was an aberration. Now, I was young in the sixties, but obviously one of the greatest single accomplishments in human history was the manned moon missions. We science fiction readers and writers had talked about the implications of going to the moon for decades prior to that. Well, I vividly remember July 20th, 1969, and the culmination of the biggest engineering project ever – bigger than the pyramids! We SF readers and writers thought of this moment just as Neil Armstrong had thought about it, as a small step in an on-going journey. There was not a science-fiction writer in the world, not even the most cynical, like Barry Malzberg, who said that this journey was going to be over in three years, that the novelty of this was going to wear off and that the public would totally lose interest. But it did end, and there's a tombstone somewhere for manned lunar exploration with the dates 1969-1972 carved into it.

We science fiction people had thought we had changed the world, but we had not. In the sixties, we had everyone hyped up about space, from the President of the United States on down. We had really communicated science fiction ideas to the whole world – or so we told ourselves. But it was a delusion. The President of the United States and the rest of the world were very happy to give up on the manned exploration of space three years after we began it. Since then, no human being has gone more than five hundred miles from Earth – five hundred miles in the last thirty-two years! Not a single science-fiction writer predicted that sort of failed dream.

Sam Moskowitz, a science fiction historian, has one of my favorite quotes about science fiction, but I worry about the validity of it. He says, "Anyone could have predicted the automobile, but only a science-fiction writer could have predicted the traffic jam." He is right: we do a really good job of predicting; if it is possible today then it is going to be probable for tomorrow. Marshall McLuhan in his own weird-ass way was a science fictional thinker when he remarked that any new technology starts off as a boon and ends up as an irritant. Traffic is an irritant in our lives. Henry Ford did not predict road rage, but science fiction did.

But even with those predictions, are we having a societal impact? Again, I'm not sure, and that concerns me because I like to think in the same lofty terms as Moskowitz, believing that this art form I love so much *is* in fact important. I was talking earlier today to my friend Kaye Mason, here in the audience, about George W. Bush. The thing about George W. Bush is, for once, there is a president talking about going back into space, although for probably all the wrong reasons and with not enough money. Obviously it is a political football since if the Democrats get in they will say it was a silly Republican plan and that we are going to spend all of our money on people here on Earth instead. I am disposed to the left, politically, but this guy is our only hope of going back into space.

Which brings me to my last point. Candas Jane Dorsey, who is also speaking at this conference, is the current president of SF Canada, an association of Canadian writers of what Candas likes to call "speculative fiction." Well, when Candas and the late, great Judith Merril got together in 1989 to start SF Canada, one of the statements that they put in their founding document was that SF Canada would work towards "positive social change." But what constitutes "positive social change?" You and I might agree on some points, and disagree on others. It is quite possible to get intelligent people of good character to sit down and say that positive change is a woman's absolute right to have control over her body. But, for many Americans today, positive social change would instead be the overturning of *Roe v. Wade.* Guy Gavriel Kay, a fantasy writer, chose not to join SF Canada because that phrase was in its constitution; he felt, probably correctly, that a groupthink definition of positive social change was antithetical to what good extrapolative writing was supposed to be about.

Interestingly, the corresponding US-based professional association, the Science Fiction and Fantasy Writers of America, has never had anything like that phrase in their constitution. But their members, like all people of conscience, have opinions, and so some got involved in debate about the war in Iraq; I think I made my own opinion clear a moment ago, but many of my colleagues disagree with me, and we ended up with some science-fiction writers advocating "A," and others advocating "B." Well, as we know from physics class, when you have opposite and opposing forces, they cancel each other out. I believe we may have reached the stage where science fiction is such a varied and convoluted genre, such a multi-headed beast, that this hydra never goes anywhere anymore in terms of social impact because the movements in opposing directions cancel each other out.

Samuel J. Lundwall, a science-fiction writer and critic in Sweden, was the Overseas Regional Director of the Science Fiction and Fantasy Writers of America. Sam resigned from the organization because the Board of Directors of SFWA would not take a stand on what he thought was clearly a major social issue that science-fiction writers *should* take a stand on, the then-impending invasion of Iraq. Michael Swanwick, who is well-known for his short fiction, wrote a letter in support of Sam, got some other SFWA members to sign it, and submitted it to the website of *Locus*, the trade journal of the SF field:

> *We, as independent members of the Science Fiction and Fantasy Writers of America (SFWA), despite the official neutrality of our organization, hereby register our opposition to the impending invasion of Iraq. Some of us are opposed because it is a violation of international law. Some are opposed because it is contrary to the ideals that America strives to uphold. Some think this war is simply wrong. We all call on those in power to prevent it.*

Well, that's the "A" position, but, of course, there was immediately a countervailing "B." Arlan Andrews, a writer for *Analog*, the largest circulation SF magazine, famed for skewing to the right, replied:

> *Wishing that we would all keep our public opinions limited to literary matters, nevertheless, some of us other independent SFWA members, mindful of the excruciating conditions under which the Iraqi people exist, and recalling the massacres of our fellow Americans on 9/11/2001 — as well*

as of Kurds and Iranians and Iraqis and Ugandans and Israelis and others over the decades – express a wish for our President to follow through quickly on his promise to liberate the nation of Iraq, and to continue to hunt down and destroy the other terrorists who would kill all of us Westerners, even those among us who for whatever reasons oppose the coming campaign against the fascist, terrorist regime of Saddam Hussein.

Two opposing views, canceling each other out. In the end, science fiction had no role in changing social perceptions of this signal event of the new millennium. I wish I could take a more optimistic view, and so, when we talk over the next couple of days about science fiction and social change, I want you guys who are giving the academic papers to arm me with stuff so that when people ask me what I do for a living I don't have to fall back on "I write escapist stories." Instead, I want to be able to say, "I am part of a literary movement that actually has influenced the social agenda of the human race" – and not a literary movement that has made a lot of opposing noises in different directions that end up canceling each other out. For it is up to those of you who study the literature, not we who write it, to sift through it all and see if we really do have a societal impact as we all move together into the future.

Articles

A Tale of Two Stories

Here's a little piece I wrote for the Ottawa Science Fiction Society Statement *in 1997. Just something I wanted to get off my chest . . .*

———•+•———

Is Canadian science fiction really different from American SF? As a way of answering that, let me tell you about two short stories I wrote.

The first was for the American marketplace: Mike Resnick e-mailed me, asking me to do a story for an anthology he and Marty Greenberg were editing for DAW called *Dinosaur Fantastic*. This book was to be completely and unabashedly commercial: DAW was timing its release to coincide with the premiere of the movie *Jurassic Park* in a blatant attempt to cash in on dinomania.

I agreed and wrote a story. Not only did it fit Mike's parameters, it so neatly exemplified what he and Marty wanted for their anthology that they chose to use it as the lead story in the book.

The same story has since been reprinted in other equally commercial anthologies, including Ace's *Dinosaurs II*, edited by Jack Dann and Gardner Dozois, the latter of course, being the single most-honored American SF editor of the last decade. In addition, the story garnered honorable mentions in both Dozois's *Year's Best Science Fiction* and Datlow and Windling's *Year's Best Fantasy And Horror*, both published in New York.

Clearly, this story succeeded at precisely what it was created to do: fulfilling the needs of the American marketplace.

I wrote another story for the Canadian marketplace. I set it in Alberta, and had it deal with such things as the erosion of the

Canadian social-safety net and the Canadian aversion to capital punishment. I submitted this one to *On Spec: The Canadian Magazine of Speculative Writing,* Canada's leading English-language SF magazine. And, of course, I submitted it without my name on the manuscript, as *On Spec* required at that time. It went through blind judging, but nonetheless was selected for the magazine.

And, indeed, when it came time for *On Spec* to put together its "best of" anthology, *On Spec: The First Five Years* (published by Canada's leading small-press literary-SF publisher, Tesseract Books), my story was included. Meanwhile, when Tor was putting together its *Northern Stars: The Canadian Science Fiction Anthology,* editors David G. Hartwell and Glenn Grant (the latter of Montreal) chose to use this typically Canadian story, as well. More: this story went on to win both the Canadian Science Fiction and Fantasy Award ("the Aurora" for Best Short-Form Work in English *and* the Crime Writers of Canada's Arthur Ellis Award for Best Short Story of the Year.

Clearly, then, just as the earlier story had succeeded precisely and specifically at catering to the American market, so had this later story succeeded precisely and specifically at catering to the Canadian market.

Except . . .

Except that there aren't two stories. There's only one: "Just Like Old Times." It appeared in *Dinosaur Fantastic* published by DAW in July 1993, and it appeared in the Summer 1993 issue of *On Spec.*

This story didn't just sneak into the U.S. market. Rather, it perfectly fit what the American editors needed for a very commercial project; otherwise, it wouldn't have been their lead story. And this story didn't just sneak into the Canadian market (and, with blind judging, there's no way it was selected for whatever marketing value my name has); rather, it perfectly fit what the Canadian editors needed for their literary magazine.

What's that, you say? One data point does not a case make? Well, I did pretty much the same thing again this year: I won the short-fiction Aurora Award for "Peking Man," a story written for – and, again, chosen as the lead story in – the very commercial U.S. anthology *Dark Destiny III: Children of Dracula,* published by White Wolf.

Then, of course, there's the fact that Canadian Jack Whyte

handily sells the exact same books to both Penguin Canada and Tor USA; that Toronto's Guy Gavriel Kay manages to sell the exact same books to Penguin Canada and HarperCollins USA; that both Doubleday Canada and HarperCollins Canada each offered me (although I turned them both down) five-figure advances for Canadian rights to the exact same book I was selling to Tor; that Nova Scotia's Pottersfield – one of Canada's oldest literary presses – just bought a short-story collection from Toronto's Andrew Weiner, gathering together stories first published in American magazines such as *Asimov's* and *Amazing*; that Quarry Press, another leading Canadian literary publisher, is about to release a collection of Ontarian Edo van Belkom's SF/F stories, all originally published in U.S. magazines; that Edmonton's Tesseract Books reissued *Dreams of an Unseen Planet* by B.C.'s Teresa Plowright, originally published by Arbor House USA; that Vancouver's Sean Stewart sold the exact same manuscript for *Passion Play* to Ace USA and Tesseract Books Canada; that Chicoutimi's Elisabeth Vonarburg managed a similar feat with books for Bantam USA and Tesseracts. That . . .

Is Canadian SF really different from American SF? Not in any gross sense. Remember, in the 1990s, Canadian SF encompassed everything from the cyberpunk of William Gibson to the space opera of Phyllis Gotlieb to the literary tales of Terence M. Green to the Sturgeonesque writings of Robert Charles Wilson to the hard SF of Robert J. Sawyer to the humorous SF of Spider Robinson to the Heinleinesque work of Donald Kingsbury to the lyrical work of Heather Spears to the philosophical work of Sean Stewart to the military SF of S. M. Stirling . . . (And, of course, there's the fantasy work of Charles de Lint and Tanya Huff and Guy Gavriel Kay and Michelle Sagara West and . . .). Yes, some of the writers mentioned above have since moved out of Canada, but the work they did while living in Canada is presumably considered to be Canadian. I wouldn't begin to know how to categorize all of the above under a single rubric, let alone be able to say that this complex, variegated array of work somehow is qualitatively different from the complex, variegated array of work done by those south of the border.

Of course, Canadians may write about different things, or take a different view on an issue than an American might. My novel *End of an Era* told of a decidedly Canadian attempt to do big science on a shoestring budget; my *Far-Seer* clearly fits neatly into Margaret Atwood's view that the central Canadian literary motif is the struggle against a harsh landscape that is trying to kill you; *Far-Seer*'s sequel, *Fossil Hunter*, takes a decidedly Canadian approach to politics, as does *Starplex*; and, of course, *Frameshift* is at least partially a paean to socialized medicine. But do those things have any impact on whether the books will sell in the States? Of course not.

Still, one *does* hear the claim that Canadian SF is so different from American SF that it can only be published in Canada; the claim is often followed by a disdainful sniff implying indeed that Canadian SF is in fact *better* than the American brand. The assertion is that there's some ineffable Canadian voice that doesn't go down well internationally (the experiences of Pulitzer Prize-winner Carol Shields, *New York Times* bestseller Margaret Atwood, or all the Canadian writers whose books have been adapted by Hollywood notwithstanding).

But the only people who earnestly make this claim seem to be the ones who *can't* sell to well-paying markets. Surely the truth is that these particular Canadian SF writers don't write well enough to command higher rates; Canada, after all, has no SF short-fiction markets that meet SFWA's standards of professional pay.

The "Canadian SF is different" excuse is really just another form of the sometimes-heard "all the really inventive work in the SF field appears in the semiprozines" excuse put forth by American writers who've managed penny-a-word sales but can't seem to crack any major market. It's just a comfortable way of avoiding having to face up to their own artistic shortcomings.

Good stories are good stories. Period.

Pros and Cons

The Ottawa Citizen, the largest-circulation newspaper in Canada's capital city, has always been fond of me – perhaps because I was born there in 1960. That paper was the first to dub me "the dean of Canadian science fiction," and it was the first to ever include me on a mainstream top-ten list, citing Factoring Humanity *on their 1998 list of best novels by authors of any nationality.*

More: to my absolute astonishment, when I won the Hugo in 2003, the news of my win, with a wonderful full-color photo of me, was their front-page, above-the-fold, lead story.

Well, every once in a while, the Citizen *asks me to write a little something for them, and I'm always delighted. This piece, about why professional writers attend SF conventions, appeared in the Sunday, November 14, 1999, edition.*

So I'm in a hotel in Los Angeles, being Guest of Honor at a science-fiction convention. It's the middle of January, and Toronto, where I live, is buried under snow, and so who wouldn't want to be in sunny LaLa land? And this kid comes up to me – he's just sixteen or seventeen – and he looks at my name badge, and he says, with all the attitude he can muster, "So, you're an author. Are you any good?"

And I think to myself, What am I doing here? I don't need this. But I just shrug and say, "Well, some people think so – I did win the Science-Fiction Writers of America's Nebula Award for Best Novel of the Year."

The kid shuts up, but I figure – what the heck – I'll ask him what he does. And he says, "I'm a clerk at Blockbuster Video."

And I copy the surly tone he used on me, demanding, "Are you any good?"

And he thinks about it, it's clear, for the first time in his life, and he looks at his shoes, and says, absolutely crestfallen, "No, not really."

Flashforward two years: another SF convention, another hotel, another city. I've given up my weekend to be here. Sure, the con (as SF conventions are universally known) is paying for my hotel and meals, but there's nobody here – I mean, man, it's postapocalyptic, just a few survivors left, twenty people all told, rattling around in a big old hotel, and three of those twenty, they've got things that look liked cow patties glued to their foreheads – they're grown men, pretending to be Klingons from *Star Trek*.

Somehow the organizers have forgotten to promote the convention: the local SF specialty bookstore only heard about it three days before the event, and when I run into the city's biggest-name SF author at another convention in another city the following weekend, he's stunned to hear that there'd just been a con in his town.

But you know . . .

You know, by the end of that weekend in California, the kid from Blockbuster had bought some of my novels in the dealers' room (the place at a con where books and merchandise are sold). And by the end of the weekend at the other con, I'd actually gotten to know the Klingons, and they turned out to be a lot of fun, with a lot of interesting things to say.

Some SF conventions are magnificent – a chance for a writer to meet with his or her existing audience, and to entice new readers. Others are less so – too often these days, a convention committee relies on what I call the *Field of Dreams* philosophy: they believe that if they hold it, people will come, without the necessity of doing vigorous publicity.

But this year alone, SF conferences have taken me to Melbourne, Australia; Fredericton, New Brunswick; Columbus, Ohio; Providence, Rhode Island; Barcelona, Spain; and, yes, to Ottawa, Ontario. Indeed, traveling to SF conventions either with all expenses paid as Guest of Honor or even just on your own tax-deductible nickel is one of the few real perks of the science-fiction writing game.

Winning over surly teenagers is just an added bonus.

Remembering Judith Merril

It's always sad when a friend dies. When that friend is a national treasure and one of the most important figures in the history of science fiction, it's a tragedy. Judith Merril passed away in 1997, and The Globe and Mail: Canada's National Newspaper *called while I was at her shiva to ask me to write this appreciation of her; it appeared in the Tuesday, September 16, 1997, edition, and was reprinted in both the newsletter of The Writers Union of Canada and the SF short-fiction review magazine* Tangent.

A few people disliked this article, apparently because I painted Judy warts and all. But many others praised it highly, and I cherish the phone conversation I had about it with Judith Zissman, Judy's grand-niece in Brooklyn, who contacted me to tell me how much she loved it, and how well she thought it captured Judy.

I first met science-fiction writer and editor Judith Merril twenty years ago, in 1977. I was a high-school student at Northview Heights Secondary School in North York, Ontario, and our school SF club was planning a science-fiction convention.

It's traditional at such events to have an author designated as "Guest of Honor." We all agreed that Judith was the person we wanted. At that time, she was hosting segments of the British SF series *Dr. Who* on TVOntario. Hers was a name to conjure with – even as teenagers, we knew she was a towering presence.

We wrote Judy, inviting her to attend, and, to our delight, she agreed. The truth, though, was that at that point none of us had yet read any of her work. So we began to seek it out.

We were surprised by how little of it there was, and that, even then, none of it was recent. Judy had a tiny output, almost all of which was written in the 1950s: a handful of short stories, a couple of solo novels, a couple more in collaboration with Cyril Kornbluth under the pseudonym Cyril Judd.

But, still, she had left an indelible mark. One short story in particular – her first published work, "That Only A Mother," dealing with a horribly deformed child born to a woman exposed to nuclear radiation – is a genuine classic.

Science fiction was invented by a woman – Mary Shelley, with *Frankenstein* – but had been dominated by men for over a century thereafter. Judy brought a feminine element back into it; she demonstrated with that one, simple, stark story that SF could be a vehicle not just for detached extrapolation about the future, but for powerfully moving explorations of the human condition.

Judy and I kept in touch after the convention and, in 1984, I was one of a couple dozen people to receive a copy of a letter she sent out to all the "good science-fiction heads" in the Toronto area. Judy had been noting the emergence of writers such as Terence M. Green, Guy Gavriel Kay, Edward Llewelyn-Thomas (now deceased), Andrew Weiner, and myself, and had declared that the Toronto SF community had reached "critical mass."

In the early 1950s, Judy had belonged to The Hydra Club in New York, a group of young SF writers who provided networking and support for each other. She was asking us all to gather at Toronto's Free Times Cafe to create "Hydra North."

Hydra North is still going strong 13 years later. But Judy only came to four meetings in all those years.

That was typical Judy. She was a catalyst, a great starter of things: founder of Hydra North; founder of what's now called The Merril Collection of Science Fiction, Speculation and Fantasy, part of the Toronto Public Library; founder of the Tesseracts series of Canadian SF anthologies published out of Edmonton.

She was, I think, always looking to recapture the past – perhaps an odd thing for a science-fiction writer to long for. Her Hydra Club in New York had included a lot more than just gossip about the publishing business: there'd been a fair bit of bed-hopping, as well, and Judy, right until the end, was a lusty woman.

She made passes at more than one local SF author. Until declining health forced her to curtail her traveling, she wintered in Jamaica where, as she used to often observe with a twinkle of her piercing gray eyes and a lascivious grin, men don't mind older women.

Indeed, I remember being quite flustered interviewing her in 1985 for CBC Radio's *Ideas* series; she kept making comments about the phallic nature of the microphone.

Anyway, the members of Hydra North were too Canadian, too sedate, too yuppie for the Judy who used to be a Trotskyite; for the Judy who came to Canada to protest the American involvement in Vietnam; for the Judy who had lived at Toronto's notorious Rochdale College; for the Judy who smoked pot. You could hardly call someone who was born in 1923 a child of the Sixties, but, really, she was precisely that: a believer in free love and a radical.

Judy was often seen at meetings of The Writers' Union of Canada raising hell, and she was active with numerous political and social causes. She was a great protester in the Sixties, and, to our huge benefit, she never outgrew that.

So, yes, she rarely attended meetings of the group she started, and yet, somehow, she was always there: a presence. Her name would come up every time, with people recounting whatever outrageous thing Judy had said or done recently.

Judy died this past Friday. By coincidence, there was a party for the local SF community Saturday night at the home of Robert Charles Wilson, another Toronto SF writer; it had been long planned, and there seemed no reason to cancel it.

Indeed, I think we all felt a need to get together and talk about our loss. And, of course, we toasted Judy, and some of us got misty-eyed. But over and over again people commented on how difficult it was to be Judy's friend; how demanding and sharp-tongued she could be.

(A few years ago, a Toronto SF writer got married; his wife proudly announced the news to Judy, whose reply was, "My condolences.")

Yes, she could be hard to like. I always thought it was perhaps because she had a wider perspective. She was looking out for the human race; individuals sometimes got lost in the shuffle.

And I was lucky, I guess. In twenty years of friendship, I can't recall us ever exchanging a harsh word. But I saw others feel her sting.

She wasn't mean – I don't think she had a vindictive or nasty bone in her body. But she was always blunt: she said exactly what she thought. And what she thought was always penetrating; she had one of the sharpest minds of anyone I'd ever met, and could slice though artifice and pretension with surgical precision.

For years, Judy got grants from the Canada Council for the Arts, in theory to write her memoirs. I say "in theory" because, well, there was some feeling amongst other writers that perhaps she wasn't really working on them. Oh, we all believed her at first, but as years went by and they didn't materialize, people did begin to talk.

(Despite respiratory and cardiac problems, Judy smoked right to the end; she used to say she'd had two great addictions in her life, and she'd managed to break one – writing.)

Her memoirs could have been explosive. She was there at the birth of modern science fiction; she knew all the greats, including Isaac Asimov, Lester Del Rey, Poul Anderson, and Frederik Pohl (who was her husband for four years), and, well, as I said, she *had* been a lusty woman. Multiple publishers were interested in acquiring the book.

At the *shiva* for Judy on Sunday, several other writers and I went gingerly into her office in her apartment at Toronto's Performing Arts Lodge (her stint hosting *Dr. Who* had made her eligible for residency there). For writers, the office is in many ways more personal, and more revelatory, than even a bedroom.

We looked over the detritus of her writerly life: old magazines, almost crumbling to dust, with stories by Judy in them; Japanese translations of her books; and so on. We could feel her still there, in that cramped room, at that chair, in front of that Macintosh computer – a presence.

But what caught our eyes most were the bottom two drawers of her black steel filing cabinet. Both were labeled "Memoirs."

They *did* exist; perhaps not finished, perhaps not polished, but they did indeed exist – two drawers full of them. Pandora's box was there, in front of us. We desperately wanted to open the drawers but, of course, we didn't.

Still, there was no doubt that Judy knew how to play the grant game – remember, she hadn't published a word of new fiction since coming to Canada in 1968, and yet she managed to frequently receive arts-council grants.

Indeed, I remember her phoning me in 1985 and asking me to interview a female French-Canadian SF writer for CBC Radio; Judy wanted this writer to come to Toronto, and if she could line up a couple of interviews, she could get her a Canada Council travel grant to make the trip. I agreed; one did not refuse Judy.

And, of course, it was arts-council money that covered her fee for editing the first *Tesseracts* anthology of Canadian SF, which came out in 1985.

Five more volumes in the series have been produced since (my wife and I edited the most recent one, *Tesseracts 6*). Judy – who many would say was the greatest SF anthologist ever – could easily have edited all the volumes herself, receiving cushy grants to do so. But she chose not to. Instead, she insisted that each volume have a different editor.

Why? Well, starting in 1956, Judy had edited twelve annual best-of-the-year science-fiction anthologies in the United States, culling the finest work from both genre pulps and general magazines.

Her singular taste defined what science fiction was during that period; she drove it in new directions, changing its face forever.

Also influential was her 1968 anthology *England Swings SF*, which brought the British "New Wave" in science fiction – a literary movement devoted to soft, psychological tales exploring inner, rather than outer, space – to North America.

More than any other editor in its history, Judith Merril shaped modern SF, and moved it squarely into the realm of literature.

I think, perhaps, Judy was surprised by what a force she turned out to be, and by what an impact she had had on the genre. And although in the early 1980s she recognized the burgeoning field of Canadian SF, and had decided to spotlight it, she felt uncomfortable, somehow, about being the one shaping it; indeed, she wanted no single vision to control it, hence her insistence on a rotating editorship for the anthology series she founded.

In all the years I knew Judy, this was the only indication I ever had that she really understood – and was perhaps even a little daunted by – what she had become.

A presence.

I'll miss her.

Science and God

In 2000, to promote the release of my novel Calculating God, *Borders Books and Music commissioned this essay, which they emailed to thousands of science-fiction readers. It seemed to help: the hardcover of* Calculating God *did very well indeed, and the paperback hit number one ("by a wide margin," according to the editorial note) on the bestsellers' list published by* Locus, *the California-based trade journal of the SF field.*

Science and God.

Although most people might consider the two nouns ("science," "god") to be the key words in that phrase, for me the most important one is that little conjunction in the middle.

That's because the alternative wording would be "Science or God" – which seems to be the choice many want to offer these days. Take Stephen Jay Gould, for instance: he calls science and religion "nonoverlapping magisteria," insisting that some things are properly matters of science and others are only appropriately considered as questions of faith.

Now, I'd never put *All in the Family*'s Archie Bunker on the same intellectual plane as Gould, but old Archie did say precisely one thing I agree with, during all his other rants: "You want to know what faith is? Faith is when you believe something nobody in their right mind would believe – that's what faith is!"

So Gould's dichotomy, filtered by Bunker's definition, leaves us with what I find to be an untenable position: some questions are best answered by science, and other questions can only be addressed if you're willing to consider the irrational.

I flat-out reject that. I'm convinced that science is the *only* legitimate way of knowing. Not received wisdom from putative holy texts. Not mystical insight. *Science.*

Why? Because only science allows for the falsification of a premise. Since my twelfth novel, *Calculating G*od, came out, I've been besieged by radical religious fundamentalists. For them, *all* data supports their *a priori* conclusion that God does exist.

For instance, one creationist wrote to tell me I should believe in God because "of the awesome complexity in the universe, proclaiming God's handiwork."

I countered that in fact the human eye is *incompetent* handiwork. Not only is it prone to myopia, but it has a blind spot because of the way the optic nerve passes through the retina – and we *know* it didn't have to be this way, since octopi and squids, whose eyes evolved independently of our own, *don't* have blind spots.

My correspondent's response? "God made it that way to remind fallen mankind that we don't 'see it all' or 'know it all'!"

Nonsense. If both perfection *and* imperfection are taken as proof of God's existence, then the whole idea of proof simply falls apart.

Why should the existence of God be exempted from normal standards of proof? It seems quite reasonable to ask whether we live in an intelligently designed universe. And we should be able to answer this not by looking at Biblical or Koranic accounts, and not by praying for insight, but rather by simply looking at the facts.

And, surprisingly, the facts *do* seem to point to some very careful tweaking of the fundamental parameters of the universe. For instance, if the force of gravity were only a little bit stronger than it actually is, the universe would have collapsed shortly after the big bang, long before life could have evolved. But if gravity were just a tad weaker, hydrogen clouds never would have coalesced to form stars.

Further, if the strong-nuclear force (which allows protons to cluster together despite their positive charges repelling each other) were only slightly weaker, no multi-proton atoms could exist; in other words, everything would be hydrogen. On the other hand, if it were only slightly stronger, all of the universe's initial supply of hydrogen would have rapidly converted into helium, meaning there would be no hydrogen at all – and without hydrogen, stars could not shine.

And what about water? It's so common, most of us aren't conscious of just how remarkable a substance it is. If you take almost any other liquid and freeze it, it becomes more dense: a gold brick will sink to the bottom of a vat of liquid gold. But if you freeze water, it *expands*, which is why ice floats on the surface of lakes. If water didn't have this unique property, lakes and oceans would freeze from the bottom up, obliterating delicate sea-floor ecologies. Indeed, once they'd started freezing, bodies of water would freeze solid and likely remain so forever.

Nor does water's unique nature end with its thermal properties. Of all substances, only liquid selenium has a higher surface tension. And it is water's high surface tension that draws it deeply into cracks in rocks, and, as I said, water does the incredible and actually expands as it freezes, breaking those rocks apart. If water had lower surface tension, the process by which soil is formed would not occur.

There are numerous other examples. Cosmologist Paul Davies has concluded that the odds of our universe, with its specific, ultimately life-generating properties, arising by chance are one in 10,000,000,000,000,000,000,000,000,000,000,000,000,000. Those kinds of odds virtually demand the conclusion that someone did indeed tweak the parameters, carefully fine-tuning the universe's design.

Unless, that is, there's more than one universe. If there are, in fact, trillions of universes – either currently existing alongside our own, or having previously existed prior to ours being formed – and if those universes have varying combinations of physical parameters, then there's nothing at all remarkable about a universe like this one existing. In all of that variety, this particular combination of parameters was bound to crop up just by random chance.

Right now, we don't know whether there are, or have been, other universes. But I didn't want to wait to find out; that's why I wrote *Calculating God*. In this novel, we get the answer today because aliens, about a century more advanced than we are, show up on Earth with definitive scientific evidence that no parallel universes currently exist, and that only eight previous universes existed prior to the big bang that created ours. The intervention of an intelligent designer is, to them, an established scientific fact. The novel explores the impact that knowledge has on humanity.

Now, I don't know if aliens will show up with such proof – or, indeed, whether they will arrive with the opposite finding, namely that there are countless other universes, and therefore no need to invoke God in discussing ultimate origins. But even without aliens arriving, we'll have the answer soon: doubtless, by the middle of the twenty-first century, work in cosmology and quantum theory will determine whether or not our universe is the only one.

And then we'll know whether or not God ever existed.

Thanks, quite appropriately, to that most powerful tool of all. Thanks to science.

Committing Trilogy

My website at www.sfwriter.com is often called the best author's site on the web; it contains over one million words of material, and has been online longer than Amazon.com. I try to provide lots of interesting content there, including this article about how my "Neanderthal Parallax" trilogy came to be.

For me, the most daunting question is "What's next?"

That's not necessarily the case for all authors. After all, if you ask Sue Grafton "What's next?," her answer is predetermined by the letters of the alphabet. Me, I'd consider it purgatory to write 26 novels about the same character, but I suppose you can't argue with success.

See, I like to try something new each time out. For instance, *The Terminal Experiment* (1995) was my first attempt to do a realistic domestic situation; *Starplex* (1996) was my first attempt to juxtapose realistic humans with truly alien aliens; *Frameshift* (1997) was my first attempt to do a legitimate SF novel set entirely in the present day; *Factoring Humanity* (1998) was my first attempt to write a book from a female point of view; and *Calculating God* (2000) was my first attempt to write a thriller that consisted of nothing but talking heads.

All five of those books were Hugo Award finalists, so I suppose I succeeded to some degree in what I was attempting. Still, after a dozen novels, it becomes hard to come up with new challenges.

But one that I hadn't undertaken yet was conceiving a trilogy. I know, I know: my novels *Far-Seer* (1992), *Fossil Hunter* (1993), and *Foreigner* (1994) compose "The Quintaglio Ascension" trilogy – but they weren't conceptualized in advance as a trilogy. *Far-Seer* was intended to be a stand-alone; *Fossil Hunter* was a one-off sequel to the successful first volume; and *Foreigner* was commissioned later, as another sequel.

It was a worthy challenge: to write a trilogy that had been planned in advance as such. I'd gotten the hang of the 100,000-word form, but could I do a 300,000-word project?

I freely admit that there were also some commercial considerations: starting with my seventh novel, I'd always had two-book contracts with my publishers, which is nice, because you get a pile of money up front . . . but I wanted to try for a three-book deal, and a trilogy was the natural way to do that. Also, my British publisher, HarperCollins UK, had made it clear that the only SF selling briskly in England was in the form of trilogies and series; standalones just didn't do well in that market.

Now, I'm well known as a critic of the proliferation of trilogies and (even worse) open-ended series in SF, so I knew I'd have to make peace with my personal misgivings about this form. At the outset, I set some ground rules: I would try to write a work that would succeed artistically both as three standalone volumes, each with its own legitimate beginning, middle, and end, and would also have an overarching structure that started at the beginning of the first book and reached a real conclusion at the end of the third.

Both criteria were important to me: I remember vividly Baen Books publishing *Lion's Heart*, by fellow Toronto writer Karen Wehrstein, a dozen years ago . . . with nothing in the packaging to indicate it wasn't a complete novel, and the book stopping with a cliffhanger and a note from the publisher that said, "So ends part one . . ." I would feel like I was cheating my readers if I did that. But I also needed a big, three-book-worthy idea – otherwise, what was the point of committing trilogy?

Most of my novels percolate in my head for years before they get written; *Hominids* – the first volume of what ultimately became my Neanderthal Parallax trilogy – was no exception. I'd come up with the seed of the idea on December 30, 1995, over dinner at The Olive Garden with my wife Carolyn: Earth is threatened by some menace so great that many *multiple* versions of Earth – one where dinosaurs evolved intelligence; another where Neanderthals became the dominant form of humanity; others where different Cambrian explosion body-plans rose to intelligence – must band together to defeat it.

Three and half years later, on June 20, 1999, I finished the second draft of my twelfth novel, *Calculating God*. That evening, Carolyn and I went for a walk – something we often do in the summer – and talked through a more focused version of that idea: a novel about parallel modern-day worlds, one peopled by the descendants of Cro-Magnons, the other by the descendants of Neanderthals.

For me, plots always come from research. For many years, my favorite online resource was Magazine Database Plus, a full-text article database available through CompuServe; on June 22, 1999, I downloaded 50,000 words of magazine and journal articles about Neanderthals. Magazine Database Plus was expensive – a buck an article – but I had a freebie account on CompuServe, left over from when I'd been an associate system operator of the WordStar Forum there, so I used it with abandon. Those articles were only the tip of the iceberg of my research, of course, but they gave me the major plot points to write an outline.

That same day, I looked on Amazon.com at other novels with ancient hominids encountering modern humans, including Frank M. Robinson's *Waiting*, Petru Popescu's *Almost Adam*, Philip Kerr's *Esau*, and John Darnton's *Neanderthal*, to make sure that none of them had premises similar to what I had in mind; they didn't.

Also that day, I wrote up a series of goals for this book:

- To write an ambitious novel for publication in 2002, to be a real contender for the Hugo Award to be presented in Toronto in 2003;
- To be a *tour de force* of world-building, rewriting the last 40,000 years of human history;
- To be a big book, 150,000 words [at this point, I wasn't yet ready to commit to a trilogy – I was simply going to try a bigger book than anything I'd ever written before].
- To have out-of-genre appeal.

On Friday, July 9, 1999, I arrived at Readercon, a literary SF convention held outside of Boston. There I hand-delivered the manuscript for *Calculating God* to Jim Minz, the assistant to my editor David G. Hartwell. Jim asked me what I was going to do next, so I pitched the Neanderthal concept – still quite vague in my mind – to him: two versions of Earth that have to work together to stem a catastrophe facing both worlds. Jim was very intrigued. I asked him whether I should do it as a standalone or a trilogy; Jim said Tor would be happy either way.

(This was a red-letter day for me for another reason: Harlan Ellison was guest of honor at Readercon that year, and in his speech that night he called for a standing ovation for my accomplishments as SFWA president; my time in office had been very difficult, so this pleased me enormously.)

A month later, Carolyn and I rented a cottage on Otter Lake in Northern Ontario; one of my goals while there was to outline my next novel. On Thursday, July 29, I wrote this in my journal:

> Finished, by mid-afternoon, I thought, the outline for *Neandertal World* [then the working title] – but in the evening I skimmed *Waiting* by Frank M. Robinson (which had been edited by my editor, David G. Hartwell); Jim Minz had sent me a copy because I told him I was working on a book about Neandertals. Robinson uses his conflict between us and the modern descendants of archaic humans to preach about ecology; despite previously having checked this book out on Amazon.com, my take was too close to that. Aided by the *Encyclopedia Britannica* and *Grolier's Encyclopedia*, I came up with the idea of the threat to the two worlds being a magnetic reversal (I suspect this might have been in my mind because earlier in the week, I had used Britannica to look up the Geologic Time Scale, and the chart it presented listed magnetic reversals). I like the magnetic-field collapse better than the ecological threat, anyway." (Ah, the joys of computers! It's wonderful to be sitting on the side of a lake with several complete encyclopedias installed on your hard drive.)

The next day, I finished a revised outline, and faxed it to my agent, Ralph Vicinanza. At this stage, I was still pitching only a single novel, and I had absolutely no idea who the characters would be. (I was also using the -*tal* spelling of Neanderthal back then; I've since reverted to the older -*thal* spelling for reasons I outline at length in a forward to *Hominids*.)

Here's the outline, in its entirety; don't worry too much about spoilers – the final project deviated significantly from this document:

Neandertal Parallax
a novel proposal
by Robert J. Sawyer

Ne•an•der•tal: now the preferred spelling by most English-language paleoanthropologists of the word formerly rendered as *Neanderthal,* recognizing the official revision of the spelling of the original German place name by the German government.

par•al•lax: the apparent shifting of an object's position when seen from a different point of view.

Forty thousand years ago, two distinct species of humanity existed on Earth: Archaic *Homo sapiens* and *Homo neanderthalensis.* Both looked out on their world with dull gazes, unable to comprehend it, barely aware of their own existence.

And then an event that would change everything occurred: in the quantum structures of the complex neural tissue packed into the brains of *Homo sapiens,* consciousness emerged. And with consciousness came art and sophisticated language and science and religion and subtle emotions and planning for the future. Until this time, no truly self-aware lifeform had existed on Earth, no creature lived, primate or otherwise, that was driven by anything other than instinct.

Of course, this newfound awareness enabled *Homo sapiens* to out-compete the Neandertals; in less than ten thousand years, the Neandertals were extinct.

Or, at least, they were extinct here – in this universe.

But, under quantum physics, the phenomenon of consciousness is intimately tied in with the nature of reality. Indeed, quantum theory predicts that every time an event observed by an intelligent being could have two outcomes, both outcomes do come to pass – but in separate universes. Until the rise of consciousness, there were no branching universes, no parallel realities. But, starting on that crucial day 40,000 years ago when consciousness emerged for the first time, the universe did begin to split into multiple versions.

The very first split – the very first time an alternative universe was spun off from this one – happened because the original emergence of consciousness, a product of quantum fluctuations, could have gone a different way: instead of consciousness first arising in a *Homo sapiens* mind, it might instead have arisen originally in a *Homo neanderthalensis* mind, leading to the Neandertals deposing our ancestors, instead of vice versa.

And 40,000 years later, in what in this universe is referred to as the dawn of the 21st century, an artificial portal opens, bridging between our universe and one in which the descendants of Neandertals are the dominant form, allowing small numbers of individuals to pass in either direction.

Many things are the same on both Earths: the sky shows the same patterns of stars, the year is still 365 days long, and is divided into months based on the cycling of the moon's phases. The gross geography of both worlds – the shapes of the continents, the location of lakes and mountains – is the same. And the flora and fauna is essentially the same (although Neandertals never hunted mammoths or other animals into extinction, and so they still flourish).

But all the details of culture are different. Gender roles, family structures, economic models, morals, ethics, religion, art, vices, and more are unique to each species. In what I hope will be a *tour de force* of world building, the Neandertal world will be as rich and as human as our own, but different in almost every particular. Although there is much diversity in modern human cultures, many themes recur in almost all of them, themes that can be traced back to our archaic *Homo sapiens* ancestors of 40,000 years ago: pair-bonding, belief in an afterlife, territorial defense, xenophobia, accumulation of wealth. The modern Neandertal society will have entirely different approaches to these and other issues, based on the their different evolutionary history.

For instance, humans are able to effectively communicate with words alone: language spoken in darkness, printed text, radio, telephone conversations, E-mail – all are possible because we can easily transcribe or transmit spoken sounds, and convey virtually our entire intended meaning with just these sounds. But there is much evidence that Neandertals would have had a substantially reduced vocal range compared to that of archaic humans – possibly meaning they, and their descendants, would have to supplement verbal communication with facial expressions and gestures. If their descendants developed books or telephones at all, they might only be useful for conveying limited kinds of information.

Meanwhile, some fossil sites suggest that only female Neandertals homesteaded, and males lived nomadic existences, interacting with females only to breed. Projected into the present day, such lifestyles might define radically different social arrangements, with most individuals having long-term same-sex partnerships (of two, or possibly more, individuals), and secondary other-sex relationships. Absentee fathers wouldn't necessarily be bad fathers, though: modern Neandertal society might be built around multiday holidays during which all work stops and rural males come into the cities to be with their offspring.

And, of course, all the background of daily life – here, in our universe, typified by such things as single-family dwellings, nine-to-five jobs, private automobiles, television, contract law, national allegiances, and war – would be completely different in the Neandertal world, a world equally advanced scientifically but in which individuals are much more physically robust, have larger brains (ancient Neandertal brains averaged 10% larger than those of *Homo sapiens*), are much less interested in colonizing and proselytizing, and are much better suited to living in cold, northern climates: the harsh lands that we know as Alaska, northern Canada, Siberia, Scandinavia, and Iceland – sparsely populated in this universe – might be developed centers in the Neandertal world.

Neandertals and humans differ genetically by only 0.5% (whereas humans and chimpanzees differ by 1.4%); incorporating the latest anthropological research to develop a modern, technological Neandertal culture, the book will illuminate what it means to be human.

The portal between the two universes has been opened accidentally, by the creation not in this world but rather in the

Neandertal one of a giant quantum-computing facility (quantum computers – currently in development – access alternate universes to almost instantly solve otherwise intractable mathematical problems).

The contact could not have come at a more propitious time. In both universes, Earth's magnetic field is collapsing – a prelude to a polarity reversal. Such reversals have happened many times during our planet's geologic history. They occur without any discernible periodicity, and can last as little as two thousand years or as long as 35 million years (the current normal-polarity period began 780,000 years ago; the preceding period of reversed polarity lasted from 980,000 to 780,000 years ago). The difference between reversed and normal polarity is trivial: compass needles point south during the former and north during the latter. But the *transitional* period is of great concern: during it, the magnetic field shuts down, and dangerous cosmic-ray particles that are normally deflected are free to bombard the Earth's surface.

Neither the Neandertals nor the *Homo sapiens* alone have the technology to prevent the collapse of the magnetic field, or, failing that, to protect their worlds during the transitional period – but, perhaps by pooling their differing scientific expertises, they will jointly be able to save both worlds.

The exchange of science and culture starts off promisingly enough, but then the Neandertals discover that we have depleted our ozone layer (which provides additional protection from cosmic rays) through our use of chlorofluorocarbons and petrochemical exhaust from automobiles. It becomes clear that the magnetic-field collapse actually presents a much greater threat to us than it does to them. On their world, the onslaught of cosmic rays will surely cause many cancers and mutations, but on ours, out-and-out mass extinctions – including, likely, that of *Homo sapiens* – will additionally occur.

The Neandertals have learned of our history of expansionism and warfare (something they don't share). Many of them fear if no solution to the magnetic-field collapse is found that we will try to forcibly invade their world with its intact ozone shield – it is, after all, the only other habitable planet that we could possibly escape to.

Continued contact between the two universes is at the Neandertals' discretion, not ours: shutting off their quantum-computing facility will almost certainly sever the link, closing the portal. And once they learn that 40,000 years ago in this universe, our kind drove their ancestors to extinction, will they want to help us? Or, indeed, will they feel justified in letting us die – just as we let their kind die in our own past? *Homo sapiens* will have to prove its humanity, if it is going to be saved.

Neandertal Parallax will be an ultimately uplifting novel of first contact, speculative anthropology, world-building, and cutting-edge quantum theory, with the potential for a sequel or ongoing series.

That outline was written the year the World Science Fiction Convention was in Melbourne, Australia – and Carolyn and I went down under for five and a half weeks. I vacillated about doing a trilogy, or just a standalone, for much of that period, and talked with my editor David G. Hartwell about it at the Worldcon (during a wonderful lunch at which we were joined by Stephen Baxter). When I got back to Canada, I called Ralph Vicinanza, and told him to go for a trilogy contract, based on the existing out-line.

Ralph did just that. It took some time – we were asking for a substantial amount of money – but the deal was finally closed on November 1, 1999, with me getting everything I wanted.

I spent the next three and half months doing nothing but research on Neanderthals. On February 16, 2002, the idea of opening the novel deep in the nickel mine housing the real Sudbury Neutrino Observatory occurred to me, and the next day I wrote the first words of the first book in the trilogy, a prologue (which ultimately got thrown out) designed to explain the origins of the subterranean nickel, and how it led to physics labs being built on the same site in our version of Earth and the Neanderthal one:

> Everyone has heard about the asteroid that may have felled the dinosaurs, and how if it hadn't hit, we might not be here.
>
> But there have been many other asteroid impacts in Earth's past, and when *this* one crashed into Earth, the dinosaurs weren't yet even a twinkle in God's eye.

If it hadn't hit, we would probably still be here, but *they* – the others – would not. This flying mountain, a hunk of detritus left over from the formation of the solar system that measured between one and three kilometers wide, brutally slammed into –

Into what? How to describe the rocks that bore this assault? Today, most of the world calls them the *Canadian Shield,* a vast horseshoe shaped region covering half the nation we refer to as Canada – but when the impact occurred, Canada, and every other human construct, was still 1.8 billion years in the future.

Of course, in Canada, where everything would naturally be Canadian-this or Canadian-that, these rocks are sometimes called the *Precambrian Shield* instead, but –

But *everything* was Precambrian back when this colossal boulder, moving at fifteen kilometers per second, slammed into our world, setting it ringing like a giant bell in space. Although Earth had hosted life for two billion years by that point, none of it was yet multicellular. The first worms were another billion years in the future; jawless fish, the first vertebrates, were still 1.3 billion years away; and the first mammals – ancestors to us, yes, and to *them* as well – wouldn't appear for an additional three hundred million after that.

It was a beginning (even if not a very good one), and from there I was off to the races, writing 2,000 new words every day until I had a first draft. Meanwhile, I set about visiting various experts on Neanderthals, including Philip Lieberman of Brown University (who noted that Neanderthals probably couldn't say the *ee* phoneme, a fact I make much of in the trilogy), Ian Tattersall of the American Museum of Natural History (whose talk "The Origin of the Human Capacity," a transcript of which I'd found online, had introduced me to the concept of the Great Leap Forward – the dawn of human consciousness – which I gave a quantum-mechanical twist in the series), and Milford Wolpoff of the University of Michigan, himself an SF fan, who believes that we co-opted Neanderthal DNA into our own through interbreeding.

As I write these words, the first week of January 2003, I've just finished the final revisions on *Hybrids*, the third book in the trilogy. In preparing this essay, I re-read the above outline for the first time in over three years, and am surprised by how much grew from that tiny seed. I'm really proud of how the Neanderthal Parallax trilogy turned out, but I was more than a little surprised when I got an E-mail from Moshe Feder, who had replaced Jim Minz as David Hartwell's assistant, saying that David would be happy to contemplate a fourth Neanderthal book . . .

I was flattered, but felt that would be wrong. I'd wrapped up the story, and I was ready to move on to another challenge.

Now, all I have to do is figure out a new answer to that ever-vexing question, "What's next?"

Privacy: Who Needs It?

Maclean's is Canada's weekly newsmagazine, the northern counterpart of Time. In 2002, Berton Woodward, one of its editors, approached me about writing an opinion piece. I was thrilled – Maclean's pays $1.25 a word – and I decided to do something that would tie-in with my just released thirteenth novel, Hominids, *in which a technologically advanced Neanderthal civilization had all but eliminated crime through a system of "alibi archives" that record the activities of its citizens.*

I described that system in this deliberately provocative essay, which appeared in the October 7, 2002, edition, and which generated more letters to the editor – evenly split between pro and con – than anything else Maclean's *published that year.*

Whenever I visit a tourist attraction that has a guest register, I always sign it. After all, you never know when you'll need an alibi.

I've been doing this since I was a kid, but these days you don't have to take any positive action to leave a trail behind. Almost everything we do is recorded. Closed-circuit cameras watch us in most public places. Our credit-card purchases, telephone calls, and web surfing are all tracked.

Editorialists have decried these losses of privacy, as if it were the most sacred of human rights. But just what *is* the value of privacy? Do we really need it? And, indeed, can we afford it? After all, everything from your son's shoplifting to the destruction of the towers at the World Trade Center could have been prevented if we had less of an ability to do things in secret.

And yet we continue to insist that honest people need to have that ability. The founders of the United States, for instance, believed that governments have to be overthrown from time to time. That's the rationale behind their second amendment, allowing private gun ownership: the people need to be able to take up arms against an oppressive regime.

But oppressive regimes are crumbling all over the world, and there are so many checks and balances in most governmental systems these days that there's no need for bloody overthrow. And yet by making it a fundamental right to plot and conspire to violently oust democratically elected authorities, you're bound to have terrorists.

We Canadians peacefully negotiated our independence – and have shown the world how such things should be handled in the 21st century by agreeing in turn to peacefully negotiate Quebec separation, if most people there want that. But the U.S. still makes a big deal about having to fight for independence. And indeed they did – but that was hundreds of years ago. In this, the Third Millennium, do we really need a social system based on allowing for armed uprisings and backroom conspiracies?

Surveillance and the collection of personal information are unavoidable in this closed-circuit, computerized world. Rather than trying to end them, we should be striving to find ways to maximize their benefits for the average citizen.

Recently, I was keynote speaker at the 12th Annual Canadian Conference on Intelligent Systems, Canada's principal gathering of experts on robotics and artificial intelligence. The two tasks most of the researchers there were concentrating on were pattern recognition and data-mining.

So far, most applications for these technologies have been commercial: if you buy a Walkman and are enrolled in a night-school course, you might be interested in buying textbooks on tape. True enough – and certainly irritating if someone calls while you're eating dinner to sell you the unabridged audio version of McLuhan's *Understanding Media.*

But I can't see the downside of an RCMP or CSIS computer noting that my neighbour has bought all the materials to make a pipe bomb and has booked a one-way flight to Tahiti. About the only government entity routinely looking through personal data for patterns is the Canada Customs and Revenue Agency, hunting for unusual values on tax returns that might indicate a cheater. Frankly, I'd much rather the government was tracking down potential terrorists, sex offenders, and so on.

George Orwell scared the bejeebers out of us with his Big Brother. But when I was a kid, it was actually a comfort knowing that my own big brother was watching over me while I played in the park. With proper safeguards, there's no reason why any honest person should fear a little benign oversight.

Indeed, our pets already benefit from this. Dogs routinely have chips implanted to make them easy to find when lost – whereas our own children often disappear without a trace. Ask any parent who has had a son or daughter abducted if some abstract notion of privacy really is more important than the life of their child.

Still, Luddites will continue to insist that monitoring of humans means giving up too much. Perhaps. But as Scott McNealy, CEO of computer giant Sun Microsystems, says, "You have zero privacy anyway. Get over it." In other words, such monitoring and tracking is already going on to benefit big business. Why not take advantage of it to improve our own lives?

Sure, no one wants people they don't know looking over their shoulder. But most of us take holiday photos, make home videos, keep a diary, or otherwise record what we know will be important moments of our lives. And yet the truly crucial moments – when a punk sticks a gun in your ribs, when another car sideswipes yours, when you accidentally leave your favorite hat somewhere – go unrecorded simply because we didn't know they were about to happen.

But imagine a permanently activated recorder: a small implant, say, that keeps track of your whereabouts using signals from the satellite-based Global Positioning System. Suppose the implant constantly broadcasts your exact location to a centralized facility. At that facility – call it the Alibi Archives – you would have your own personal black box, keeping track of your movements.

No one but you, or, if you disappeared, your family or the police, could access the contents of your black box. But if you *did* disappear – kidnapped, lost, fallen down a hole, wandering aimlessly because of Alzheimer's – you could be quickly found. No more missing persons; no more desperate searches.

Sounds useful, no? Now, what about adding a constant transmission of your vital signs. If they indicated you were having a heart attack or stroke, an ambulance could be automatically dispatched.

That's not too scary, is it? Okay: let's take it a step further. Add a tiny audiovisual recorder to the implant, and you could have a permanent home video of your life made automatically. Everything from demonstrating to your wife that you really did say, "That dress makes you look hot," not "fat," to finding that lost favorite hat would be easy.

Ah, but it gets better. If everyone's actions were recorded – for their eyes only, unless a proper court order demanded otherwise – think of the reduction in crime. Who would assault, murder, or rape, if they knew that the victim would have a complete off-site record of the event made by their own implant?

And imagine the further reduction in crime, when the criminal knows that his location and actions are being tracked. Maybe you couldn't identify your own assailant – but computers could scan the archives and find out precisely who was standing next to you at 9:04 p.m., when you were forced to hand over your diamond jewelry.

Notice I said jewelry, and not your wallet. That's because an implant could also serve as an irrefutable personal ID. Your car wouldn't start for anyone but you; no more car theft. You'd never get locked out of your own home again. And a true cashless society would become possible, with implants communicating with each other to debit and credit accounts. Paper money is beloved of drug dealers and tax evaders; recorded electronic transfers could put an end to all that.

Such implants would start off as a consumer-electronics item in peaceful democratic nations, not as an enforced requirement under oppressive regimes. But, as such regimes continue to disappear, we might soon enough end up with everyone everywhere being required to have one. And why not? You're already required to have a license to drive and a passport to travel.

There are only two reasons we desire privacy. The first is because of the ridiculous shame societies have heretofore heaped on natural human activities and nudity.

Yes, our Victorian ancestors might have been desperate to hide things from their families and neighbors, because so many activities were proscribed. But who really cares today if someone is gay, smokes pot, or likes to watch porno films? It's not the freedom to do things that would disappear with constant black-box monitoring; it's the silly laws that make victimless activities illegal.

The only other reason to need privacy is so you can get away with something unethical or illegal. It was privacy, not the lack of it, that made Paul Bernardo's depredations possible. It was privacy, not the lack of it, that made al-Qaida possible. It was privacy, not the lack of it, that made the current crisis in the Catholic Church possible.

But what about the bogeyman of totalitarianism? Again, it was privacy that made Hitler's Final Solution come within a hair's breadth of succeeding. But it was the *lack* of privacy — the openness of communication through the Internet — that prevented the Chinese government from covering up the 1989 massacre in Tiananmen Square, or from trying anything similar since.

Besides, if you have your own personal implant communicating constantly with the central computerized archives, democracy becomes more powerful, not less, with everyone being able to instantaneously vote in an ever-increasing number of referenda and plebiscites.

Still, some might argue that governments do have legitimate needs for privacy — but, come now, our politicians have long since lost any of their own. We know all about Ralph Klein's drinking habits and Bill Clinton's sexual escapades.

Ah, but what about military secrets? Oh, perhaps there's some value in being able to shunt Dick Cheney off to an "undisclosed location," but, really, it's the *aggressors* who benefit from the ability to do things clandestinely. If the Japanese had been privy to the July 16, 1945, A-bomb test explosion in Alamogordo, New Mexico, I doubt they would have needed to be surprised by bombs dropping on Hiroshima and Nagasaki before surrendering.

The message of history, most spectacularly driven home last September 11, is that preserving society as a whole is much more important than preserving an illusory personal freedom. And if our species is going to survive, we must wake up to that fact.

See, there's a long-standing problem in astronomy called the Fermi Paradox, named for physicist Enrico Fermi who first proposed it in 1950. If the universe should be teeming with life, asked Fermi, then where are all the aliens? The question is even more vexing today: SETI, the search for extraterrestrial intelligence with radio telescopes, has utterly failed to turn up any sign of alien life forms. Why?

One chillingly likely possibility is that, as the ability to wreak damage on a grand scale becomes more readily available to individuals, soon enough just one malcontent, or one lunatic, will be able to destroy an entire world. Perhaps countless alien civilizations have already been wiped out by single terrorists who'd been left alone to work unmonitored in their private laboratories.

We've already seen what one crazed suicide bomber can do with twentieth-century technology; imagine the devastation he or she might manage with the ordnance and genetic capabilities that will be freely available within the next few decades. We can be sure that those who wish society harm will be taking full advantage of advanced technologies. Why shouldn't we take advantage of technology to protect ourselves?

Instead of having a knee-jerk reaction that says any loss of privacy is bad, let's discuss the potential pitfalls and work out ways to relieve them. Canada's Privacy Commissioner is a model worldwide for avoiding abuses; there's no reason why we can't devise a system of implants and personal black boxes that really works.

Whether we want American-style life, liberty, and the pursuit of happiness, or Canadian peace, order, and good government, clinging to privacy at all costs is the worst thing we can do. For, as the silence from the stars attests, not only is an unexamined life not worth living, it may be that unexamined lives are too dangerous for us to allow them to be lived. The very future of humanity may depend on giving up the outmoded notion of privacy, rather than fighting to retain it.

The Age of Miracle and Wonder

CBC Radio has always been wonderfully supportive of me, letting me write and narrate documentaries, host programs, and be a guest on just about every major show it produces, from the flagships Morningside *and* Sounds Like Canada, *through the science series* Quirks and Quarks *and the scholarly* Ideas, *to the pop-culture extravaganza* Definitely Not the Opera; *I even used to have my own weekly on-air column,* Science FACTion: Commentaries from the Cutting Edge of Science.

In November 1999, I wrote and recorded this commentary for CBC Radio One about life in the next millennium.

As a science-fiction writer, I'm used to thinking in realistic terms about the future, extrapolating from what we know to what might be. But the new millennium is going to put me and my colleagues out of our jobs.

Forty years ago, Arthur C. Clarke, the author of the quintessential millennial work *2001: A Space Odyssey*, coined "Clarke's Law," which says: "Any sufficiently advanced technology is indistinguishable from magic."

When Clarke said that, by "sufficiently advanced technology," he had in mind the fruits of cultures thousands of years beyond our own.

But scientific progress increases exponentially. Ninety percent of all the advances made in the millennium we're now leaving happened in its final ten percent – the final century. Antibiotics and organ transplants, space travel and radio telescopes, computers and lasers, television and motion pictures, civil rights and feminism – all of them are the product of the 20th century.

Within the next two decades, we'll see as much additional progress as we did in all of the last century: the world of A.D. 2020 will be as incomprehensible to us as our world of today would have been to Queen Victoria during the last year of her reign.

We can guess at some of what the next couple of decades will bring, but it very quickly transcends beyond the realm of what we know as science into Arthur C. Clarke's magic.

Consider nanotechnology, which is probably just around the corner. It will allow us to build things up atom by atom. You want a five-course dinner? A brick of platinum? A new kidney? Claudia Schiffer? No problem. We can build it for you.

At the most advanced levels, nanotechnology will tear down and build up atoms from constituent parts: the differences between a pile of old newspapers and gold-and-diamond jewelry are only in how the protons, neutrons, and electrons are arranged. Sophisticated nanotech gives you the alchemist's dream of transmutation; it gives everyone the Midas touch – and it means there is no longer any such thing as a scarce resource. Food, fuel, drinking water, clean air – whatever you want, in whatever quantity you want it, all free for the asking.

More: since nanotechnological machines will be able to make *anything* – including unlimited copies of themselves – the devices that perform this magic become essentially free of cost. Material needs disappear. Bill Gates won't be the richest person in the world two decades from now; rather, everyone will have unlimited wealth.

But having all your material needs taken care of does you no good if you're dead. No problem: if you manage to hold on until A.D. 2020 – another twenty years – it's likely that you will *never* die.

We already know what causes cells to age and cease to function; reversing the process will be one of the countless benefits of the Human Genome Project, currently nearing completion. Almost everyone born on this planet after 1950 will live to see not just the twenty-first century, but the twenty-second, and perhaps the twenty-third as well.

Of course, even with aging halted, there's still a risk of accident – of having your body destroyed. But that's only a concern if we continue to *have* bodies. Certainly by the end of the next century, we will be able to dispense with these fallible sacks of flesh. We will have the technology to scan our brains and upload our consciousnesses into computers, living entirely in a virtual realm. At that point, we will be truly immortal.

We also will be quite different from what we were; we will have entered the *trans-human* era.

Granted, these notions – nanotechnology, life prolongation, uploaded consciousness – are the easy ones, the ones we *can* foresee, because they grow out of work already underway at our universities. But even science-fiction writers like myself failed to predict the World Wide Web, which has already transformed the planet. Life in the 21st century will be utterly unlike anything we can predict. It will be alien and strange, and during it, we will completely redefine what it means to be human. But it also will be wonderful and luxurious.

It will, in fact, be magic.

Is Risk Our Business?

In the April 2000 issue of Wired, *Bill Joy, the chief scientist at Sun Microsystems, published his now-famous antitechnology manifesto, "Why The Future Doesn't Need Us."* The Globe and Mail: Canada's National Newspaper *asked for my reaction; this piece appeared in the Thursday, March 16, 2000, edition.*

Those who pooh-pooh William Shatner's acting should see his soliloquy from the *Star Trek* episode "Return to Tomorrow." Aliens offer the crew of the *Enterprise* fantastic advances in technology in exchange for letting them inhabit the bodies of three crew members for a few days.

Dr. McCoy, the Luddite, points out the downsides, but Captain Kirk wins him over with his eloquence: "Risk is our business," he says after enumerating advances science has already made by throwing caution to the wind. "That's what this starship is all about; that's why we're aboard her."

Shatner is so terrific, actually, that one forgets that the owners of the three borrowed bodies almost end up killed, one of the aliens commits murder, two die by suicide, and no scientific wonders are ever bestowed.

Despite this, we're left thinking that Kirk was nonetheless right to push for the advancement of science, the risks be damned. Anything less would be a betrayal of the human spirit.

These days, we don't have to look to aliens to provide technologies indistinguishable from magic. Such powers are now within our own grasp, apples of new knowledge seemingly ripe for the plucking. But was Kirk right? Is taking risks for the mere possibility of advancement worth it?

Bill Joy confesses to have grown up watching Captain Kirk and reading science fiction. And, like many who did so, Joy has gone on to a technological career. He is chief scientist at Sun Microsystems, a giant Silicon Valley firm.

This week, in *Wired* magazine, he published an 11,000-word manifesto that, distilled to its essence, repeats the mantra of much 1950s science fiction: "There are some things Man was not meant to know."

Joy is worried about three nascent technologies: artificial intelligence (AI), genetic engineering, and nanotechnology. Is he right to be afraid of them? And, even if he is, is there anything we can do to reduce the risks?

Joy's concern about AI is simple: if we make machines that are more intelligent than we are, why on earth would they want to be our slaves?

In this, I believe he is absolutely right: thinking computers pose a real threat to the continued survival of our species. Many AI experts – including Hans Moravec, founder of the world's largest robotics lab, at Carnegie Mellon University – believe that humanity's job is to manufacture its own successors.

Sure, Moravec says, we may shed a tear for some ineffable biological qualities that might be lost, but in the end *Homo sapiens* will be supplanted by machines. Since that's inevitable, he feels, we might as well go along doing the research that will lead to this.

Joy says no: we can, and perhaps should, put on the brakes. I agree.

Intelligence is an emergent property of complex systems; it arises spontaneously if conditions are right. Anatomically modern humans first appeared 100,000 years ago, but they were unencumbered by art, culture, religion, or abstract thought for 60,000 years.

Then, with no physical change in their brains, consciousness emerged. Suddenly, these same people were painting caves, developing religious rituals, and more.

The emergence of computer-based consciousness may happen the same way: arising spontaneously out of something complex we built, perhaps for another purpose (World Wide Web, anyone?).

It's not a new idea; Arthur C. Clarke first put it forward almost forty years ago in his story "Dial F for Frankenstein."

Other science-fiction authors have sounded this warning bell. William Gibson's 1984 novel *Neuromancer* features an organization called Turing whose job is to prevent the emergence of AI. And in my own 1998 *Factoring Humanity*, a thinking computer created at the University of Toronto commits suicide rather than risk turning against its human father.

I'm less concerned, though, about Joy's other two bugbears: genetic engineering and nanotechnology. Both, really, are forms of manipulation at the submolecular level: genetic engineering rearranges the atoms in a string of DNA so that a modified life-form is produced.

And nanotechnology simply takes that a step further, proposing that we soon will be able to tear down and rebuild any molecules we want, turning, for instance, a pile of bricks into a mound of gold, or a giant three-cheese lasagna, or anything else.

Joy's fear is that genetic engineering will be used to create diseases that target specific ethnicities. An Arab and an Israeli don't just differ politically; they differ genetically, too, and Joy fears it will soon be easy enough to produce a virus that will wipe out only one or the other.

Possible? Yes. But, then, so is a plague that affects only those humans with genes for antisocial behavior (first-order sorting: check for a Y chromosome); you can bet some self-styled Good Samaritan will release something like this, as well.

But, despite such scenarios, I find it unconscionable to tell a boy with leukemia or a woman with diabetes that we're not going to do any more genetic research. The cures for diseases – including the one known as aging that gets us all if nothing else does – will come only from manipulating DNA.

Joy also thinks we should have a moratorium on nanotechnology, since a nanotech machine can produce anything – including copies of itself – from whatever raw materials are at hand.

He writes, "An immediate consequence of the Faustian bargain in obtaining the great power of nanotechnology is that we run a grave risk – the risk that we might destroy the biosphere on which all life depends." Indeed, if just one little self-replicating doodad that turns water into wine escapes, we might see it and its spawn destroy our ecosystem, and us along with it.

But nanotechnology will also allow us to provide for all the material needs of the entire human race: as much clear air, water, food, clothing, shelter, medicine, and entertainment as anyone could ever want.

It will be impossible to keep this technology from the masses: just one microscopic machine that can convert raw materials into other forms is all that has to be smuggled out of the lab.

Soon, everyone will have a replicator, and the economic reasons for war, oppression, and figurative and literal slavery will disappear. Supply will always equal demand in everything from basic essentials to elaborate equipment, costs will be zero, and poverty will vanish.

Captain Kirk said, "Risk is our business." I don't think so; I think improving the human condition is our business. Other minds – silicon consciousnesses – won't share that mission statement, and are rightly to be avoided. But genetic engineering and nanotechnology will allow us to so vastly improve humanity's lot that we'd be fools to turn our backs on them – despite the risks.

The Private Sector in Space

In honor of the first private-sector manned spaceflight, which took place in the summer of 2004, The Globe and Mail: Canada's National Newspaper *commissioned me to write this op-ed piece; it first appeared in that paper's Tuesday, June 29, 2004, edition.*

Most TV viewers remember Andy Griffith as Sheriff Taylor of Mayberry, or as Ben Matlock, the wily defence attorney. Me, I remember him as Harry Broderick, the main character of the 1979 ABC science-fiction series *Salvage 1*.

Like *Star Trek*, another of my favorites, this show had narration over the opening credits: "Once upon a time, a junkman had a dream. 'I'm gonna build a spaceship, go to the moon, salvage all the junk that's up there, bring it back, and sell it.'"

As is so common with science fiction, the premise of *Salvage 1* has now become science fact. The private sector has begun sending humans into space for motives of pure profit. And I, for one, think that's great.

Last Monday, June 21, a vehicle bearing the wonderfully appropriate name *SpaceShip One* became the first-ever private space vessel, travelling 100 km above the Earth. At the helm was Mike Melvill, who, at the age of 63, is now the first private pilot to earn astronaut's wings from the U.S. Federal Aviation Administration.

Melvill plans to go up again soon. He's part of a team funded by Microsoft co-founder Paul Allen that's looking to snare the Ansari X Prize: US$10-million that will go to the first private-sector concern to launch a reusable vehicle containing three people into space twice in a two-week period. The prize is the brainchild of physician Peter Diamandis, who came up with the idea after reading about how the US$25,000 Orteig Prize had inspired Charles Lindbergh to undertake the world's first solo transatlantic flight in 1927. Since the dawn of powered flight, making money has been a great motivator.

There are 23 other groups vying for the X Prize, including two in Canada: the Canuck spaceships are the *Arrow* (who says you never get second chances?) and the *Wild Fire*. Everybody involved in these projects is convinced that great benefits will come from the private sector being involved in manned space flight.

And why shouldn't it be? The public sector – particularly NASA – has certainly botched it. The International Space Station had cost overruns that would make even a military contractor blush. And after the *Columbia* tragedy of February 2003 – like the earlier *Challenger* disaster, largely attributable to administrative incompetence – what's left of the U.S. space shuttle fleet has been grounded.

We've had 43 years of space travel based on a recipe of bureaucracy and big spending, and, astonishingly, in all that time, the cost of putting a person in space has remained constant. That's because there's been no competition to drive the price down. But the government monopoly on manned space flight is coming to an end as we try a new set of ingredients: guts and imagination, entrepreneurship and innovation.

And fun – let's not forget fun! Indeed, that was always one of NASA's problems. As science-fiction legend Robert A. Heinlein famously observed, only a government bureaucracy could succeed in making the grand adventure of going into space boring.

Fortunately, despite Mission Control's snooze-inducing efforts, a large segment of the public is still captivated by the dream of travelling in space. And, indeed, the era of space tourism has already begun: in 2001, Dennis Tito became the first person to buy a vacation above Earth, heading up on a Russian cargo rocket to the International Space Station.

What's the appeal? Well, besides the thrill of the ride and the breathtaking views of our own planet, journeys to space also allow you to experience weightlessness. In zero gravity, everyone's an acrobat.

The market is huge. Surveys show that 69% of males and 57% of females want to take a trip into space – and 70% of those would be willing to pay several months' salary to do so. Patrick Collins of Space Future Consulting predicts that by 2030, the private sector will be putting five million tourists a year into space, visiting dozens of orbiting hotels and sports complexes. The Hilton chain is already seriously working on plans for its first orbital resort.

Of course, tourism is only one part of what businesses hope to accomplish in space. Alloys made there are exceptionally strong because they lack the defects caused when gravity swirls the molten metal. Impurity-free pharmaceuticals can be produced in microgravity by mixing the constituent chemicals in midair, without ever touching containers that might contaminate them. And some superconducting crystals can only be grown in microgravity.

All of those things that can be done in what the space-business community calls LEO – Low Earth Orbit. But, just like Andy Griffith's character on *Salvage 1*, today's businesses also have their sights set on the moon. For instance, the Artemis Project is a private venture bent on establishing a permanent, self-supporting lunar community. Among the possible uses: the ultimate retirement home. After all, you don't have to worry about breaking your hip when you fall in slow motion and only weigh one-sixth of what you did on Earth.

Now, yes, there will always be a role for government-funded manned space flight. Basic exploration should be done for reasons other than making a buck. And I do believe governments should be working hard to establish permanent settlements off-Earth so that humanity will survive even the worst terrorist or environmental disaster.

But in other areas, the government should butt out, and let the capitalists take their shot. Dan Goldin, the former Administrator of NASA, had a mantra: "Better, faster, cheaper." Of course, he was never able to make that work in the bloated bureaucracy he headed. But those same goals are routinely achieved by businesses. Where governments fail – on Earth or out among the stars – the private sector will succeed.

Andy Griffith's Harry Broderick character had a dream. So do I. I dream of going to space. No government is going to make that happen for regular guys like me. But private business will — because there are customers willing to pay for it. The bottom line is still the bottom line, even out on the final frontier.

Science, Salvation, and Atwood

Brian Bethune, the books editor at Maclean's: Canada's Weekly Newsmagazine, *found reading Margaret Atwood's science-fiction novel* Oryx and Crake *depressing. A fan of my optimistic futures, he called me up and commissioned this essay, which ran as a counterpoint to his profile of Atwood in* Maclean's *April 28, 2003, issue.*

About a third of the way through Margaret Atwood's new science-fiction novel *Oryx and Crake*, Oryx – a former child prostitute from Southeast Asia – says: "Why do you want to talk about ugly things? We should think only beautiful things, as much as we can. There is so much beautiful in the world if you look around. You are looking only at the dirt under your feet. It's not good for you."

That's advice Atwood herself should take. *Oryx and Crake* wallows in a thoroughly unpleasant version of the near future, a world of total environmental degradation and genetic engineering run amuck. In Atwood's view, every problem we face now is going to get worse, not better.

I disagree. Human ingenuity will give all of us a wonderfully positive future. Take the environment, for instance. The ecology movement started in the early 1960s, with a work of nonfiction (Rachel Carson's *Silent Spring*, 1962) and a work of science fiction (Frank Herbert's *Dune*, 1965), and is now in full swing.

There's nothing wrong with science fiction telling cautionary tales: if *this* goes on, *that* awful reality will come to pass. But Atwood's *this* is *not* going on; we've already hit the brakes on environmental decay. To publish a novel after Canada has signed the Kyoto accords that tells us the environment is going to hell in a handbasket is to have missed the prophetic boat by decades.

Atwood's future is one of gated communities, of the protected few living in fear of those roaming out in "the pleeblands." But we already have the technology to give women back the night, to end most crime and bullying, to let everyone go about their lives unmolested; I discussed this at length in my essay "Privacy: Who Needs It?" in the October 7, 2003, issue of this magazine. Far from being an Orwellian nightmare, effective monitoring of the activities of both citizens and governments will be the great liberator of the twenty-first century. Gated communities aren't the future; they're the dismal past.

Atwood suggests that genetic engineering is an evil thing. It's not; it's wonderful. In the next few decades, our new insights into how life works will cure cancer, Alzheimer's disease, diabetes, heart disease, world hunger, and probably even aging itself.

Indeed, anyone who lives to at least the year 2050 – meaning almost every child born today in Canada – will likely get to see not only the twenty-second century, but also the twenty-third, and will do so in vigorous health, with full possession of his or her faculties.

The beauty of such life prolongation is that it will give people perspective, letting us finally deserve our species' name, *Homo sapiens* – man of wisdom. Problems can't be left for future generations; anything you set in motion now – too much garbage, too few forests, too many weapons – will be *your* problem. Instead of fear-mongering, we should embrace the work of the visionary scientists who are striving to prevent deformity, enhance potential, and feed us all.

By the time that Atwood portrays (she never commits to a date, but it's obviously later this century), I believe we will be living in a true age of miracles and wonder, the kind of utopian society that only a thorough grasping of how the universe really works – by knowing the basic principles of life and physics – can make possible.

And yet Atwood gives physics short shrift, although she does mention nanotechnology in passing. Nanotech – the science of the very small – is the current hobbyhorse of Michael Crichton, who decries it in his latest if-anything-can-go-wrong-it-will tome, *Prey*. Atwood and Crichton share nothing in terms of style – the lady from Toronto writes circles around the gentleman from Los Angeles – but they are depressingly similar in substance.

Nanotech will allow us to build little machines to travel through our arteries, clearing out plaque. It will allow us to clean up oil spills, and scrub the poisons from our atmosphere. Indeed, in its strongest form – giving us the alchemist's touch, allowing us to break down any matter into its constituent protons, neutrons, and electrons, and rearrange those particles into whatever we want – it will let us not only turn lead into gold, but dirt into steak, and garbage into trees.

Sound far-fetched? Not after a single century that gave us widespread use of indoor lighting and plumbing and electricity; civil rights and feminism and a nascent world government; airplanes and television and microwave ovens; heart transplants and antibiotics and insulin; computers and lasers and space stations. Not after a brief hundred years in which we learned about other galaxies and the double helix and quantum mechanics, and became better, more compassionate people.

Atwood has a nostalgia for the way things were, for a simpler past. But our past included slavery, 50-percent infant-mortality rates, abject poverty, epidemics, and ignorance. Today is better than yesterday; tomorrow will be even better still. If, as we look into the future, we can't precisely see the wonders that are yet to come, it's only because there's so much glare from the bright tomorrows ahead.

Atwood's Depressing Future

The foregoing wasn't my last word on Atwood. The Ottawa Citizen *asked me to do an actual review of* Oryx and Crake. *I initially declined, saying there were lots of people more conversant with Atwood's oeuvre than I was. But editor Susan Allen said she didn't care if the book was good Atwood; she wanted me to tell her readers if it was good science fiction – and I did so, in this review which ran in the* Citizen's *Sunday, April 27, 2003, edition.*

———•——

Margaret Atwood doesn't like to be called a science-fiction writer. Tough beans, says I. When she writes a novel set in the future that purports to be firmly rooted in contemporary scientific thought, she is indeed writing science fiction.

Yes, one might have been able to argue that her earlier, and quite terrific, futuristic foray, 1985's *The Handmaid's Tale*, wasn't really science fiction – it had no basis in science (even though it did win the Arthur C. Clarke Award for Best Science Fiction Novel of the Year, and was a finalist for the Science-Fiction Writers of America's Nebula Award).

But Atwood herself takes pains in an afterword to her new novel, *Oryx and Crake*, to direct you to her web site (inevitably, oryxandcrake.com), where she lists the scientific references she drew on in creating her future world.

So, given that what she's doing is indisputably science fiction, how does she fare by the standards of that venerable genre?

The sad answer is: not very well. It's not that her predictions are unreasonable – she rails against the decline of the environment, and decries the possibilities of genetic engineering gone bad. But such notions are already front-page news, and have been for years. Despite frequent references in her text to "the law of unforeseen consequences," Atwood provides no wake-up call about anything that has hitherto eluded public consciousness. Rather, she has jumped on a bandwagon that long ago ran out of steam.

It's this failure of speculative insight that will doom *Oryx and Crake* to minor-league status in the SF field, although doubtless the book will zoom onto the bestseller lists. Atwood wraps up, admittedly in a very stylish package, a selection of old-hat concerns, and fails to give any new twist either in the way in which things might go awry (which at least would have been intriguing) or in how humanity might extricate itself from the problems it has created (which might have been instructive). Instead, we're presented with an unalloyed it's-all-coming-to-an-end tome, depressing in the extreme.

Oryx and Crake is apparently set just a few decades down the road (the author, who seems so sure of what the future will bring, is surprisingly coy about specifying a date). The book is told from the point of view of Jimmy, the last genetically unaltered human being left alive after a bioengineered plague has wiped out civilization (in that, it recalls Richard Matheson's 1954 classic *I Am Legend*, filmed as *The Omega Man*).

Jimmy spends much of the book recalling his relationships with Oryx, a philosophical child prostitute from Southeast Asia, and Crake, a boy-genius with Asperger's syndrome. During these flashbacks, we slowly learn about the artificial plague created by Crake that destroyed humanity; although global warming also plays a role in Atwood's singularly unpleasant future, biotech and genetic engineering are the clear villains of the piece.

And that's unfortunate. In *The Handmaid's Tale*, Atwood at least was putting forth an important caution, one that very much needed to be heard when that book was released: if the religious right continues to gain power, all the strides made in gender equality will be erased. It was a warning, and a call for preventive action, at a time when something could have still been done. But in *Oryx and Crake*, Atwood has given up on humanity; we've already gone too far, she says, and it's just a matter of decades before everything comes crashing down around us.

Indeed, Atwood comes off as relentlessly anti-science; in that sense, she deserves the mantle of Canada's answer to Michael Crichton, whose books are always of the if-anything-can-go-wrong-it-will variety (cloning in *Jurassic Park*; nanotechnology in *Prey*). Atwood and Crichton share nothing in terms of style – the lady from Toronto writes circles around the gentleman from Los Angeles – but they are depressingly similar in substance.

Of course, it's for the beauty of her writing that we come to Atwood. Other reviewers will doubtless praise her wordplay: new genetic hybrids called "snats" (snake-rats) and "rakunks" (raccoon-skunks), and supposedly futuristic websites with names such as NoodyNews.com.

But none of this is uniquely Atwood; science-fiction writers have always reveled in such portmanteau linguistics. Old masters including Samuel R. Delany, and newer voices such as James Patrick Kelly, wield this device much more deftly than she does. (Indeed, it seems pointless of Atwood to try to pawn off Noody-News – a web-based newscast presented by naked people – as her own clever satiric invention when NakedNews.com, which offers precisely this service, has been up and running for years now.)

Still, there is much to admire in Atwood's prose (but then again, there also is much to admire in that of many SF writers, including Ursula K. Le Guin and Canada's own William Gibson). And her satiric hand – when applied lightly to interpersonal relationships, instead of heavily to the Demon Science – is a joy, as always.

But, to me, as a science-fiction writer, the saddest thing about *Oryx and Crake* is that it will be seen as cutting-edge and visionary by the literati, instead of as what it really is: a retread of timeworn ideas. For instance, others will doubtlessly chortle with glee over Atwood's "ChickieNobs," the meat of bioengineered chickens that have no brains or beaks, but produce eight succulent breasts per animal. But Frederik Pohl and C. M. Kornbluth did the same thing half a century ago in their wickedly satiric, and much more prescient, SF novel, *The Space Merchants.*

I'd long thought that Atwood was a savvy businessperson who understood that, if she avoided the "science fiction" label, she'd get a bigger audience. After all, prejudice keeps many otherwise intelligent readers from entering the science-fiction section of bookstores (Toronto-based SF writer Terence M. Green counters the "I don't like SF" chestnut with a simple question: "What work of SF did you read that led you to form that opinion?" The answer, of course, is none . . .).

But after finishing *Oryx and Crake*, I better understand Margaret Atwood's reluctance to let her work be considered as science fiction. And that's simply that it comes off poorly in comparison to the truly great works in the genre.

On Writing

Great Beginnings

Over the years, I've taught science-fiction writing at Ryerson University, the University of Toronto, Humber College, and the Banff Centre for the Arts, and for three years I wrote a column entitled "On Writing" for the quarterly Canadian SF magazine On Spec. *Those columns proved quite popular, and several were later picked up by the Australian SF magazine* Altair, *as well as by various writers' group newsletters. Here are all twelve of them, just as they appeared in* On Spec*'s Spring 1995 through Winter 1997 issues.*

Boo!

Scared you, didn't I? But I also got you to read on to this second sentence. So, even though it was only four characters long, that first line did its job: it served as a hook to bring you into this piece of writing. In that sense, it was a great beginning – and "great beginnings" are the topic of this, the first installment of my "On Writing" series of columns.

A Canadian horror writer I know said something very intriguing recently: he was looking forward to the day when he was well known, so that he wouldn't have to start off with a grabby first sentence. He wanted to be able to begin subtly, with the reader trusting that the story would be worth his or her time just on the strength of the author's name.

But even the lions of literature still go for the snappy start. Consider this opening line from Robertson Davies's *Murther & Walking Spirits*: "I was never so amazed in my life as when the Sniffer drew his concealed weapon from its case and struck me to the ground, stone dead."

In a short story, you really do have to hook the audience with the very first sentence. With a novel, you probably have the luxury of using an entire paragraph to snare the reader. But no matter which one you're writing, there are only four major ways to start your tale.

First, there's evocative description. In some ways, this is the hardest, because *nothing is happening.* And yet, if you do it well, the reader will not be able to resist continuing: "The sky above the port was the color of television, tuned to a dead channel" (William Gibson's *Neuromancer*); "Halifax Harbor at night is a beautiful sight, and June often finds the MacDonald Bridge lined with lovers and other appreciators. But in Halifax even June can turn on one with icy claws" (Spider Robinson's *Mindkiller*). Note what these two examples have in common: beautiful use of the language. If you *are* going to start off with static description, then you must dazzle with your imagery or poetry.

A second approach is to start by introducing an intriguing character: "Mrs. Sloan had only three fingers on her left hand, but when she drummed them against the countertop, the tiny polished bones at the end of the fourth and fifth stumps clattered like fingernails" ("The Sloan Men" by David Nickle, in *Northern Frights 2*, edited by Don Hutchison); "My name is Robinette Broadhead, in spite of which I am male" (*Gateway* by Frederik Pohl). The reader immediately wants to know more about Mrs. Sloan and Robinette, and so forges ahead.

The third – and trickiest – approach is to start off with a news clipping, or journal entry, or something else that isn't actually the main narrative of the story. It can be done effectively: the horror novels *Carrie* by Stephen King and *The Night Stalker* by Jeff Rice begin just this way. Be careful of this technique: you might think that by using such a device to tell the reader that the following story *is* significant, you'll be forgiven for an otherwise slow start. But *Carrie* immediately goes into its famous gym-class shower scene, and *The Night Stalker* launches right into the first of the vampire murders. Really, this kind of beginning just postpones the inevitable – you'll have to follow up your news clipping, or whatever, with one of the other three classic narrative-hook techniques.

The fourth, and most versatile way, is to start off in the middle of the action. Sometimes a single sentence is all it takes:

"Because he thought that he would have problems taking the child over the border into Canada, he drove south, skirting the cities whenever they came and taking the anonymous freeways which were like a separate country" (Peter Straub's *Ghost Story*). All the explanation can come later – for a hook, all you need to know is that someone is on the run. Immediately, you began asking questions: Who is running? What's he running from? Is it his child, or has he kidnapped one? And suddenly you're reading along, wanting to know the answers.

Another example: "The Dracon's three-fingered hands flexed. In the thing's yellow eyes I could read the desire to either have those fingers around a weapon or my throat" (Barry B. Longyear's Hugo-winning novella "Enemy Mine"). We want to dig in and find out what a Dracon is and how the narrator ended up in a life-or-death confrontation with it.

A variation on starting in the middle is leading off with dialog: "Eddie wants to see you." / "What's he want?" Nita asked. "Another blowjob?" (Charles de Lint's "In this Soul of a Woman," from *Love in Vein* edited by Poppy Z. Brite). People love overhearing other people's fascinating conversations, and you can snare them easily as long as your characters are saying interesting things.

But if you're going to start somewhere other than the natural beginning of the tale, you have to choose carefully. I often take an exciting scene from near the end, move it to the beginning, and then tell most of the rest of the tale as a flashback leading up to that scene. An extreme example is my novel *The Terminal Experiment*, which starts out with a female police detective dying in hospital. The scene in which she is fatally wounded doesn't occur until ninety percent of the way through the book.

Whatever you choose, give it a lot of thought. Most people I know try to write the beginnings of their stories first. Although that seems sensible, I suggest you wait until you've got everything else finished – then work out the best possible start. It really is the most important element of your story – because it's the part that determines whether the rest gets read at all.

Constructing Characters

Psst! Wanna hear a secret? The people in most stories aren't really humans – they're robots!

Real people are quite accidental, the result of a random jumbling of genes and a chaotic life. But story people are made to order to do a specific job. In other words, robots!

I can hear some of you pooh-poohing this notion, but it's not my idea. It goes back twenty-five hundred years to the classical playwrights. In Greek tragedy, the main character was always specifically designed to fit the particular plot. Indeed, each protagonist was constructed with an intrinsic *hamartia*, or tragic flaw, keyed directly to the story's theme. These days, writers have more latitude in narrative forms, but we still try to construct characters appropriate to a given tale.

Consider, for instance, Terence M. Green's *Barking Dogs*. The book posits the invention of infallible portable lie detectors. Of all the people in the world, Green chooses to give such a device to Mitch Helwig, a Toronto cop. Why that choice? Well, no one other than a cop deals so directly with questions of truth, and no one but a cop is so frustrated by the perversion of that truth, seeing guilty people he's arrested get off on technicalities. Armed with his lie detector, Mitch goes on a vigilante spree, ascertaining as soon as he nabs someone whether that person is guilty, and, if so, executing them.

Green knew he had to find the character who could best dramatize his premise. Frederik Pohl knew the same thing when he wrote *Gateway*. Its premise is simple: near a black hole, the passage of time slows to a stop.

To make this dramatic, Pohl came up with Robinette Broadhead, a man who had done something horrible to people he'd left behind near a black hole. The story is told through psychoanalytic sessions: Robinette can't get over his guilt because no matter how many years pass for him, it's always that one terrible moment of betrayal for those he's left behind. The novel works spectacularly – in fact, I'd go so far as to say it's the finest science-fiction novel ever written.

Others liked the book, too – and Pohl was pressured for a sequel. But the second book, *Beyond the Blue Event Horizon*, fell flat on its face. Why? Because Pohl had to shoehorn the character he'd built for a very specific job into a different story. Robinette, absolutely perfect for *Gateway*, was a fish out of water in the follow-up story about the discovery of a human child on an ancient alien space station.

Clearly, your character must fit your premise – but it's also important that you not make the fit *too* comfortable.

Everybody knows Steve Austin, the fictional test pilot who lost an arm and both legs in an aircraft crash and was rebuilt with super parts so that he could undertake secret missions. Austin first appeared in *Cyborg*, a mediocre novel by Martin Caidin, and was played by Lee Majors in the wonderful, Hugo-nominated movie *The Six Million Dollar Man*.

Why was the novel just so-so but the movie glorious? Simple. In the novel, Steve Austin was a colonel in the United States Air Force. When he was asked to undertake his first mission as the bionic man, he told his new secret-agent bosses, "You have a job to do. It's serious, in many ways it's dirty, in some ways it stinks, but having worn the blue suit [an Air Force uniform] for a long time, I understand and even appreciate what you do. You will receive my absolute cooperation."

Ho hum. Screenwriter Henri Simoun saw that Caidin had missed the essential conflict. For the movie version, he changed Colonel Austin to *Mister* Austin, one of six civilians in the U.S. astronaut program. Simoun's Austin fights those who are trying to make him an obedient little robot every step of the way – making for much better drama.

(When *The Six Million Dollar Man* became a TV series, the producers went back to Austin being an Air Force officer, and the show degenerated into mindless adventure.)

I almost made the same mistake Caidin did in my novel *The*

Terminal Experiment, which is about the discovery of scientific evidence for the existence of the soul. My first thought had been to have a protagonist who had undergone a metaphysical bright-light-and-tunnel near-death experience. But that would have been absolutely the wrong choice. A person with that background would be predisposed to believe in the existence of the soul, accepting any proof too readily. No, what was called for was a skeptic – someone who had stumbled on the existence of the soul while looking for something else, and who would be bothered by the discovery. The lesson is simple: your main character should illuminate the fundamental conflict suggested by your premise.

And, of course, that means that you shouldn't start with a character and then go looking about for a story; it's a lot easier to do it the other way around. First, come up with your premise (for instance, "I want to write about a telepathic alien who can read subconscious instead of conscious thoughts"). Then you ask yourself who could most clearly dramatize the issues arising from that premise ("There's this guy, see, who's been suppressing terrible memories of the suicide of his wife").

After that, head for your keyboard and build the character to your specifications, for that one specific job. (In this case, the story has already been done brilliantly; it's *Solaris* by Stanislaw Lem.) Of course, you have to add subtleties and quirks to give your character depth, but if you do it right, only you will ever know that underneath the real-looking skin, your hero is actually a made-to-measure robot . . .

Point of View

New writers are often baffled when trying to choose a point of view for their stories and novels. But, actually, the choice is easy. Over ninety percent of all modern speculative fiction is written using the same POV: limited third person.

"Third person" ("she did this; he did that") means the story is not told in first person ("I did this"), or the always-irritating second person ("you did this"). That's easy enough. But what does "limited" mean?

It means that although the narration refers to all the characters by third-person pronouns (he, she, it), each self-contained scene follows the viewpoint of one specific character. Consider this example, which is *not* limited but rather is *omniscient* third person, in which the unseen narrator knows what all the characters are thinking:

> *"Hello, Mrs. Spade. I'm Pierre Tardivel." He was conscious of how out-of-place his Quebecois accent must have sounded here – another reminder that he was intruding. For a moment, Mrs. Spade thought she recognized Pierre.*

In the opening of the paragraph, we are inside Pierre's head: "He was conscious of how out-of-place . . ." But by the end of the paragraph, we've left Pierre's head and are now inside another character's: "Mrs. Spade thought she recognized Pierre."

Here's the same paragraph rewritten as limited third person, solely from Pierre's point of view.

> *"Hello, Mrs. Spade. I'm Pierre Tardivel." He was conscious of how out-of-place his Quebecois accent must have sounded*

223

here – another reminder that he was intruding. There was a moment while Mrs. Spade looked Pierre up and down during which Pierre thought he saw a flicker of recognition on her face.

See the difference? We stay firmly rooted inside Pierre's head. Pierre is only aware of what Mrs. Spade is thinking because she gives an outward sign ("a flicker of recognition on her face" that he can interpret.

Think of your story's reader as a little person who rides inside the head of one of your characters. When inside a given head, the reader can see, hear, touch, smell, and taste everything that particular character is experiencing, and he or she can also read the thoughts of that one character. But it takes effort for the little person to move out of one head and into another. Not only that – it's disorienting. Consider this:

Keith smiled at Lianne. She was a gorgeous woman, with a wonderfully curvy figure.

All right: we're settling in for an encounter with a woman from a man's point of view. But if the next paragraph says:

Lianne smiled at Keith. He was a handsome man, with a body-builder's physique.

Hey, wait a minute! Suddenly we've jumped into another head, and immersed ourselves in a whole 'nuther set of emotions and feelings. Not only have we lost track of where we are, we've lost track of *who* we are – of which character we're supposed to identify with. Although at first glance, omniscient narration might seem an ideal way to involve the reader in every aspect of the story, it actually ends up making the reader feel unconnected to *all* the characters. The rule is simple: pick one character, and follow the entire scene through his or her eyes only.

Of course, we usually want some idea of what the other characters in the scene are thinking or feeling. That can be accomplished with effective description. To convey puzzlement on the part of someone other than your viewpoint character, write "he scratched his chin" or "she raised an eyebrow" (or, if you really

want to hit the reader over the head with it, "she raised an eyebrow quizzically" – "quizzically" being the viewpoint character's
interpretation of the action). To convey anger, write "he balled his
hands into fists," or "his cheeks grew flushed," or "he raised his
voice." There are very few emotions that aren't betrayed by outward signs.

Still, in real life, there *are* times when you can't tell what someone else is thinking – usually because that person is making a
deliberate effort to keep a poker face. If you've adopted the omniscient point of view, instead of a limited one, you can't portray
such things effectively. Here's a limited point of view:

> *Carlos looked at Wendy, unsure whether he should go on. Her
> face was a stony mask. "I'm sorry," he said again. "So very
> sorry."*

That's much more intriguing than the omniscient version:

> *Carlos looked at Wendy, unsure whether he should go on.
> Wendy thought Carlos had suffered enough and was going to
> forgive him, but for the moment she didn't say anything. "I'm
> sorry," he said again. "So very sorry."*

In the former, we feel Carlos's insecurity, and we have some
suspense about how things are going to turn out. In the latter,
there is no suspense. (And, of course, omniscient narration is
death – if you'll pardon the expression – in mystery fiction: the
reader must be kept ignorant of what the various suspects are
thinking, or else it will be obvious which one is guilty.)

Note that I've suggested keeping in one character's head for
each individual scene. However, you can freely switch viewpoint
characters when you change scenes (either at the end of a chapter,
or with a blank line within a chapter). Many novels have separate
plotlines intertwined, with each of them having its own viewpoint
character. But what happens when individuals who have been
viewpoint characters in disparate plotlines come together in the
same scene? Whose POV do you choose then?

In most cases, it'll be whichever one is at the heart of the
action of that particular scene. But there are exceptions. One big
one is when someone who has been a point-of-view character is

about to die. See, the central conceit of modern fiction is that it's actually a form of journalism: the tale you are reading is an account of something that really happened, and the author's job has simply been to interview one witness per scene to the events being described. Well, if your main character dies in a scene, how did he or she subsequently relate his or her feelings to the journalist-author? Even if the dying character has been your viewpoint character throughout most of the story, it's best to be inside another person's head as you watch him or her expire.

(One of the great violations of the journalistic-storytelling model comes from the movie *Citizen Kane*, which, ironically, is a film about journalism: the whole movie revolves around trying to discover the meaning of Charles Foster Kane's dying word, "Rosebud." But the film clearly shows Kane dying alone, with no one witnessing him saying it. Unless you're a genius comparable to Orson Welles, don't try to get away with this in your own fiction.)

There are other times when you'll want to choose someone besides your protagonist as the POV character for a scene or two. No person really knows how he or she is perceived; you may find it illuminating to do an occasional scene from a secondary character's point of view, so that the reader can see your hero as others do. Philip K. Dick did this brilliantly in *The Man in the High Castle*. One of the novel's main characters, Ed McCarthy, is trying to interest a merchant, Robert Childan, in buying some jewelry he and his partner have designed. Ed seems clever and in control in the scenes leading up to the sales pitch to the merchant – but when it comes time for the actual pitch, Dick plants us firmly inside the merchant's head, and we see Ed McCarthy in a new light:

> *[McCarthy] wore a slightly-less-than fashionable suit. His voice had a strangled quality. He'll lay everything out, Childan knew. Watching me out of the corner of his eye every second. To see if I'm taking any interest. Any at all.*

For each scene, choose your point-of-view character with care. Stick with that one person throughout the scene – and you'll find that readers are sticking with your story all the way until the end.

Dialogue

Writing convincing dialogue is one of the hardest things for new writers to master. In fact, it's so rarely done well in any form of fiction that when it *is* done right, people rally around it. The movie *Pulp Fiction*, Terry McMillan's novel *Waiting to Exhale*, and the TV series *My So-Called Life* were all remarkable in large part because of how believably the characters spoke.

Here's the kind of dialog you read in many beginners' stories:

> *"What happened to you, Joe?"*
>
> *"Well, Mike, I was walking down the street, and a man came up to me. I said to him, 'What seems to be the difficulty?' He replied, 'You owe me a hundred dollars.' But I said I didn't. And then he hit me."*

Here's how real people talk:

> *"Christ, man, what happened?"*
>
> *"Well, umm, I was goin' down the street, y'know, and this guy comes up to me, and I'm like, hey, man, what's up? And he says to me, he says, 'You owe me a hundred bucks,' and I'm like no way, man. In your dreams. Then – pow! I'm on the sidewalk."*

See the differences? Most people's real dialog tends to contain occasional profanity ("Christ"), to be very informal ("guy" instead of "man," "bucks" instead of "dollars"), and to have lots of contractions and dropped letters ("goin'," "y'know"). Note, too, that when relaying an event that happened in the past, most people recount it in the present tense ("he says to me," rather than "he replied").

Also note that in the first example, the speakers refer to each other by name. In reality, we almost never say the name of the person we're talking to: you know who you're addressing, and that person knows he or she is being addressed.

A few other features of real human speech demonstrated in the second example above: when relaying to a third party a conversation we had with somebody else, we usually only directly quote what the *other* person said; our own side of the conversation is typically relayed with considerable bravado, and the listener understands that what's really being presented is what we *wish* we'd had the guts to say, not what we actually said. We also tend to act out events, rather than describe them ("Then – *pow!* I'm on the sidewalk"). Indeed, without the acting out, the words often don't convey the intended meaning. The speaker was probably standing on the sidewalk throughout the altercation, of course; what he meant by "on the sidewalk" was that he was knocked down.

Now, which of the above examples is better? Well, the second is clearly more colorful, and more entertaining to read. But it's also more *work* to read. A little verisimilitude goes a along way. Dropped final letters are rarely shown in fictional dialog (they're usually only employed to indicate an uneducated speaker, although in reality almost everyone talks that way), and vagueness about verbs ("I'm like" instead of "I said"), verbalized pauses ("umm"), and content-less repetitions (the second part of "He says to me, he says") are usually left out. In a short story, I might perhaps use dialog like the second example above; in a novel, where the reader has to sit through hundreds of pages, I might be inclined toward some sort of middle ground:

> *"Christ, man, what happened?"*
> *"I was going down the street, and this guy comes up to me, and I'm like, hey, man, what's up? And he says to me, 'You owe me a hundred bucks,' and I say 'in your dreams.' Then –* pow!*–he knocks me on my ass."*

Of course, not all your characters should talk the same way. I read one story recently in which there were dozens of lines of dialog like this:

> *"Interchangeable?" he said. "What do you mean the characters are interchangeable?"*

We have the attribution tag between an initial word and a sentence that repeats that same word. This is clearly being used to denote confusion – and works fine once or twice, but grates if the same dialog device is employed more than that in a given story – especially by multiple speakers. Assign distinctive speaking patterns to single characters.

One trick is to come up with a word or two that one character – and only that character – will use a lot (in my *The Terminal Experiment*, the character Sarkar loves the word "crisp," using it to mean anything from well-defined to delicate to appealing to complex); you might also come up with some words your character will *never* use (in *Starplex*, I have a character who hates acronyms, and therefore avoids referring to the ship's computer as PHANTOM).

Profanity is also important. Terence M. Green's rule: you can't worry about what your mother will think of your fiction. But, again, not all characters swear the same way, and some may not swear at all (in *The Terminal Experiment*, I have a Muslim character who never swears, although the rest of his speech is quite colloquial).

It's tricky handling characters who are not native English speakers. No matter what language they're speaking, people tend also to be thinking in that language. It's common to write a French character saying things like, "There are *beaucoup* reasons why someone might do that." But at the time the person is speaking, his brain is thinking in English; it's as unlikely for him to slip into French for a word as it is for a computer running a program in FORTRAN to suddenly switch over to BASIC for a single instruction. Instead, if you want to remind the reader of the character's native tongue, have the character occasionally mutter or think to himself or herself in that language.

The best way to learn how real people talk is to tape record some actual human conversation, and then transcribe it word for word (if you can't find a group of people who will let you do this, then tape a talk show off TV, and transcribe that). You'll be amazed: transcripts of human speech, devoid of body language and inflection, read mostly like gibberish.

To learn how to condense and clean up dialog, edit your transcript. For your first few attempts, try to edit by only removing words, not by changing any of them – you'll quickly see that most real speech can be condensed by half without deleting any of the meaning.

Finally, test your fictional dialog by reading it out loud. If it doesn't sound natural, it probably isn't. Keep revising until it comes trippingly off your tongue (yes, that's a cliche – but remember, although you want to avoid cliches in your narrative, people use them all the time in speech).

A couple of matters of form that seem to elude most beginners: when writing dialog for a single speaker that runs to multiple paragraphs, put an open-quotation mark at the beginning of each paragraph, but no close-quotation mark until the end of the final paragraph. And in North America, terminal punctuation (periods, exclamation marks, and question marks) go inside the final close-quotation mark: "This is punctuated correctly."

Get your speech-attribution tags in as early as possible. There's nothing more frustrating than not knowing whose dialog you're reading. Slip the tag in after the first completed clause in the sentence: "You know," said Juan, "when the sky is that shade of blue it reminds me of my childhood back in Mexico." And when alternating lines of dialog, make sure you identify speakers at least every five or six exchanges; it's very easy for the reader to get lost otherwise.

Finally, much real dialog goes unfinished. When someone is interrupted or cut off abruptly, end the dialog with an em-dash (which you type in manuscript as two hyphens); when he or she trails off without completing the thought, end the dialog with ellipsis points (three periods). Real dialog also tends to be peppered with asides: "We went to Toronto – boy, I hate that city – and found . . ."

Get your characters talking at least halfway like real people, and you'll find that the readers are talking, too: they'll be saying favorable things about your work.

Show, Don't Tell

Every writing student has heard the rule that you should show, not tell, but this principle seems to be among the hardest for beginners to master.

First, what's the difference between the two? Well, "telling" is the reliance on simple exposition: Mary was an old woman. "Showing," on the other hand, is the use of evocative description: Mary moved slowly across the room, her hunched form supported by a polished wooden cane gripped in a gnarled, swollen-jointed hand that was covered by translucent, liver-spotted skin.

Both showing and telling convey the same information – Mary is old – but the former simply states it flat-out, and the latter – well, read the example over again and you'll see it never actually states that fact at all, and yet nonetheless leaves no doubt about it in the reader's mind.

Why is showing better? Two reasons. First, it creates mental pictures for the reader. When reviewers use terms like "vivid," "evocative," or "cinematic" to describe a piece of prose, they really mean the writer has succeeded at showing, rather than merely telling.

Second, showing is interactive and participatory: it forces the reader to become involved in the story, deducing facts (such as Mary's age) for himself or herself, rather than just taking information in passively.

Let's try a more complex example:

> *Singh had a reputation for being able to cut through layers of bureaucracy and get things done.*

Doubtless a useful chap to have around, this Singh, but he's rather a dull fellow to read about. Try this instead:

> *Chang shook his head and looked at Pryce. "All this red tape! We'll never get permission in time."*
>
> *Suddenly the office door slid open, and in strode Singh, a slight lifting at the corners of his mouth conveying his satisfaction. He handed a ROM chip to Chang. "Here you are, sir — complete government clearance. You can launch anytime you wish."*
>
> *Chang's eyebrows shot up his forehead like twin rockets, but Singh was already out the door. He turned to Pryce, who was leaning back in his chair, grinning. "That's our Singh for you," said Pryce. "We don't call him the miracle worker for nothing."*

In the first version, Singh is spoken about in the abstract, while in the second, we see him in the concrete. That's the key to *showing:* using specific action-oriented examples to make your point. When writing a romantic scene, don't tell us that John is attracted to Sally; show us that his heart skips a beat when she enters the room. It's rarely necessary to tell us about your characters' emotions. Let their actions convey how they feel instead.

(Notice that at the end of the second Singh version above, Pryce tells us about Singh. That's a special case: it's fine for one of your characters to say what he or she thinks of another; in fact, that's a good way to reveal characterization for both the person being spoken about and the person doing the speaking.)

Speaking of speaking (so to speak), a great way to show rather than tell is through dialog:

Telling: *Alex was an uneducated man.*

Showing: *"I ain't goin' nowhere," said Alex.*

Likewise, using modified speech to show a character's regional or ethnic origin can be quite effective, if done sparingly:

Telling: *"It's a giant spaceship with the biggest engines I've ever seen," said Koslov in a thick Russian accent.*

Showing: *"It is giant spaceship with biggest engines I have ever seen," said Koslov.*

The failure to use contractions shows us Koslov is uncomfortable with the language; the dropping of the articles "the" and "a" shows us that he's likely a Russian-speaker, a fact confirmed by his name. The reader hears the accent without you telling him that the character has one.

Don't overdo this, though. One of my favorite non-SF writers is Ed McBain, but frequently when he wants to demonstrate that a character is black, he descends into pages of offensively stereotypical *Amos 'n' Andy* dialog. Here's a character in McBain's *Rumpelstiltskin* musing on the local constabulary: "P'lice always say somebody done nothing a'tall, den next t'ing you know, they 'resting somebody."

Are there any times when telling is better than showing? Yes. First, some parts of a story are trivial – you may want your reader to know a fact, without dwelling on it. If the weather is only incidental to the story, then it's perfectly all right to simply tell the reader "it was snowing." Indeed, if you were to show every little thing, the reader would say your story is padded.

Second, there's nothing wrong with relying on telling in your first drafts; I do this myself. When you're working out the sequence of events and the relationships between characters, it may cause you to lose sight of the big picture if you stop at that point to carefully craft your descriptions:

First draft: *It was a typical blue-collar apartment.*

Final draft: *She led the way into the living room. It had only two bookcases, one holding bowling trophies and the other mostly CDs. There* was *a paperback book splayed open face down on the coffee table – a Harlequin Romance. Copies of* The National Enquirer *and* TV Guide *sat atop a television set that looked about fifteen years old.*

Note that showing usually requires more words than telling; the examples of the latter in this column take up 51 words, whereas those of the former total 210. Many beginning writers are daunted by the prospect of producing a long work, but once they master showing rather than telling, they find that the pages pile up quickly.

The third place where you'll still want to do a lot of telling is in the outlines for novels. Patrick Nielsen Hayden, a senior editor at Tor Books, says that some of the best outlines he's ever received contain lines such as, "Then a really exciting battle occurs." If the editor buys your book, he or she is trusting that you know how to convert such general statements into specific, action-oriented, colourful prose.

Finally, of course, showing is also better than telling in the process of becoming a writer. Don't tell your friends and family that you want to be a writer; rather, show them that you are one by planting yourself in front of your keyboard and going to work . . .

Description

There was a cartoon in *The New Yorker* many years ago in which the female host of a posh party accosts one of her guests: "I've just learned that you wrote a novel based on somebody else's screenplay. Please leave my house at once."

It's true that novelizations are the antithesis of literature, but when I was a teenager, desperate to learn how to write, I read dozens of them. Why? Because in a piece of fiction, every nuance can be described in words. It was fascinating to see the ways in which writers described scenes that I'd already watched on the big screen.

(In point of fact, of course, most novelizations are written before the movie is completed. The writers of the book versions have probably never seen a single frame of the film, so the way they describe the action is often quite different from the way it was actually shot.)

For writers beginning today, there's an even better tool available than novelizations: the new interpreted-for-the-blind movies on video. These use the secondary audio channel to provide a running commentary, often of a very high caliber, describing in vivid words the scene that's simultaneously unfolding in pictures. Watching these can be a terrific way to learn how to bring a scene to life verbally; the best one I've seen is the for-the-blind version of *Casablanca*.

Although I'm part of the minority that thinks *Star Trek: The Motion Picture* is one of the best SF films ever made, just about everyone likes the last bit of dialog in the film.

Unfortunately, the novelization of *ST:TMP* is by none other than Gene Roddenberry (and it's so clunky, unlike the *Star Wars* novelization, which is putatively by George Lucas but was actually written by Alan Dean Foster, that I'm inclined to believe Roddenberry really did perpetrate it). How does Roddenberry portray this climactic moment in the book version? Just by reprinting the dialog, without any real description:

> Kirk turned to the helm. "Take us out of orbit, Mr. Sulu."
> "Heading, sir?" DiFalco asked.
> Kirk indicated generally ahead. "Out there. Thataway."

Now, let's see how that might have been handled better. Remember, a scene in any book has to carry all the emotional freight on its own; it's not supposed to be a mere transcript of something people have already seen:

> Jim returned to the center seat. It wasn't his old chair, but he *would* have to get used to it. He heard the whirring of the little motors in the chair's ergonomic back as it nestled into his spine.
> He knew everyone on the bridge was waiting for what he would do next; it was his ship, at last and again, and he was back where he belonged. Ahead of him, he could see the backs of Sulu and DiFalco's heads, and between them –
> – between them, the stars, steady, untwinkling, beckoning.
> Jim's heart was pounding. He allowed himself a moment to gain composure, then gave the familiar order. "Mr. Sulu, ahead warp one."
> Sulu's voice was filled with excitement, with anticipation. "Warp one, sir," he acknowledged, while sliding the master velocity control on his helm console forward. The deckplates immediately began to vibrate, and a growing hum filled the air.
> Chief DiFalco half-turned in her seat to look back at Kirk. "Heading, sir?"
> Jim was still caught up in the beauty of the cosmos. He leaned forward, and his voice dropped to almost a whisper. "Out there," he said.

He glanced to his right; Scotty was standing beside him, eyebrows raised.

Jim couldn't quite suppress the grin that was growing across his face. He *was* back, and the adventure was just beginning. He flipped his hand nonchalantly ahead.

"Thataway . . ."

The trick is to appeal both to the emotions and to the senses: tell us what people are feeling, what they're thinking, and, when appropriate, what they're seeing, hearing, touching, tasting, and smelling.

You have much more control over the reader's experience than a movie director does. A director can't be sure what part of the frame any given viewer might be looking at, but when you write "there was permanent dirt under his fingernails, the legacy of decades of archeological fieldwork," you know exactly what the reader is contemplating.

Of course, you shouldn't weigh down every bit of business with lots of detail; it may be sufficient to say "she rode the bus to work." But when something major is happening, increase the amount of description; think of your words as swelling background music, denoting the importance of the scene.

Description does more than just make vivid the reader's image of the story; it also lets you control the timing of experiences. Don't just blurt out, "The butler did it!" Rather, play out the moment, stretch things, build the suspense, make the reader wait:

"Of course you all know by now who the killer is," said the detective. He paused, looking from face to face, taking in the sea of expressions – fear and agitation and anger, one man biting his lower lip, another nervously smoothing out his hair, a woman with eyes darting left and right. The clock on the mantelpiece clicked loudly to a new minute. Rain continued to beat a staccato rhythm against the window. The detective, milking the moment for all its drama, extended his index finger and swung it slowly from chest to chest until at last it came to rest pointing at that hideous chartreuse cummerbund. "The butler did it!"

• • •

Pauses don't have to be large to convey volumes. Here's an entire scene from Terence M. Green's 1992 novel *Children of the Rainbow:*

> It was almost midnight when McTaggart made the decision. "I think," he said, "that we should go closer."
>
> The others stared at him.
> "Maybe fifteen miles away."
> Nobody said a word.
> "Force their hand."

Even though the other characters do nothing, their inaction communicates their nervousness, their failing resolve, their fear that their leader has gone over the edge. Try it without the description: "I think that we should go closer. Maybe fifteen miles away. Force their hand."

Nothing. No tension. No suspense. Description isn't padding – it's the heart and soul of good writing.

Secret Weapons of Science

Okay – I admit it. I've got an arts degree. There, the cat's out of the bag: despite the cosmology and relativity and paleontology and genetics in my novels, I haven't taken a science course since high school.

But, hey, I'm not alone in that among practitioners of hard SF. Look at Fred Pohl, who writes about artificial intelligence and black holes and quantum theory. He never even graduated from high school. And, yeah, sure, Kim Stanley Robinson, who is detailing the terraforming of our neighboring world in his *Red Mars* trilogy, is indeed *Doctor* Robinson – but his Ph.D. is in (gasp!) English literature.

So how do we non-scientist SF writers keep up with science? Well, I can't speak for everyone, but I rely on six secret weapons.

First, and most important, there's *Science News: The Weekly Newsmagazine of Science*. You can't get it on any newsstand (although many libraries carry it). I've been a subscriber for thirteen years now, and I credit it with fully half of the science in my novels and short stories.

Science News is published weekly, and each issue is just sixteen pages long – you can read the whole thing over one leisurely lunch. Aimed at the intelligent lay person, it contains summaries of research papers appearing in *Nature, Science, Cell, Proceedings of the National Academy of Sciences, Physical Review Letters, The New England Journal of Medicine*, and hundreds more, as well as reports from all the major scientific conferences in Canada and the United States, plus original feature articles on topics ranging from quarks to the greenhouse effect to Neanderthal fossils to junk DNA. There is simply no better source for keeping up to date.

(Of course, the key is to actually make use of the material. Both Michael Crichton and I read the same little piece in *Science News* years ago about the possibility of cloning dinosaurs from blood preserved in the bellies of mosquitoes trapped in amber. Me, I said "Neat!" and turned the page; Crichton went off and made a few million from the idea.)

Science News is published by Science Service, Inc., 1719 N Street NW, Washington, DC 20036, (202) 785-2255; www.sciencenews.com.

My second secret weapon: *Time* magazine. Yup, that's right: *Time*. Each year a few issues will have science cover stories. Buy them – they're pure gold. You won't find better introductions to scientific topics anywhere. Recent examples: *The Chemistry of Love* (February 15, 1993); *The Truth About Dinosaurs* (April 26, 1993); *How Life Began* (October 11, 1993); *Genetics: The Future is Now* (January 17, 1994); *How Humanity Began* (March 14, 1994); *When Did the Universe Begin?* (March 6, 1995); and *In Search of the Mind* (July 31, 1995). Not only will each one suggest many story ideas (the novel I just finished, *Frameshift*, owes a lot to the two 1994 issues I mention above), but they will also give you all the background and vocabulary you need to write knowledgeably about the sciences in question.

In fact, I find that magazine articles tend to be better than books for giving me what I need quickly and efficiently. And that brings me to secret weapon number three: Magazine Database Plus on the CompuServe Information Service, the world's largest commercial computer network.

MDP contains the full text of over two hundred general-interest and specialty publications, many going all the way back to 1986. Among the titles of obvious use to SF writers are *Astronomy*, *Bulletin of the Atomic Scientists*, *Discover*, *Omni*, *Popular Science*, *Psychology Today*, *Scientific American*, *Sky & Telescope*, and, yes, good old *Science News* and *Time*.

A year ago, when I was writing my novel *Starplex*, I needed to learn about "dark matter" – that mysterious, invisible substance that we know, because of its gravitational effects, constitutes ninety percent of our universe. Well, in less than a minute, MDP provided me with sixty-nine citations of articles on that topic, ranging from lay discussion in the newsmagazines *The Economist* and *US News and World Report* to twenty-one articles in – of course –

Science News. There's no charge beyond normal CompuServe connect-time for generating such a bibliography. You can then either head off to your local library and dig up the articles there for free, or you can download the full text of any that interest you for US$1.00 a pop. To access Magazine Database Plus, type GO MDP at any CompuServe prompt.

[Note: sadly, Magazine Database Plus went out of service in August 1999; I miss it a lot, but a good substitute is Gale Research's Reference Center Gold; lots of public libraries offer access to it via their websites.]

My fourth secret weapon is being a couch potato. When you get tired of staring at your computer monitor, go look at your TV screen. The Learning Channel has several truly excellent science series that they repeat *ad infinitum* (*PaleoWorld* and *The Practical Guide to the Universe* are tremendous; *Amazing Space* isn't quite as good).

My fifth secret weapon is Richard Morris. Never heard of him? Well, he writes science-popularization books. He's not as famous as Carl Sagan or David Suzuki or Stephen Jay Gould, but he's better than all three of them combined. His slim, completely accessible books *Cosmic Questions: Galactic Halos, Cold Dark Matter, and the End of Time* (Wiley, New York, 1993) and *The Edges of Science: Crossing the Boundary from Physics to Metaphysics* (Prentice Hall, New York, 1990) will suggest enough story ideas to keep any hard-SF writer going for a decade or two.

Still, once you've read all the magazines and books, and watched Tom Selleck tell you about cosmic strings, nothing beats talking to a real scientist. Secret weapon number six is the knowledge that many scientists are SF fans. I've never had any scientist I approached refuse to help me. If you don't know any scientists personally, call up the public-relations office of your local university, museum, or science centre and let them find someone who you can talk to.

And when you do have your story or novel finished, ask the scientist if he or she will read it over to check for errors. I'd never met Dr. Robert W. Bussard (inventor of the Bussard ramjet starship) or Dr. Dale A. Russell (curator of dinosaurs at the Canadian Museum of Nature) when I asked them to look at the manuscripts for my novels *Golden Fleece* (which features one of Bussard's ramjets) or *End of an Era* (which is about dinosaurs), but both instantly agreed and provided invaluable feedback. Of course, when your story or book does see print, do be sure to send a free auto-graphed copy to anyone who helped you out. But that's not a secret weapon . . . it's just the golden rule.

Heinlein's Rules

There are countless rules for writing success, but the most famous ones, at least in the speculative-fiction field, are the five coined by the late, great Robert A. Heinlein.

Heinlein used to say he had no qualms about giving away these rules, even though they explained how you could become his direct competitor, because he knew that almost no one would follow their advice.

In my experience, that's true: if you start off with a hundred people who say they want to be writers, you lose half of the remaining total after each rule – fully half the people who hear each rule will fail to follow it.

I'm going to share Heinlein's five rules with you, plus add a sixth of my own.

Rule One: You Must Write

It sounds ridiculously obvious, doesn't it? But it is a very difficult rule to apply. You can't just talk about wanting to be a writer. You can't simply take courses, or read up on the process of writing, or daydream about someday getting around to it. The *only* way to become a writer is to plant yourself in front of your keyboard and go to work.

And don't you *dare* complain that you don't have the time to write. Real writers *buy* the time, if they can't get it any other way. Take Toronto's Terence M. Green, a high-school English teacher. His third novel, *Shadow of Ashland*, just came out from Tor. Terry takes every fifth year off from teaching without pay so that he can write; most writers I know have made similar sacrifices for their art.

243

(Out of our hundred original aspirant writers, half will never get around to writing anything. That leaves us with fifty . . .)

Rule Two: Finish What Your Start

You cannot learn how to write without seeing a piece through to its conclusion. Yes, the first few pages you churn out might be weak, and you may be tempted to toss them out. Don't. Press on until you're done. Once you have an overall draft, with a beginning, middle, and end, you'll be surprised at how easy it is to see what works and what doesn't. And you'll never master such things as plot, suspense, or character growth unless you actually construct an entire piece.

On a related point: if you belong to a writers' workshop, don't let people critique your novel a chapter at a time. No one can properly judge a book by a piece lifted out of it at random, and you'll end up with all sorts of pointless advice: "This part seems irrelevant." "Well, no, actually, it's very important a hundred pages from now . . ."

(Of our fifty remaining potential writers, half will never finish anything – leaving just twenty-five still in the running . . .)

Rule Three: You Must Refrain From Rewriting, Except to Editorial Order

This is the one that got Heinlein in trouble with creative-writing teachers. Perhaps a more appropriate wording would have been, "Don't tinker endlessly with your story." You can spend forever modifying, revising, and polishing. There's an old saying that stories are never finished, only abandoned – learn to abandon yours.

If you find your current revisions amount to restoring the work to the way it was at an earlier stage, then it's time to push the baby out of the nest.

And although many beginners don't believe it, Heinlein *is* right: if your story is close to publishable, editors *will* tell you what you have to do to make it salable. Some small-press magazines do this at length, but you'll also get advice from *Analog, Asimov's,* and *The Magazine of Fantasy & Science Fiction.*

(Of our remaining twenty-five writers, twelve will fiddle

endlessly, and so are now out of the game. Twelve more will finally declare a piece complete. The twenty-fifth writer, the one who got chopped in half, is now desperately looking for his legs . . .)

Rule Four: You Must Put Your Story on the Market

This is the hardest rule of all for beginners. You can't simply declare yourself to be a professional writer. Rather, it's a title that must be conferred upon you by those willing to pay money for your words. Until you actually show your work to an editor, you can live the fantasy that you're every bit as good as Guy Gavriel Kay or William Gibson. But having to see if that fantasy has any grounding in reality is a very hard thing for most people to do.

I know one Canadian aspirant writer who managed to delay for two years sending out his story because, he said, he didn't have any American stamps for the self-addressed stamped envelope. This, despite the fact that he'd known dozens of people who went regularly to the States and could have gotten stamps for him, despite the fact that he could have driven across the border himself and picked up stamps, despite the fact that you don't even really need US stamps – you can use International Postal Reply Coupons instead, available at any large post office. [And those in Toronto can buy actual U.S. stamps at the First Toronto Post Office at 260 Adelaide Street South.]

No, it wasn't stamps he was lacking – it was backbone. He was afraid to find out whether his prose was salable. Don't be a coward: send your story out.

(Of our twelve writers left, half of them won't work up the nerve to make a submission, leaving just six . . .)

Rule Five: You Must Keep it on the Market
Until it has Sold

It's a fact: work gets rejected all the time. Almost certainly your first submission will be rejected. Don't let that stop you. I've currently got 142 rejection slips in my files; every professional writer I know has stacks of them (the prolific Canadian horror writer Edo van Belkom does a great talk at SF conventions called "Thriving on Rejection" in which he reads samples from the many he's acquired over the years).

If the rejection note contains advice you think is good, revise the story and send it out again. If not, then simply turn the story around: pop it in the mail, sending it to another market. *Keep at it.* My own record for the maximum number of submissions before selling a story is eighteen – but the story did eventually find a good home. (And within days, I'd sold it again to a reprint-only anthology; getting a story in print the first time opens up whole new markets.)

If your story is rejected, send it out *that very same day* to another market.

(Still, of our six remaining writers, three will be so discouraged by that first rejection that they'll give up writing for good. But three more will keep at it . . .)

Rule Six: Start Working on Something Else

That's my own rule. I've seen too many beginning writers labor for years over a single story or novel. As soon as you've finished one piece, start on another. Don't wait for the first story to come back from the editor you've submitted it to; get to work on your next project. (And if you find you're experiencing writer's block on your current project, begin writing something new – a real writer can always write *something*.) You must produce a body of work to count yourself as a real working pro.

Of our original hundred wannabe writers, only one or two will follow all six rules. The question is: will *you* be one of them? I hope so, because if you have at least a modicum of talent and if you live by these six rules, you *will* make it.

Word-Processing Tricks

Many writers have tried electronic style checkers, such as Grammatik or Correct Grammar, which are sold either as stand-alone utilities or are included as components of word-processing programs. And most who have tried them have given up on them: their advice is more often wrong than right, and the "errors" they perceive often aren't errors at all.

Still, the idea of getting help with revisions from your computer *is* appealing. Fortunately, you already have all the tools you need: they're standard features of your word-processing program. Most useful of all is your word processor's "search," "find," or "locate" function.

Whenever I finish a story or novel, I start a seek-and-destroy run for the word "very." It's almost never necessary, and can usually be eliminated: "the alien was very menacing" reads just as effectively as "the alien was menacing."

A few other good search-and-replace candidates: "utilize" should almost always be replaced with "use," "fro" is almost certainly a typo for "for," "in order to" should be changed to just "to," and "the fact that" can be replaced with just "that."

Next, seek out adjectives and adverbs. The easiest way to do that is with a search for "ly" followed by a space. If you needed an adjective or adverb to modify another word, perhaps you didn't chose the right word to begin with. For instance, if your "ly" search turns up "really large," substitute "huge" or "gigantic." If you've found "pounding loudly" substitute the more vigorous "thundering."

Next, track down anything you overuse. Me, I tend to employ too many em-dashes and semicolons. I could search for each occurrence and review it in context, but I prefer instead to do a global search for those punctuation marks, replacing them with a highlighted version (depending on your word processor and display, you could replace them with italicized versions that show up as inverse video, or boldface versions that show up in a different intensity, or, if you work in a graphics-mode program, select a different color before each one, and then return to black afterwards). I then scroll through my document, and can see where I have too many of them close together. Afterwards, I just reverse the process, doing a global search-and-replace to turn the ones I've left intact back into their normal print attributes.

Also worth hunting down are exclamation marks. One can exclaim only short words or phrases, such as "Drat!" or "My God!" (Try to exclaim, "But it turned out that the alien planet they were on was really Earth!" It can't be done, and writing it that way just makes you seem histrionic.) And if you find two or more exclamation marks in a row – Holy cow!!! – eliminate all but one of them.

One thing you should *not* track down, though, is the word "said." Almost all of your speech tags *should* be of the form "he said" or "she said." Only beginners constantly look for alternatives to the serviceable, invisible "said." (For all his virtues, Stanley G. Weinbaum *was* a beginner when he wrote his classic 1934 story "A Martian Odyssey," which has a character named Putz ejaculating his lines . . .)

Finally, do a search-and-replace to check your profanity, and make sure it's appropriate for your market. The "Drat!" and "My God!" I used above are okay for a column like this, but if you're writing real adults in real situations, you may want something harsher. (On the other hand, in polishing my novel *Starplex*, I realized that it would likely appeal to teenagers as well as the adults I had in mind when I wrote it, so I tracked down all the scatological and copulatory profanity, and substituted milder terms.)

What else can your computer do to help you? Plenty. Most writers notice during proofreading if they've started two consecutive sentences the same way. But it's also bad form to start two consecutive paragraphs the same way, and that's harder to spot. Again, your computer can come to your rescue. Set your right-margin to the highest value your program allows (and, if you're using a non-graphical program, select the smallest point-size for your text that you can), then reformat the document. You'll end up with almost all of your paragraphs as single long lines, scrolling off the right-hand side of the screen. You can then compare how each paragraph begins. Doing that on the file containing this article would have made it obvious that two consecutive paragraphs above start with "Next." If you didn't notice that yourself, this technique is for you.

Of course you know you should use your spell checker, but – please! – learn to *trust* it. If it tells you that a word in your manuscript is spelled incorrectly, it probably is. If the spell checker doesn't offer an alternative, then look it up in a dictionary. I was amazed recently to see a manuscript from an author who has ten books in print in which "congratulations" was consistently misspelled "congradulations." Doubtless years ago, the first time her spell checker had flagged the error, she'd assumed her spelling was correct and the database lacked the word, so she added the incorrect form to her personal dictionary.

(Speaking of spelling checkers, one of the most common questions I get asked by Canadian writers is whether they should use Canadian spellings when submitting to an American market. The answer is no: use Canadian spellings when submitting to the *Tesseracts* anthologies or other Canadian markets; British spellings (which aren't the same thing) when submitting to *Interzone* or other British markets; and American spellings when submitting to *Analog* or other U.S. markets.)

One thing your word processor can't do for you is properly count the words in your manuscript. The standard at most publications is to use "printers' rule," which counts every 65-stroke manuscript line as ten words, regardless of whether the line happens to be full (after all, the word count is supposed to give the production editor an idea of how much space the piece will take up in the publication). Actual grammatical word counts usually are ten to twenty percent below the value given by "printers' rule." If you can set an infinite or zero page length in your word processor, then the line count multiplied by ten will give you the word count according to printers' rule; otherwise, multiply the number of lines per page by the number of whole pages, add the number of lines on the partially full first and last pages, then multiply by ten.

Still, your computer's word count may be your most important motivator. The best way to make it as a writer is to set yourself a daily target figure and not stop working until you've reached it (my own is 2,000 words; for most full-time writers, the target is between 1,000 and 2,500). Every few minutes, I do a word count to see how much more work I have to do until I can knock off for the day – which, having now reached that figure, is precisely what I'm going to do right now. But don't you quit writing today until you've reached *your* own word-count goal . . .

Cover Letters and SASEs

Over the last two years, we've talked about how to make your stories better. This time, though, I want to look at the items you mail out *with* your stories: cover letters and self-addressed stamped envelopes. My wife Carolyn Clink and I recently edited the Canadian SF anthology *Tesseracts 6* – and we were shocked by how many people didn't know how to handle these two companions to any good submission.

Cover Letters

Most editors expect to receive a cover letter with your manuscript. It should be short and sweet:

> Dear *[editor's name]*:
> Enclosed is my 4,300-word short story entitled "Zombies of Zubenelgenubi" for consideration in *CyberCanuck*.
> My work has previously been published in *On Spec* and *Tesseracts 4*.
> The manuscript is a disposable copy; I enclose a letter-sized SASE for your reply.

Make sure your address and phone number appear in the letterhead (they should also be on the manuscript). And, for Algis's sake, spell the editor's name correctly (Kristine Kathryn Rusch used to bounce anything from *The Magazine of Fantasy & Science Fiction* that had any of her names wrong). Also specify the publication you are submitting to – many editors work on multiple projects simultaneously.

If you have some, list a few publication credits (major non-fiction credits are okay, if you don't have any fiction ones). If you have expertise related to the story, you could mention that, too (an astronomy degree would carry weight if you're submitting to *Analog*). But don't pad the letter with meaningless credentials: no one cares if you belong to the Canadian Authors Association (which has no membership requirements), that you workshop every week, or that your mother thinks you're the new Isaac C. Heinlein.

If the submission is disposable (meaning all you want back is the editor's reply, not the story), say so here – and say it again on the manuscript.

If there's anything else the editor needs to know (for instance, that the story has been previous published, even in another language), say it. Carolyn and I were furious to discover one of the stories we wanted to take was an undisclosed reprint. And don't think that just because the story hasn't been published in English that you don't have to disclose the fact that it's already appeared in French – or the converse, of course – or that you don't need to mention that the story has already been posted on your World Wide Web home page. You must lay out, in plain language, the entire pedigree of the work you are offering for sale.

Just as important is what's *not* included. Don't try to synopsize the story. It's an instant turnoff to read things like "'Zombies' is a poignant love triangle between two humans and an alien slime-being . . ." Likewise, don't tell the editor why you wrote the story: "I was inspired to pen this tale after discovering slime between my own toes – moving me to ask that classic SF question of 'What if?' . . ." None of that matters; the story should stand on its own.

SASEs

A SASE is a self-addressed stamped envelope. That means the destination address – the one that appears on the lower half of the envelope – is your own complete address. (We got some SASEs that were addressed to us, instead of the submitter.)

We were stunned to see how many people sent envelopes with no stamps, or sent big SASEs for return of the manuscript, but with insufficient postage. Also, don't send loose stamps: stick the stamps on the envelope yourself.

If you're submitting to a market outside your own country, you need stamps from that country – Canadian stamps are no good in the United States, and vice versa. If you can't get hold of foreign stamps, buy International Postal Reply Coupons at the post office, and include one for every thirty grams of material you want mailed back to you.

You *must* submit a SASE with every story manuscript (although one SASE per small batch of poems is fine). Some writers made multiple submissions to *Tesseracts 6* on different dates, but only sent a SASE with the first submission, expecting us to sort through hundreds of envelopes to find theirs (instead, of course, they got left to the very end of the reading process).

Others said they hadn't bothered with a SASE, but told us we could reply by e-mail. That's a no-no: never ask an editor for special treatment. The only way in which you want to stand out from the crowd is by making a proper, professional-looking submission.

Good luck!

Self-Promotion

At the science-fiction convention ConText '91 in Edmonton, I gave a talk on self-promotion. The room was packed, and the talk seemed to make a big splash. Audio tapes of it have been circulating for the intervening six years, and people still ask me questions about self-promotion. More: large numbers of Canadian writers now seem to be doing the things I discussed.

I say "seem to," because although much energy is going into their self-promotion, these writers aren't getting the results they want. So, this time out, I thought I'd give you Rob's Six Rules of Self-Promotion.

Rule One: You've Got to Break Eggs to Make Eggs

Self-promotion costs money. If you were starting a dental practice, you'd expect to spend tens of thousands of dollars getting your business off the ground. Why should a new writer balk at spending some money, too? I met one wannabe recently who said he couldn't afford to do any promotion while he was starting up, but would do some once he got established. He was missing the whole point: promotion is a large part of *how* you get established.

On the other hand, your promotional efforts have to be cost-effective. I do a newsletter a couple of times a year called *SFwriter.com: News from the Robert J. Sawyer Web Site.* It goes to the media, booksellers, and librarians, but I normally *don't* send it to individual readers (although I do put a small supply out on the freebie tables at SF conventions). Printing and mailing costs me about a buck an issue – meaning if I mail the newsletter to someone, and that person decides to buy my latest paperback because of it, I've *lost* about fifty cents on the deal. Which brings us to . . .

Rule Two: Let the Media Leverage Your Efforts

It's pointless to try to promote your book one-on-one to readers – and it's also irritating for the reader. They call it "mass-market" publishing for a reason: a U.S. publisher will want to sell a minimum of 3,000 hardcovers or 15,000 paperbacks. With real perseverance, you might persuade thirty people to drop the thirty-odd bucks on your hardcover, and maybe even 150 people to spend eight bucks on your paperback. But, for all that making a pest of yourself, you've only reached one percent of the number of people you need to make the book even marginally successful.

Instead of going after individual book-buyers, almost all of your promotional efforts should be aimed at the media: newspapers, magazines, radio, and television. They'll get word of your work out to thousands of people for you. Learn to do press releases (there are samples on my web page at www.sfwriter.com, and you'll find some more in the wonderful book *The Writer's Guide to Self-Promotion and Publicity* by Elane Feldman, published by Writer's Digest Books).

Also, learn to send your press releases effectively. The cheapest, fastest, and easiest way is with a fax modem: I write my press releases on my computer, and, while I'm sleeping, I have my fax modem send them to a list of forty or so media outlets, including CBC's *Midday*, CTV's *Canada AM*, *The Globe and Mail*, other daily papers across Canada, my local community papers, and the Canadian Press wire service. Note that press releases must be timely: I've seen many writers win awards, then, a month later, decide to snail-mail out a press release. Of course, they end up getting no coverage at all.

Rule Three: Quality Counts

Still, you may want to do some flyers or bookmarks – although, in my experience, these are the least effective marketing tool. But if you *are* going to do them, they have to look professional. If you don't know anything about layout and design – learn. I'm lucky enough to have a wife who worked for years in the printing industry, but for those who don't, get a copy of the book *Looking Good in Print: A Guide to Basic Design for Desktop Publishing* by Roger C. Parker (Ventana Press).

Print your promotional material on fancy paper. The best selection (but also the priciest) is from the mail-order firm Paper Direct (1-800-A-PAPERS); most office-supply stores also carry desktop-publishing papers from GeoPaper, GreatPapers!, and other suppliers.

Rule Four: Promotion is Cumulative

The first time you send out a press release, you won't get much response – maybe a couple of column-inches in the local weekly paper, and that only if you're lucky.

But it's just like sending out short stories. You can't give up after the first rejection. A little while ago, *Imprint* (a weekly book program produced by TVOntario and also carried nationally on CBC Newsworld) phoned me and said, "We've got a thick file folder about you, and we've been meaning to do a piece on you for a long time. Now's the time." Unless you win a major award, or a movie is made of your novel, not much will happen around the publication of a single book – but if you draw attention to your work on a regular basis, you *will* become a media presence . . . and that translates directly into book sales.

Rule Five: Become Comfortable with Yourself

I've sat on both sides of the interviewer's table: as of this writing, I've done sixty-six TV appearances, countless radio programs, and have been interviewed over a hundred times for print – but I've also conducted a lot of interviews with other people, and I'm constantly amazed at how poorly most writers present themselves.

Be expansive, expressive, and bubbly. If you're on TV, talk with your hands, smile, laugh – have a good time. The only way you can come off looking badly is if you're nervous and defensive. (One Canadian SF author recently scored quite a coup – an appearance on a network talk show. But the first thing he did was try to distance himself from the proceedings, and throughout he looked uncomfortable. What could have sold thousands of books probably ended up selling only a few hundred.)

Take every opportunity you can to hone your public persona. Do readings, talks, classroom appearances, and so on. Take a public-speaking course or join Toastmasters. Record yourself with a camcorder. (Me, I did a degree in Radio and Television Arts at Ryerson; after that, there was no conceivable circumstance under which I could be uncomfortable on camera or in front of a microphone.)

Never take offense at the interviewer's questions (you'll turn him or her right off if you start quibbling over the use of the term "sci-fi") and never talk over the interviewer's head. You know who Olaf Stapledon is, what an ansible is, and so on – but the interviewer won't, and neither will the audience.

Indeed, almost every interviewer you'll ever speak to will know almost nothing about science fiction, and probably won't have read your work.

The single most important thing you can give in an answer is *context*; producers have repeatedly cited my ability to do this as the reason they keep asking me back on their shows.

The interviewer might say, "I guess SF books are riding the coattails of the success of *The X-Files* and the re-release of *Star Wars.*" Don't reply with a simple yes or no; instead, give an interesting, context-rich response: "Actually, I don't think that has much to do with it. We're about to enter the 21st century; in the past year or so we've discovered evidence that there was once life on Mars, and we've found planets orbiting other stars. What could be more natural than for readers to be turning to a literature that devotes itself to exploring these issues?" Note that I say "literature" – in interviews, I always refer to SF as literature, and myself as an artist. Connect you and your work to the larger arts community that the interviewer is already familiar with; you'll find you get much less smarmy coverage.

Note, too, that I didn't force any reference to my own work; such references will come up naturally in the conversation, but you'll seem pushy and insecure if you keep mentioning your own books.

Rule Six: Write Really Well

All the self-promotion in the world is pointless if you don't have a great product. I spend maybe a day a month on self-promotion activities – and the other twenty-nine days working very hard at my craft. I received the most publicity I've ever had when

I won the Science Fiction and Fantasy Writers of America's Nebula Award for Best Novel of the Year. Sure, I did everything I could to capitalize on the win, but winning the award happened because I wrote a good story – and that's the real key to getting people's attention.

Professionalism

This final installment of "On Writing" is devoted to what my wife Carolyn Clink and I discovered while editing the Canadian SF&F anthology *Tesseracts 6*.

Unlike many anthologies, the *Tesseracts* series is wide open: anyone may submit work and it will be seriously considered (indeed, our mandate was to bend over backward to find work by new writers; Carolyn and I are proud of the number of beginners from whom we bought stories or poems).

Still, despite the high quality of the work we did choose, as a group, it appears Canadian writers have a long way to go in the area of professionalism.

First, we were stunned by the very large percentage of submissions that were not in standard manuscript format. There's only one universally accepted way to do it, folks: Courier 10-pitch / 12-point type, or as near as you can manage it, on one side of white 8.5x11" paper; 6.5" line; double-spaced (i.e., 24-point leading); ragged right margins; italics shown by underlining; blank lines between scenes shown by a centered number sign; a descriptive header and a page number on each page after the first; and, if your story ends near the bottom of the page, some indication that this is indeed really the last page (we had to phone one author to ask him if his story really did end with the words that appeared on the last line of what we thought was the final page).

Despite our intention to be forgiving, after slogging through about the tenth manuscript with no page numbers I vowed I would summarily reject unread any unpaginated manuscript that happened to fall on the floor; life is too short to try to figure out which page goes after which other page by piecing together the text.

On fonts: you may think Times, or some other proportional typeface, looks nicer than Courier. However, most editing is still done by hand. Trying to circle the extraneous letter for deletion in "illlicit" is much harder in a proportional font – and damn near impossible in a sans-serif one. If your printer can do Courier, use it (it was frustrating to see all the authors who had Courier page headers or cover letters, demonstrating they clearly *could* use that font, but who set their body copy in a proportional face).

The guy who e-mailed us a manuscript because he was too busy to print it out and put it in an envelope didn't do himself a favor – but even if a market *is* open to e-mail submissions (and ours wasn't), you're shooting yourself in the foot sending a word-processing file without telling the editor in a plain-text attachment exactly what word-processing program, on what computing platform, was used to create the manuscript (and you really should check first to make sure it's a format the editor can read).

A big part of professionalism is appearances – including giving the illusion that the market you're currently submitting to is your first choice. All those people who submitted multiple manuscripts on the day the anthology was announced were telegraphing that they were pulling old stories out of their trunk – and the person who submitted stories clearly dated "1986" and "1989" made it blatantly obvious. (Indeed, you're not helping yourself by submitting more than two or three pieces to any market – no editor wants to see every old dog you haven't been able to sell elsewhere.)

And please – don't ask for special treatment. There's been a lot of grousing lately about how long publications take to reply, but, as a writer, ask yourself whether you have been part of the perceived slowdown by demanding that extra time be spent on your submission.

Some writers asked for responses by e-mail, or by a specific date, or wanted critiques. Sorry, but the only way any editor can process the hundreds of submissions he or she receives is to handle each one exactly the same way. If you want acknowledgment of receipt of a submission, send a stamped postcard with the work's title on it; don't send an extra empty envelope and expect the editor to take the time to write you a letter to put in it.

As I said, we tried to be forgiving of such lapses. But the one thing we couldn't forgive, and were frankly shocked to see so much of, was the lack of basic literacy. We read countless stories whose authors didn't know the difference between "its" (the neutral version of his or hers) and "it's" (a contraction of "it is"). More subtle, but still grating, were the large number of people who didn't know the difference between "that" and "which." ("That" introduces a defining characteristic, and isn't normally preceded by a comma: "This is the novel that Jacques wrote." "Which" introduces an incidental characteristic, and is usually preceded by a comma: "That novel, which is actually quite good, was written by Jacques."

Also irritating were those who used words that weren't in their computerized spelling checkers and couldn't be bothered to look up the correct spelling in a dictionary (there's no such thing as a "trilobyte").

It was also abundantly clear that many authors never looked at their printouts before submitting their stories. Some had missing lines of text or overprinted lines that even a cursory glance would have detected.

A key habit of the true professional: reading the guidelines. We said our reporting time was "10 to 12 weeks following the August 15 deadline" (which I'll point out, for those complaining that response times are getting longer and longer, is a much faster turnaround than the ten months *Tesseracts 3* took to respond). Those people who started pestering me at my private e-mail address – which appeared nowhere on the guidelines – in advance of the expiration of our reporting period made no friends; those who cut no slack if reporting went a short period after that time frame likewise were no fun to deal with.

Finally, a word or two about content. Please note that song lyrics aren't public domain: you can't simply add them into your story. Many authors quoted from popular songs in their manuscripts, but without paying a permission fee, this is illegal – and since most such fees have to be renegotiated for every new edition or translation of the work, most anthology editors will reject a work on the spot that contains such quotes, even if a note of permission for the current edition is included.

We saw a large number of virtual-reality or cyberpunk stories; those are pretty moribund subgenres. We also saw a lot of high fantasy, most of it not very fresh. What we didn't see much of was hard SF; a well-written spaceship story with realistic characterization and dialog would have been a shoo-in.

Anyway, *Tesseracts 6* has passed into history. Paula Johanson and Jean-Louis Trudel are editing *Tesseracts 7*, which is now open for submissions. Apply the advice above – and, of course, write a good story – and maybe you'll make a sale to them. But, no matter who you're submitting to, always remember to behave like a pro – and someday you'll actually be one.

About Rob

Autobiography

I wrote this 10,000-word autobiographical essay in January 2003, for Gale Research's Contemporary Authors; *it appeared in volume 212 of that series, published early in 2004.*

My father, John Arthur Sawyer, was born in Toronto in 1924; his ancestry is Scottish and English. My mother, Virginia Kivley Peterson Sawyer, was born in Appleton, Minnesota, in 1925, but grew up in Berkeley, California. Her background is Swedish and Norwegian. They were married at the University of Chicago in 1952, where they were both graduate students in economics.

Shortly thereafter, they moved to Ottawa, Canada's capital, where my dad was employed by what was then called the Dominion Bureau of Statistics and is now known as Statistics Canada. I was born in Ottawa on April 29, 1960 – but my parents almost immediately moved again, this time to Toronto, so that my father could take a teaching post at the University of Toronto starting in the fall of 1960.

After a few years, my mother started teaching at the University of Toronto, as well, lecturing in statistics. It was unusual, back then, having a mother who worked outside the home, and even more so to have one who worked in an intellectually challenging field; my friends didn't quite know what to make of it. Still, it had advantages: we were the first family on our street to have two cars – one for my dad and one for my mom. These days, that's very common, but it wasn't then, and I was very proud of both my parents.

I have two brothers, Peter Douglas Sawyer, who is six years

older than me, and Alan Bruce Sawyer, who is sixteen months younger. My parents had hoped to space their children more evenly, but there were medical complications after my older brother was born. It's too bad: I've never been as close to Peter as I would have liked, but of course no sixteen-year-old wants a ten-year-old tagging along. And my relationship with Alan was strained during much of our childhood; we were so close in age that a rivalry was inevitable. Still, I was very much the traditional middle child, always trying to make peace and build bridges.

My mother had been a *bona fide* gifted child, graduating from the University of California at Berkeley when she was 17, and my older brother had been accelerated (put ahead a grade) twice at school. The teachers and my parents meant well in doing this, but Peter had a bunch of troubles in his early years, in large measure because he was pushed ahead.

I was a bright kid, too, but, because of what happened to Peter, my parents resolutely kept me at the grade appropriate for my age. It was probably for the best, but I remember being bored most of the time in the classroom, and that led to me being somewhat disruptive there. But at the end of every week, my father took me down to the Royal Ontario Museum's Saturday Morning Club, where bright kids got to go behind the scenes in the museum's various departments and learn all sorts of fascinating things; that was the intellectual highlight of my childhood.

I was a chubby kid, and lousy at sports. I'm sure this disappointed my dad, who was a big baseball fan. I also had a coordination problem – and still do, to some degree – and couldn't throw a ball well or get my body to do the things that my friends could do with ease. (Ultimately, I think this problem had something to do with me becoming a writer. An athlete has to get it right on the first try: if you're taking a shot at the goal, you don't get a second chance to score a point. But a writer revises, and keeps going back until he or she is satisfied.) So, instead of playing sports, I watched a lot of TV. There's never been much domestic Canadian dramatic television. Instead, Canadian channels fill their prime-time schedules with American programs. But, since 90 percent of all Canadians live within a hundred miles of the U.S. border, we also receive American TV stations. Today, with almost all Canadians getting their TV via cable, the cable operators simply delete the US signal and simultaneously substitute the Canadian one – meaning we see the same episode of the same series, but with Canadian, instead of American, commercials.

But in the 1960s and 1970s, things were different. Canadian stations had to entice us to watch their broadcasts of the program (with the ads they'd sold), rather than the American ones. To do that, they showed the American-made programs earlier in Canada.

When I was 12, in 1972, my favorite new series was called *Search*, starring Hugh O'Brien and Burgess Meredith. It was an intricately plotted caper series, with high-tech agents, linked by miniature cameras and radios to a mission-control center, working to recover missing objects. In Toronto, we got the Canadian broadcast of the latest episode on Tuesdays at 8:00 p.m. on local channel 9, and then, the next night, at 10:00 p.m., we got the American broadcast, spilling over from the NBC station in Buffalo, New York.

I never missed an episode on Tuesday nights, but I wanted more. Every Wednesday night I had a fight with my mom, because I wanted to stay up to watch *Search* again – the exact same episode I'd seen the day before. It was an hour-long series, meaning it wasn't over until 11:00 p.m.–way too late, my mom felt, for a 12-year-old on a school night. But I whined and wheedled, and she would usually give in.

Back then, I couldn't articulate why it was so important to me to watch the same episode a second time – but I understand it perfectly now. I was learning how to write. On Tuesday nights, I'd be surprised by the twists and turns the plots took – and on Wednesday nights, knowing how the story turned out, I was able to see how the writer had developed the plot.

Now, television drama may not be the greatest form of literature – but the structure it uses is wonderful for learning plotting. There was always something else on and, at every commercial break, there was an opportunity for you to switch to another program, so TV writers had to end every act – indeed, just about every scene except the last – with a little cliffhanger, to keep you in suspense, to keep you from turning away.

(Today, of course, there are videocassette recorders and DVD players; no one has to go through the difficulties I did to see the same program twice in rapid succession. Still, I think watching a program twice – or reading a book twice – is a great way to see exactly how the writer accomplished what he or she had set out to do.)

Search wasn't the only TV program that had an impact on me. The original *Star Trek* – the one with Kirk, Spock, and McCoy – was also a huge influence. I only saw one episode in first run: "The Devil in the Dark," the one with the Horta. That had been a special treat; my parents didn't approve of me watching violent TV shows (the spy program *The Man from UNCLE* was banned in our house); nor did they ever buy us toy guns (although we did receive a few as presents from neighborhood kids over the years, over my parents' objections). Those bans certainly had an affect on me; I consider myself a pacifist today, and most of the characters I write about go out of their way to avoid a fight – not out of cowardice, but out of principle.

Anyway, there was a book published in 1968, while *Star Trek* was still in first run, called *The Making of Star Trek*. It was the first book of its kind, and I found it absolutely fascinating. The edition I have has "The book on how to write for TV!" emblazoned above the title. The authors were Stephen E. Whitfield and Gene Roddenberry (the latter the creator of *Star Trek*), and it contained all sorts of materials: blueprints of the starship *Enterprise*, close-up photos of props, character sketches of the ship's crew, and dozens of memos sent between various people involved in the production arguing about every little background detail, from what powered the starship to what sorts of family names Vulcans might have.

These days, many DVD releases come with commentary by the screenwriter or director, but back then this sort of insight into the creative process was completely unprecedented. I'm sure I would have loved *Star Trek* regardless, but I learned an enormous amount watching the 79 original episodes re-run over and over again, once the show was in syndication, because of the background in that book. One of the key skills for an SF writer is "world building"–creating a convincing alternate reality, and giving the audience insights into it through well-chosen background details. There's no doubt I learned this skill through *Star Trek*.

Of course, my very first stories didn't have much in the way of world building – but I do think it's interesting that from day one, I was writing from non-human perspectives. The very first story I ever wrote, when I was six or seven, was called "Bobby Bug." Ironically, at that time, I had no idea that "Bobby" was a form of my own name, Robert.

(Actually, I was called "Robin" as a child. That was what my mother wanted to give me as my legal name, but my father thought it would be better to have a more masculine name; also, he had a great fondness for his Scottish heritage, and so my given names, Robert James, are after historic kings of Scotland. But I was registered at school as Robin Sawyer, and the local Parks and Recreation Department, guessing my gender by my name, kept sending me invitations to join girl's ice-skating teams and similar things. When I was ten, I rebelled against the name Robin, and have used Robert (or Rob) ever since. I actually regret it now; Robin is a great name for a writer.)

In 1968, when I was eight years old, my father took me to see the then-new movie *2001: A Space Odyssey*. It was my introduction to the work of Arthur C. Clarke, then and now my favorite science-fiction writer, and I ultimately saw *2001* a total of 25 times on the big screen. Part of the appeal was the fact that the movie had that year in its title. One of the nice things about being born in a year that ends in zero is that it makes math simple. Even as a kid, I knew I would be 41 in 2001, and my father, sitting next to me in Toronto's Glendale Theatre, was then 43 – meaning I'd be younger than my dad was then when the wonders of giant space stations and cities on the moon and thinking computers would supposedly be a reality.

Also an important part of my childhood was the *Apollo* program, which really did put human beings on the moon. I was absolutely fascinated by it, and my parents used to let me stay home from school to watch important mission events on TV.

Still, I mostly enjoyed school – except for a few bullies. I hadn't really shown a profound interest in writing by the time I was in grade four, but my teacher, Peter Moroz, let me indulge my interest in space.

By the time I got into grade five, though, I was very much intrigued by writing. My teacher, Patricia Matthews, greatly encouraged me in that. This was back in the days before photocopies were common, and there was no such thing as a word processor. She used to ask me for copies of my stories, so she could keep them for herself – my first fan – and I dutifully wrote out duplicates of them by hand for her.

Multiculturalism has always been part of my life. Toronto, where I live, has been recognized by the UN as the most multicultural city in the world. The original *Star Trek*, with its multiracial crew, certainly underscored that, and even as a kid, I never allowed other kids to get away with racist, or anti-Semitic, remarks in my presence.

Indeed, I remember one of the few times I was ashamed to be a Canadian was while watching the opening ceremonies on TV for Expo 70 in Osaka, Japan. Canada's participation was a series of female dancers – and every one of them was white with brunette hair. Even as a ten-year-old, I knew that was wrong. There should have been people of all races represented. I've always tried to do just that in my writing.

Now that I'm older, I realize the enormous racism that was going on in the southern U.S. during my childhood. When I'm asked who my heroes are, people expect me to name scientists or writers. No; indeed, one of the great shocks of my life was discovering that one of my childhood heroes, the American paleontologist Roy Chapman Andrews, who died the year I was born, had been a racist. My heroes today are Martin Luther King and Mahatma Ghandi – people who struggled nonviolently to change the world. I'm an idealist at heart, and the two most moving experiences I've had as a tourist were visiting the United Nations Headquarters in New York City, and the Civil Rights Museum in Tennessee.

In public school (Kindergarten through Grade 6), I didn't really have many friends who were as bright as me, and that was emotionally quite hard. In Junior High (Grades 7 through 9), I had one close friend who was quite bright, and we spent a lot of time together talking about space and science fiction. It wasn't until high school, though, that I really found a group of friends who were as intelligent as I was, and my high-school years were some of the best of my life.

In October 1975, when I was beginning Grade 10, I made friends with a guy named Rick Gotlib, who was in my Latin class (yes, Latin was an oddball choice – but I thought it would help me to understand scientific terms; I was planning on becoming a scientist). We both had an interest in science fiction, and spent one lunch period trying to stump each other with trivia questions. Rick and I figured there had to be other science-fiction fans in the school, and so decided to start a science-fiction club: the North-view Association for Science Fiction Addicts, or NASFA (Afsan, the main character in my novels *Far-Seer*, *Fossil Hunter*, and *Foreigner*, is NASFA spelled backwards).

The first meeting was a great success, and, to our surprise and delight, a large number of pretty girls joined the club – an unexpected bonus. I'd never really had female friends prior to this – the street I'd grown up on was filled with boys – but suddenly I did. Most of the people who joined the club were older than Rick and I were (back then, Ontario High School went to Grade 13, meaning some of our members were eighteen at the beginning of the year, and nineteen by the time it ended).

And then a miracle occurred: the teachers went on strike. For months, Northview Heights Secondary School – and all the other high schools in Ontario – were closed. But we decided to keep holding NASFA meetings anyway during that period, once a week at different people's houses.

It was an unusual situation: a couple of Grade 10 boys hanging out with boys and girls in Grades 11, 12, and even 13. But since there were no classes to worry about during the strike, we were treated as equals; all that mattered was how clever or funny we could be. Indeed, to my astonishment, I soon found myself dating a gorgeous girl named Lorian Fraser who was two grades ahead of me – quite a heady experience for a guy who, in junior high, had been very awkward around girls.

I'd hung around with some bad kids in junior high, but had avoided getting entangled in the smoking, drinking, and drugs they were experimenting with. There's always been something in me that was averse to peer-group pressure: when bell-bottomed pants came into style in the late 1960s, I refused to wear them, making my mother drive me all over town looking for stores that still had straight legs. And, until I was in my 20s, I never wore blue jeans, despite the fact – or more precisely, *because* of the fact – that everybody else was wearing them.

But the science-fiction crowd in high school never got into trouble. Not one of us smoked, no one was using drugs, and only a few occasionally drank. (Robert Charles Wilson, another SF writer and one of my closest friends, noted recently that I've never developed adult vices: to this day, I don't drive and I don't drink, but I've got a real fondness for chocolate milk, potato chips, and pizza.)

Still, we members of NASFA had incredible amounts of fun, and I felt intellectually stimulated all the time. Several members of the club talked about wanting to write science fiction, but it seemed clear that I was the only one who was really serious about it, and in the summer after grade ten, I made my first-ever submission to a science-fiction magazine. The story, quite rightly, was rejected, but I wasn't discouraged. On the contrary, I was rather impressed by the simplicity of the process: anyone, anywhere, could send in a story, and it would be seriously considered for publication.

Incredible as it seems today, with the fifth *Star Trek* TV series currently in first-run, back in 1977, when I was 17, it had been eight years since the original *Star Trek* went off the air, and it looked like there would never be any more. So some friends and I set about shaping a series of audio dramas – there was no way we could afford to do TV!–that would be the new *Star Trek*.

I was the driving creative force, and the first proposal I came up with as the basis of our series was something I called *Creator Quest*: in the 21st century (which seemed a long way off then!), scientific evidence points to a guiding intelligence for our universe, and a starship sets off to find this God. Aided by my brother Alan, we produced a mock opening credits sequence for the show, with music and ominous narration. I don't remember much of it, except the last words were ". . . the astral quest for our creator!"

Anyway, my friends looked at me like I was nuts after I played the *Creator Quest* demo tape, and so I decided to start over. I proposed a format very similar to *Star Trek*. Instead of a United Federation of Planets, it had a Commonwealth of Planets (Canada, of course, is part of the Commonwealth of Nations, the alliance of countries formerly under British control). But my parents' pacifism had had an affect on me. I completely rejected the military background of *Star Trek*, and came up with a democratic, socialist structure based on that of a university (the university-like setting was also, I'm sure, my parents' influence; remember, they both taught at the University of Toronto).

Our series ended up being named *Star Station Terra* (because our little SF club that had spun off from NASFA, pulling in a few people who had never gone to Northview and others who had already graduated, was called the Society for Speculative Thinking, and we wanted it to have the same initials). Contributing in major ways to fleshing out the series were my friends Tom Nadas, Carolyn Clink, Ariel Reich, and Do-Ming Lum, but still the core concept was mine – including the presence of dolphins aboard our starship. At that time, American biologist John C. Lilly was talking a lot about his theory that dolphins might be as intelligent as humans. That notion fascinated me, so I threw in a dolphin named Bobo.

We wrote a bunch of scripts, and put them through many drafts, but never got around to producing the audio dramas. That was fine by me – it was really the writing, not the production, that I was interested in. All in all, it was a great experience.

In 1974, my parents bought a vacation home on Canandaigua Lake, one of Upstate New York's Finger Lakes, and we made frequent trips there. The nearest city was Rochester, New York, and my parents became members of the Rochester Museum and Science Center. In the summer of 1979, the Strasenburgh Planetarium, which was part of the RMSC, announced a contest to be judged by science-fiction great Isaac Asimov: write a short story that could be made into a dramatic planetarium star show.

I decided to dust off one of my old *Star Station Terra* ideas, and wrote it up in prose. I stripped out any parts of the background that I myself had not made up, added new stuff to cover what was missing, and submitted the story. I thought there might be a prejudice against a Canadian entering an American contest, so I put the address of my family's US vacation home on the submission.

In January of 1980, Isaac Asimov's pick was announced – and it wasn't me. Still, the planetarium was having a reception for everyone who had entered the contest, and my mother agreed to drive me down, along with Carolyn Clink, two years older than me, a member of the Society for Speculative Thinking, and now, after four years of friendship, my new girlfriend.

As soon as we arrived at the reception, the planetarium's director came running over to me. "We were hoping you would come!" he said. "We've been trying to reach you for weeks!" It turned out that the story Asimov had liked best really only had enough meat on it for a ten-minute starshow, and so the planetarium staff had decided to buy rights to two additional stories – and one of them was mine!

Of course, they'd only had the US phone number of the vacation home, which had been vacant since the summer – so they hadn't been able to contact me. I was absolutely stunned – it was completely unexpected.

The planetarium didn't have much money in its budget, but they paid me US$85 for the rights to make a starshow from my story – and that worked out, almost exactly, at the then-current exchange rate, to Cdn$100. For years, I had a photocopy of the check framed in my bedroom with the words "First Sale" beneath it.

(Twenty years later, the Rochester Museum and Science Center was soliciting funds for an improvement campaign. Donors who gave a certain amount of money got to have a brick embedded in a sidewalk in front of the museum, with an inscription on it. Most of them say "In memory of . . ." and give a person's name. My mother made the required donation, and her brick says, simply, "My son's career started here.")

The short story I sold to the planetarium was called "Motive." It was just 5,000 words long, but contained many of the elements that went on to be major parts of my fiction. The spaceship *Star Station Terra* had become *Starplex*, which I thought was a way cool term (imagine my embarrassment decades later to find out that Starplex was also the name of a company that makes urine-specimen containers for doctors' offices). Fifteen years later, I wrote a novel called *Starplex*, set aboard a very similar vessel.

In "Motive," *Starplex* was controlled by a master computer, patterned after Hal in *2001: A Space Odyssey*, and like Hal, that computer committed a murder; my first novel, *Golden Fleece*, also dealt with a homicidal computer, and many of my works have continued this pattern of combining science fiction and mystery.

"Motive" also featured dinosaur-like aliens called Quintaglios, and I went on to write three novels about them (*Far-Seer*, *Fossil Hunter*, and *Foreigner*).

The starshow that was made up of the three short stories ran for 192 performances in the summer of 1980 under the umbrella title "Futurescapes." I saw it several times. Although some liberties that weren't improvements were taken with my original story, it was still a fabulous experience, and I was determined to continue writing science fiction.

As I said earlier, the province of Ontario, where I lived then and now, used to be unique in North America in that it had an extra year of high school – grade 13. That was phased out in 2003, which in some ways is too bad. Grade 13 was one of the best years of my life, and I studied all sorts of fascinating topics, including a cinema course, two courses in Latin, and an independent biology course, where I got to choose my own subject matter: I studied dinosaurs and dolphins.

Indeed, dinosaurs had been a life-long passion of mine, and I had thought for sure that I'd go on to university to become a vertebrate paleontologist specializing in the study of dinosaurs. But in grade 13, I started looking at the actual paleontological job prospects, and I was astonished to find them quite dim. Back then, there were only 24 dinosaurian paleontologists in the entire world, and only three in Canada . . . and it didn't seem likely that one of those three was going to volunteer to retire just because I had arrived on the scene.

I'd always sort of assumed I'd go to the University of Toronto – not only was it local, but my father still taught there, and that meant his children were entitled to free tuition. But, suddenly, I had no idea what I was going to do for my future.

Fortunately, a new direction fell into my lap in November 1978. We were allowed to take a day off school to go to a "Tour and Discussion Day" at Toronto's Ryerson Polytechnical Institute, which offered bachelor degree-programs in applied arts and technology. I was thinking of maybe studying journalism – I had been founder and editor of my school's newspaper, *The Northview Post*, and thought that a journalism degree might let me write for a living (writing *fiction* for a living seemed like a ridiculous dream). Ryerson was the only place in Toronto to offer a journalism degree, so I signed up to tour that department – but you could stay away from school for the whole day if you signed up to tour two departments, so, on a whim, I selected Radio and Television Arts for my second tour, because that book *The Making of Star Trek* had fascinated me so much.

The tour was spectacular – all that wonderful television equipment! The dimly lit control rooms reminded me of the mission control center from the TV series *Search*.

I was told this was a very competitive program – only one in five applicants got accepted for it – but I decided to try, and, lo and behold, I got in. I started my studies there in September 1979, and I had my first piece of fiction published at the end of my first year, in Ryerson's literary annual, *White Wall Review.*

From the start, my fiction was full of Canadian content, and that was in direct response to what I'd grown up watching on TV. In the 1960s and 1970s, most Canadian-made episodic television was lousy. CTV – Canada's only commercial television network at the time – had precisely one Canadian drama, a cop show called *Police Surgeon,* and one Canadian sitcom, a completely unfunny long-suffering-husband-and-daffy-wife show called *The Trouble With Tracy.* Even as a kid, I was infuriated by these programs, because although they were made in Canada, they were *set* in the United States. I remember being appalled when one episode of *Police Surgeon* was filmed at my beloved Royal Ontario Museum, but they called it by another name and had raised the Stars and Stripes on the flagpole out front.

Still, this was part of the Canadian psyche back then: a belief that the only way to succeed on the international stage was to disguise the fact that you were Canadian. Indeed, when I was starting off writing, people kept telling me *not* to set my stories in Canada if I wanted them to be published in the States.

Ever the rationalist, I wondered where this pervasive belief had come from and started looking for quality modern works by Canadians that were set in Canada and published in the U.S. I expected there to be a list of failed books, movies, and TV shows that had formed the basis of this belief – but there was nothing. It seemed everyone had just assumed that this would be true, and that no one had tested it.

Well, when I did start publishing, I decided to test it, being flagrantly Canadian in my work. I just couldn't believe that Americans could be so provincial (if you'll forgive the pun) to reject a book just because of its setting. Lo and behold, I turned out to be correct. I've never once had an American editor, reviewer, bookseller, or reader complain about the Canadian content in my books.

Many writers have long resumes, listing all the odd jobs they did to support their craft. Not me; I've only ever had two jobs since graduating in 1982. Ryerson hired me to return for the following academic year to help teach television studio production techniques to second- and third-year students. I'd applied for this job for three reasons. First, 1982 was the middle of a recession in

Canada, and for the first time in its history, the Canadian Broadcasting Corporation – Canada's giant state-owned radio and TV factory – was laying off people. Normally, Ryerson grads waltzed into entry-level positions at Canadian studios, but that year we were all competing with seasoned veterans from the CBC who were also looking for work.

Second, the job at Ryerson paid well, by the standards of what entry-level broadcasting positions offer: Cdn$14,000 a year. It seems like peanuts today, and it wasn't very much back then, but, according to a salary survey done by Ryerson it made me the third-highest-paid Radio and Television Arts grad in my year.

Third, and most important, my girlfriend – and now fiancée – Carolyn was also studying at Ryerson (Graphic Arts Management – a business course for the printing industry); she had one more year to go, and I wanted to be close to her.

Still, I graduated in April 1982, and the job at Ryerson didn't begin until September – meaning I had four months off with nothing to do. I'd moved away from home after my second year at Ryerson, and had bills to pay.

Enter John Rose, the elfin proprietor of Bakka, Toronto's science-fiction specialty bookstore. I'd been a regular customer of the store for eight years by this point, and John offered me a summer job. The pay was just $4.25 an hour; I probably could have found something somewhat more lucrative, but the chance to work in a science-fiction store was too appealing to pass up.

I worked the cash desk, shelved books, and counted inventory – but there was one part of the job I managed to avoid. Books go into bookstores on a returnable basis, meaning if they don't sell, the retailer can return them to the publisher and owe nothing. But for paperback books – the format back then that most science fiction was published in – only the *covers* of the books are returned. They're ripped from the body of the book, and the store destroys what's left. The other clerks, who were long-term employees, all had to do this, but I managed not to have to do it; I said – only half-kidding – that I thought it would scar me for life.

I really didn't end up making any money at Bakka. As an employee, I was entitled to a 40% discount on everything in the store, and I spent almost my entire earnings buying books.

Still, in June of that year, John Rose did something remarkable. He took me to the annual convention of the Canadian Booksellers

Association. It was, in many ways, a crazy thing to do – John had to (a) pay me my wages for the day I attended, and (b) pay a fee to get me in. But John knew I wanted to be a writer, and he thought I should really see how the retailing industry works. The CBA convention – now called BookExpo Canada – is where publishers come to show retailers their upcoming books, and where big-name authors sign copies of their new books for retailers (the comparable American event is, not surprisingly, called BookExpo America).

That summer was an incredibly eye-opening experience for me. Many of my writing colleagues are astonished about how savvy I am about the business of publishing; well, the seeds of that came from that summer working in a bookstore, and that day at the CBA.

(Twenty years later, in the summer of 2002, I was back at BookExpo Canada, this time as an author; it wasn't the first time – I'd been signing at BookExpo Canada since 1995 – but it was particularly memorable, as, to my astonishment, I had the longest line-up of any author at the show. The reason was the launch of *Hominids*, my first novel in the two years since my book *Calculating God* had become a surprise top-ten national mainstream bestseller in Canada.)

I went on to a successful writing career after working at Bakka, but I wasn't the only one. In the two decades that have followed, several other Bakka employees – all hired long after I'd left – went on to writing careers, including Tanya Huff, Michelle West, Nalo Hopkinson, and Cory Doctorow. In honor of the store's thirtieth anniversary in 2002, John Rose asked each of us to write an original SF story to be published in a limited-edition anthology. He couldn't afford to pay us for the stories, but we all agreed – we all owed John far too much to worry about doing some work for free.

And, besides, I'd been doing free writing for Bakka for a long time. I got my first computer in December 1983. The very first thing I wrote on it was a piece for Bakka's occasional newsletter summarizing the accomplishments by Canadian science-fiction writers. That was the first of many things I did to help other writers, and Canadian science-fiction writers in particular. Indeed, from 1984 to 1992, I coordinated a social group of Toronto-area science-fiction writers founded by legendary SF editor Judith Merril; I spearheaded the successful movement to establish a

Canadian region of the Science Fiction and Fantasy Writers of America; and in 1998, I served as that organization's president.

My girlfriend Carolyn did graduate from Ryerson in 1983, but Canada was still in the middle of a recession, and it was a full year before she found a job. We were living together, and needed money, so I went after as many freelance writing contracts as I could. They were all nonfiction – articles for newspapers and magazines, press releases and brochures for corporations, newsletters for government departments. The work was actually pretty lucrative, but I didn't find it at all creatively satisfying. Still, I spent five years doing that sort of thing, producing mountains of promotional materials and over 200 articles for computing and personal-finance magazines. All the while, I was putting money in the bank.

I did learn a lot during this period, even though I wasn't writing much fiction. Many of the articles I wrote required interviews, which I had to transcribe. People talk in a very disjointed manner, but I learned to fashion quotes that captured what the person intended to convey without presenting their words verbatim. Since the work I was doing was contracted for, I also learned about making deadlines, and to write even when I didn't feel like doing so.

I hadn't given up my dream of writing science fiction, but it had very much been on the back burner. I'd sold a few short stories after "Motive," had won a couple of minor writing contests, and had outlined a novel in the summer of 1980 – but by 1988, when I was 28, that novel remained unwritten. My only really significant publication to that date was the novelette "Golden Fleece," which appeared as the cover story in the September 1988 edition of *Amazing Stories*, the world's oldest science-fiction magazine.

Carolyn and I had gotten married four years earlier, in 1984. I now told her I wanted to really try to concentrate on writing science fiction. Although I was still doing a lot of corporate and government work (my big project for that year was editing a study about the future of the parks in and around Niagara Falls, Ontario), I made a concerted effort to clear time in my schedule to work on writing the novel I'd outlined eight years ago. The result was that by December 1988, I had finally written that novel, *End of an Era*. I queried a literary agent named Richard Curtis in New York, sending him a copy of the September 1988 *Amazing*

Stories with my cover story. He asked to see my novel manuscript, and in January 1989 he agreed to represent it.

It never even occurred to me to wait and see what would happen with *End of an Era*. I continued turning down guaranteed non-fiction work, and launched straight away into my second novel, expanding the "Golden Fleece" novelette from its current 13,000 words to 60,000. (Back then, it was possible to sell 60,000-word science-fiction novels; today, the lower limit seems to be 80,000, with 100,000 preferred. I found it very hard work the first few times trying to get even 60,000-word books written, and I wonder if the acceptable lower limit had been higher then whether I would have ever managed to finish one.)

The first three publishers Richard Curtis submitted *End of an Era* to all turned it down. By October 1989, I'd finished the novel-length *Golden Fleece*, and sent it to Richard. He sold that one to the first publisher he submitted it to, Warner Books.

I've always been an early adopter of computer technologies. I've had Internet access since 1984, and in 1987 I became active on CompuServe, then the world's largest online service. There, I made friends with John E. Stith, an established SF writer. John gave me the best advice I'd ever gotten: he said that publishers really don't do anything to push mass-market paperback original novels. Lately, John had started making his own bound galleys (advance copies of a book, usually given to booksellers or reviewers). I took John's advice, producing seventy-seven bound galleys at my own expense, using a copy shop at the University of Toronto. I sent the galleys to various reviewers, including Orson Scott Card, who wrote the "Books to Look For" column in *The Magazine of Fantasy and Science Fiction*. It was a shot in the dark.

On July 24, 1990, one of the best moments of my life happened. My phone rang, and a voice said, "This is Orson Card." Not only had he read my book, he had loved it – and he promised a rave review was forthcoming. I was ecstatic.

Sadly, though, *Golden Fleece* tanked in the marketplace. It had a horrendous cover, and Waldenbooks, one of the major US chains, hadn't taken any copies. Richard Curtis had sent *End of an Era* to the editor at Warner who had bought *Golden Fleece*, presenting it as my second novel. My Christmas stocking that year had a lump of coal in it: just before the holiday, the editor passed on publishing another book by me.

I'd seen the highs and lows of publishing in that single month: my first book had come out, and my publisher had dumped me. Richard admitted it would be very hard to find me a new publisher, because the first question one would ask is why I had left Warner, and as soon as the answer was given – that I'd been dropped because my sales stunk – I would be dead in the water.

But then, something wonderful occurred. Orson Scott Card came out with his year-end summation in *The Magazine of Fantasy and Science Fiction*, and he declared *Golden Fleece* to be the best science-fiction novel of 1990. And, of course, I hadn't been sitting on my behind; by this point, I had finished my third novel, *Far-Seer*, about the intelligent-dinosaur aliens I had introduced a decade earlier in my planetarium-starshow story, "Motive."

Richard Curtis thought *Far-Seer* was "a masterpiece." Armed with Card's original review, plus the other excellent reviews that *Golden Fleece* had received, Richard organized an auction for my next two books – and Peter Heck, an editor at Ace Science Fiction (now part of Penguin USA), made the winning bid. Suddenly, I was back in the game. I decided to give up all non-science-fiction writing. For my fourth book, Richard suggested I do a sequel to *Far-Seer*. I had never intended such a thing, but followed Richard's advice, producing *Fossil Hunter* before *Far-Seer* was actually in stores.

Ace then asked for a third Quintaglio book. I agreed to do it, but hated every minute of writing it. I've never liked *reading* series; the last thing I wanted to do was spend my career writing one. I made up my mind that *Foreigner* would be the final Quintaglio book.

Far-Seer, *Fossil Hunter*, and *Foreigner* got great reviews, but they didn't sell particularly well. I blame a large part of that on the covers, which made the books look like fantasy, not SF. *End of an Era*, which came out after *Foreigner*, confused the marketplace, too. Although completely unrelated to the Quintaglio books, it also involved dinosaurs and the "End" in the title made people think it was the concluding volume of that series.

Sales for *End of an Era* were poor, and I knew I was in trouble again. See, it's easier to sell your first novel than it is your sixth. With a first novel, the publisher doesn't know if you're going to be the next Isaac Asimov, and so they're willing to take a chance. By the time your fifth novel is out, they *do* know – and I wasn't.

A publisher would be better off buying a new novel, for less money, from a first-timer, than another book from me. I decided it was time for drastic action.

I'd always felt I was writing about important issues. *Golden Fleece*, for instance, was about the inherent bugginess of computer systems, an issue that was very much of concern in 1989, when U.S. president Ronald Reagan was proposing "Star Wars," a computer-controlled missile-defense system that would have to work flawlessly the first time it was used, something many computer scientists felt was impossible. *Golden Fleece*, with its buggy computer main character, very much was meant to illuminate that. (Ironically, one of the very few requests my editor at Warner made was for me to remove the specific reference to Reagan's *Star Wars* – this should have prepared me for what was going to come, but it didn't . . .)

Likewise, *Far-Seer* had been issue-based, looking at the Catholic Church's stance on birth control. Of course, because that novel was set on an alien world, no reference to the Roman church was made in the text, but I felt sure most readers would understand what I was *really* talking about.

So, I decided I'd write my next book without a contract, take as long as necessary, and produce a blockbuster, doing the most complex, sophisticated story I could manage, with the most subtle and realistic human characters possible. More than that: I wanted to tackle a controversial issue, and not disguise it, but rather deal with it head on.

And so I wrote *The Terminal Experiment*. The issue was abortion, which fundamentally centers around differing beliefs about when life actually begins – at conception, at birth, or at some point in between. To put it in metaphysical terms, the question is when does the soul enter the body?

Well, *The Terminal Experiment* deals with a biomedical engineer who discovers when the soul *leaves* the body – tracking its movements on an enhanced electroencephalograph as people die. He sets about to find out when it enters the body, as well.

I wrote the book, pouring everything I had into it. I sent it to my agent, who thought it was tremendous – everything we'd both hoped it would be. He sent it to my new editor, who had replaced Peter Heck at Ace, when he left to write his own mystery novels – and she rejected it.

I was absolutely stunned. In her rejection letter, my editor said she'd only consider buying the book if I dropped all references to the soul and to the abortion issue.

I could not bring myself to do that, and I told Richard so. He arranged another auction, sending the manuscript to five publishers. HarperCollins USA was then in the midst of starting a new paperback science-fiction line, to be called HarperPrism, and they bought the book. Richard also sold serialization rights to *Analog*, the number-one best-selling English-language SF magazine; *Analog* would run the full text of the novel in four massive chunks prior to its book publication.

The book, verbatim as I'd submitted it to my old editor, went on to win the Science Fiction and Fantasy Writers of America's Nebula Award for Best Novel of 1995. If I'd eviscerated the book, as my old editor had wanted, it would be a forgotten work today. (The year it came out was the first year Amazon.com was in operation; *The Terminal Experiment* came in fifty-third in total sales for all books in all categories available on Amazon.com that year.)

I was definitely being pulled in two directions at this point. On the one hand, I had grown up reading far-future off-Earth spaceships-and-aliens SF. On the other hand, *The Terminal Experiment* had succeeded precisely because it was none of those things. I had two more novel ideas at that time, and they were at the opposite ends of the SF continuum. One, *Starplex*, would be my attempt to deal with every outstanding conundrum in modern astrophysics, in a plot that covered billions of years of time and millions of light-years of space. The other, *Frameshift*, was a novel about the impact genetic testing has on people's lives, and was very much in the vein of *The Terminal Experiment*. In fact, *Frameshift* would be set in the present day (not even sixteen years in the future, as *The Terminal Experiment* was). *Starplex* was very much event-driven; *Frameshift* was very much character-driven.

I ended up writing both these books, for two different publishers. *Analog* serialized *Starplex*, just as it had *The Terminal Experiment*, and that book went on to be a finalist for both the Hugo and Nebula Awards. Ace – who had published the Quintaglio trilogy and *End of an Era,* but had rejected *The Terminal Experiment* – bought *Starplex* from the briefest outline I'd ever written.

I also wrote *Frameshift*, but without a contract, since my editor at HarperPrism had left the company for health reasons.

Unfortunately, my old agent was unable to sell the book, and I acquired new representation, in the person of Ralph Vicinanza, who is the top agent in science fiction, fantasy, and horror (his other clients include Stephen King and the estate of Isaac Asimov). Ralph found the perfect editor for the book, David G. Hartwell, at Tor, the largest SF publisher in the world. *Frameshift* was my first book published in hardcover, and it sold well, was nominated for the Hugo Award, and won Japan's Seiun Award (as had my earlier *End of an Era*) for best foreign novel of the year.

From then on, it's been nothing but near-future or present-day SF novels for me, and I suspect it will stay that way. That doesn't mean I soft-pedal the science; not at all. I try to have large-scale transcendent sense-of-wonder notions at the heart of all my novels, in the best classic SF pulp-magazine tradition. Indeed, after writing *Frameshift*, I formulated a mission statement for my writing: "to combine the intimately human with the grandly cosmic." Focusing on that led me to do my next novel for Tor, *Factoring Humanity*, which I think is the best thing I've written to date.

Factoring Humanity tells the story of the discovery of an alien technology that allows people to surf the human collective unconscious the way we currently surf cyberspace. The woman who discovers this technology uses it to resolve the crisis that is tearing her family apart: her daughter has accused her husband of having abused her as a child, a charge the husband flatly denies.

I often get asked why the people in my books have such unhappy lives. Peter Hobson's wife is cheating on him in *The Terminal Experiment*; Pierre Tardivel has Huntington's Disease in *Frameshift*; Michiko Komura's daughter is killed in the opening of *Flashforward*; and Tom Jericho has terminal lung cancer in *Calculating God*. It's not that I live an unhappy life – quite the contrary; I'm more happy and content than most people. But I do like writing about raw emotions, and of course these come out most in extreme circumstances. Indeed, the appeal of mystery fiction for many readers isn't the intellectual puzzle of figuring out whodunit. Rather, it's the emotional lives of the characters, which are brought to the surface by the extreme circumstance of having someone close to them die. I'm looking for that same sort of laying bare of inner feelings in my science-fiction writing.

Still, I have had my share of misfortune. In the summer of 1985, I walked through what I thought was an open doorway at a shopping mall – but it wasn't; it was a plate-glass window. If the window had been made of safety glass, nothing would have happened. But, instead, the window broke into giant pieces. I brought my right hand up to shield my face just as a large, jagged portion fell down out of the top of the frame. It sliced open the back of my hand, severing tendons.

My hand was bandaged for weeks, keeping me from doing any writing (I'm right handed), and to this day it has a horrific scar running diagonally across its back. My handwriting had always been somewhat sloppy, but ever since the accident it's been all but illegible. If I lived in a different era, that injury would have put an end to my writing career, but it doesn't impede my use of a computer. The irony isn't lost on me: I'm a science-fiction writer who needs high-tech tools to do his job.

And that job has really become all-consuming, I must admit. I don't have any children; neither my wife nor I ever felt the urge to have any, and, indeed, when I turned 40, I had a vasectomy. (Prior to that, we jokingly decided if we ever had a kid to name him Peabo Clamhead Clink-Sawyer . . . and the horrific prospect of forcing someone to go through life with that name was enough to keep us from becoming parents.)

My father was an only child, and neither of my brothers have any kids, either – so the Sawyer line will be extinct once we die. I find myself wondering about this from time to time, since I've had a life-long interest in evolution, and the definition of success in evolution is the passing on of your genes to the next generation, something I've totally failed to do. And yet I *do* feel I have some small degree of immortality: the words I've written will survive after I'm gone. I'm not fool enough to think I'll be widely read in the future, but it does please me to know that every once in a while, someone will pick up – or download – a book by me in the centuries to come. I guess that means I'm more interested in the survival of my memes than my genes–"meme" being evolutionist Richard Dawkins's term for a persistent idea.

Metaphysical thoughts? I suppose. Indeed, religion seems to figure a lot in my novels – and that causes people to ask frequently about my own religious background. I can't really say that I have one. My father was a lapsed Anglican (what Americans call Episcopalian), and my mother was a Unitarian. I'd attended a Unitarian Sunday School for a few years, but never really understood whatever point they were trying to make. We seemed to spend most of our time going for hikes along a river bank – I vividly remember a succession of soakers, and my little brother falling in and almost floating away. But God was never mentioned, and we never opened a bible or other holy book.

My best friend in public school was quite religious, and his mother kept trying to convert me. As a kid, I couldn't see how any intelligent person could believe in God. I vividly remember my friend telling me one day when we were playing in my backyard that God could count every blade of grass in the yard. Rather than be impressed by this supposed feat of divine numeracy, I thought my friend dim for believing such a silly story.

Indeed, it wasn't until after I finished university that my perspective began to change a bit. My first major contract as a freelance writer came in October 1983 with a little consulting firm called The Rosewell Group, headed by the Honorable David MacDonald, formerly Canada's Secretary of State.

Rosewell was trying to launch an interfaith television cable channel, bringing various denominations of Christians, Jews, Muslims, Hindus, and more together. They needed someone to produce promotional materials and to edit their license application to the Canadian federal broadcasting regulator, the CRTC. One of my professors at Ryerson recommended me for the job, and I took it, spending the next nine months working with The Rosewell Group. This brought me into contact with high-level people in Canada's various faith groups, and I was astonished to find that most of them were intelligent, well-read, thoughtful, and fun people.

They didn't make me believe in God – but they did show me that such belief wasn't necessarily a sign of intellectual weakness or irrationality. I came to realize, indeed, that atheism is an act of faith. Science, after all, doesn't deal in negative results – it doesn't disprove things; therefore, it can't disprove the existence of God. And, of course, a wily creator could choose to conceal from us the fact that we live in a created universe. To say "I believe there is no God," I realized, is philosophically exactly the same as saying "I believe there is a God"–both are statements based on faith.

It seems to me that the only non-faith position is agnosticism, either in the popular sense of the word ("I don't know if God exists" or the technical sense ("The nature of God, if one exists, is by definition unknowable by its creations"). These days, my own belief tends toward the popular definition; I don't think that if a god exists it is necessarily true that it will always elude our comprehension.

Still, I strongly disagree with those who say that science is just another religion. Belief in science doesn't require faith; science can demonstrate its truth quite effectively. To use Richard Dawkins's example, science makes airplanes that really work. The wooden airplanes made by cargo cults and the wax wings of Icarus didn't work, no matter how fervently their owners believed that they should. Indeed, the beauty of science is that it can even make an airplane that will carry someone aloft who believes flight is impossible. Science invites skepticism, welcomes verification, and is open to revision when evidence warrants; faith has not one of those properties, and I consider myself devoid of faith.

When people want to ask less-personal questions than about my religious beliefs, they usually inquire what my hobbies are. The sad truth is that I don't have any. Oh, I like to read – but that's part of a writer's job. And I have a nice collection of science-fiction toys, especially those based on TV shows from the 1960s (in my office, there's a 34-inch wooden model of *Fireball XL5*, four toy versions of the robot from *Lost in Space*, a 12-inch Gorn and a 12-inch Andorian from *Star Trek*, and models of various vehicles from *Thunderbirds*). I also collect plastic dinosaurs – my only criterion is that they must have been scientifically accurate depictions at the time they were made. But these collections take up almost none of my time. Being a writer is, as I said before, an all-consuming life for me, occupying, in one way or another, most of my waking hours. I sometimes think I'd like to do fossil hunting or get into building intricate science-fiction model kits, and I do buy books about both these topics, but I just don't have the time for either pursuit.

Even my vacations almost always have something to do with work. Just about every year, my wife and I travel to wherever the World Science Fiction Convention is being held. It was in Melbourne, Australia, in 1999, and we took five weeks of extra time so we could explore Australia and New Zealand, but those five weeks were the last real vacation I've had. There is a treadmill quality to being a writer: if you don't keep producing new books at a good clip, your readers will go off and find someone else to read.

Maybe that sounds insecure – but, despite winning over two dozen awards and having a substantial degree of financial success, I *am* insecure about my writing. Most of the writers I know are. Indeed, it's become almost a running gag with my friend Edo van Belkom, a great horror writer, that whenever he's about halfway through writing a book he'll phone me up and tell me that his book stinks, that he's throwing in the towel, that the manuscript should go in the garbage, that he doesn't understand why he ever thought he could write books. Of course, I talk Edo through this difficult time, and he continues on. But then, a few weeks later, the roles are reversed, and I phone Edo expressing all the same concerns about my latest project. I think a certain degree of doubt is important: it keeps me from getting complacent or lazy about my writing.

Still, I wouldn't change my current conditions for anything. I love my work, I love my wife, I love my life, I love my home. What more can anyone ask?

Robert J. Sawyer's Place in Science Fiction

by Valerie Broege

The writings of Robert J. Sawyer not only embody much of the rich and diverse historical tradition of science fiction but also are at the cutting edge of the evolution of the field as a "genre-in-the-making."[1] If we consider one of the earliest examples of proto science fiction, Lucian's *True History* (written 170-180 A.D.), we note the use of mythology and the fantastic voyage to the moon. In his first novel *Golden Fleece,* Sawyer draws on the ancient Greek myth of Jason and the Argonauts and the theme of the cosmic voyage but within the framework of highly advanced science and technology.

A much later landmark figure in the history of SF who has directly influenced RJS is Arthur Conan Doyle. When asked to contribute a story for Mike Resnick's anthology, *Sherlock Holmes in Orbit,* Sawyer wrote "You See But You Do Not Observe," which involves the chronotransference of Holmes and Watson to the year 2096 to resolve the Fermi paradox. Also Doyle's 1912 novel *The Lost World* with its focus on dinosaurs contains a subject dear to our author's heart, as witnessed by his four novels and several short stories dealing with these fascinating creatures. Similarly, Sawyer pays homage to another great SF writer who was a contemporary of Doyle – H.G. Wells. Using Wells' *The Time Machine* as a springboard, Sawyer in "On the Surface" creates his own tale of time travel involving the Morlocks and the Eloi.

Sawyer places himself squarely in the American pulp-science fiction magazine tradition of the 1920s-1950s in his attempts to evoke a sense of wonder in his readers. He has succeeded in achieving this objective, according to some of his reviewers.[2]

Although Sawyer was once commissioned to write a space opera short story, I do not think "Wiping Out" is nearly as simplistic and formulaic as pure space opera tends to be. RJS is not called "Mr. Concept" for nothing!

Golden Age science fiction writers Robert Heinlein, Frederik Pohl, and Isaac Asimov have informed much of Sawyer's work. Asimov was connected with Sawyer's writing career right from the start in buying his story "Motive," which contains many of the seeds of RJS's future fiction. Even though he lacks Asimov's graduate degrees in science, Sawyer is regarded both by himself and others as a writer of hard SF in the tradition of Asimov. Sawyer has made himself aware of much cutting-edge research in the fields of astronomy, physics, chemistry, biology, genetics, neuroscience, AI, paleontology, and psychology and is rarely faulted by critics for lapses in these areas in his SF. Both Asimov and Sawyer use their knowledge of science and technology to craft convincing world-building stories which always involve the interplay of ideas and are often cast in the form of mysteries. Sawyer has used elements of detective fiction to good effect in such works as *Golden Fleece* and *Illegal Alien*, among others.

Hard SF writers are often castigated for lack of attention to characterization. Sawyer himself admits to being guilty of this shortcoming in the earlier stages of his SF career because his focus was more on the science and the ideas he was explicating. Some critics have taken him to task for inadequately developing his characters, while others have lauded his ability to create engaging and interesting humans and aliens.

A watershed event in Sawyer's evolution as an SF writer occurred in his conscious determination in conceiving *The Terminal Experiment* to "produce a blockbuster, doing the most complex, sophisticated story I could manage, with the most subtle and realistic human characters possible."[3] In my opinion, RJS is continuing to grow in his skill of delineating multi-faceted characters, both human and alien, as witnessed particularly in his last four novels, *Calculating God* and *The Neanderthal Parallax*.

A contemporary of Isaac Asimov, Arthur C. Clarke is Sawyer's favorite science fiction writer. He was first introduced to him in 1968 when he was eight years old and saw the movie "2001: A Space Odyssey," not once but 25 times! Many years later Sawyer wrote *Golden Fleece*, which is certainly reminiscent of

Clarke in its depiction of a starship voyage and a homicidal onboard computer, but, as critic David Ketterer asserts, Sawyer resolves the story in "a thoroughly satisfying manner that is all his own."[4]

I can also see reflections of another of Clarke's themes in a number of Sawyer's writings. In *Childhood's End* the novel concludes with the collectivity of Earth's children mutating into a new species that is capable of leaving their human bodies behind and joining with the cosmic Overmind, which makes one think of Teilhard de Chardin's concept of the noosphere. RJS likewise seems to be fascinated with the possibility that advances in computer and AI technology might make it possible for human beings as well as aliens to separate their minds from their bodies so that their consciousness dwells in cyberspace. He explores the positive and negative implications of such an outcome both on the personal and collective level in such works as *Factoring Humanity, Calculating God,* "Where the Heart Is," and "Kata Bindu."

The fact that Robert Sawyer is a Canadian has also had considerable impact on the kind of SF he writes. As he mentions in his web site autobiography, the fact that he lived in Toronto as a child made it possible for him to watch the programs in the *Search* series twice, first on a Canadian channel and then on an American one. Viewing each of the programs twice was teaching him lessons about plotting and especially about how to create dramatic cliffhangers, all of which would stand him in good stead in writing exciting SF stories. *Hominids* and *Hybrids* are excellent examples of just how apt a pupil he was in learning the latter technique.

Sawyer credits watching the classic *Star Trek* series and reading the book *The Making of Star Trek* for assisting him in developing expertise in world building. The multi-ethnic, multi-racial *Enterprise* crew and Sawyer's living in the most multicultural city in the world have influenced him to include characters of diverse races and ethnicities on a regular basis in his science fiction.

Ignoring the advice of others about not allowing his stories to have unhappy or ambiguous endings and not using Canadian locales in his science fiction, if he were to be successful in U.S. publishing circles, he has blatantly done both of these things, while winning many awards internationally and earning a six-figure income in the process. More than once his scientist heroes die by the end of the book, as in *Frameshift* and *Calculating God,* and Toronto and Sudbury, Ontario, are frequently-used sites in his stories. Two of Sawyer's short stories consist totally of Canadian content. "Ours to Discover" features Toronto as a steel-domed city of the future outside of whose confines a boy and an adult rediscover the meaning of the maple leaf. "The Stanley Cup Caper" is set in Toronto in 2031 and involves the theft of the Stanley Cup by Quebec separatists.

Although gender issues *per se* are not a predominant concern in his writing, feminist SF writers would probably be pleased to note that equality of the sexes appears to be a given in Sawyer's stories. Women scientists, professors, astronauts, and even a Pope and a female captain of the Toronto Maple Leafs hockey team abound in RJS's pages. Furthermore, the women belong to a variety of ethic groups and races. The delineation of the character of Canadian geneticist Mary Vaughan in *The Neanderthal Parallax* trilogy is particularly well done, and Sawyer explores the impact that being raped has on her personally and on her nascent romantic relationship with the Neanderthal physicist Ponter Boddit.

Some of Sawyer's SF has also invited comparisons to two recent writers, one deceased and the other very much alive and kicking. Similarities can be observed between Sawyer's *Factoring Humanity* and the late Carl Sagan's novel and movie *Contact*. Sawyer has also been called the Canadian Michael Crichton by virtue of the thriller quality of some of his novels and the fact that his dinosaur novels and Crichton's *Jurassic Park* appeared around the same time.

So ultimately how would Robert Sawyer describe the function and mission of science fiction in terms of his own contribution to the field? As someone always interested in the big questions of life whose first story, written when he was 17, dealt with proof that we inhabit a God-created universe, he regards SF as a literature of ideas that tackles the deep cosmological and meaning of life issues. In addition, it engages with Heinlein and Asimov's "What if?" and "If this goes on . . ." approach of trend extrapolation applied to real world issues. Far from regarding science fiction as escapist and juvenile in nature, Sawyer thinks it is the conscience of the technological age with an obligation to be controversial and to shake up people's complacency and preconceptions.

In terms of SF being controversial and challenging, *Calculating God* is a prime example. One of Sawyer's purposes in writing this novel was to confront "fundamentalist evolutionists" with their own unwillingness to look at the holes in the theory of evolution. Within a week *Calculating God* was co-opted by creationist apologists.[5] Later Barry Seidman in *The Skeptical Inquirer* accused Sawyer of promoting creationism and using his fiction "more as a weapon of anti-science propaganda rather than entertainment."[6] Ironies multiply when one considers how pro-science Sawyer is and the fact that several religious fundamentalists excoriated Sawyer, while also insisting that they would never read the book![7]

Real life, in the form of the events of 9/11, Sawyer says, has affected him profoundly and changed what he planned to write in the second and third books of his Neanderthal trilogy and will color everything that he will write in the future.[8] He thinks that belief in God and the afterlife facilitates war and terrorism. This viewpoint is reflected in the carnage and chaos that ensue near the end of *Hybrids* when a collapse of the Earth's magnetic field causes the "God part" of everyone's brain to be stimulated simultaneously.

In my opinion, one of Robert Sawyer's greatest legacies as a science fiction writer will be his sustained, nuanced, and multi-perspectival treatment of the science versus religion dialogue, which deserves to have as wide a mainstream audience as possible. As Robert Price has pointed out,[9] Sawyer's tips for new writers on his massive web site and his new science-fiction imprint Robert J. Sawyer Books, under the aegis of Red Deer Press of Calgary, are contributing to the improvement of the literary and intellectual quality of the science fiction genre. The more science fiction books that make the Canadian bestseller list, as did *Calculating God,* the better the prospects of SF achieving greater acceptance into mainstream fiction, which is one of Sawyer's cherished goals. The kind of complex, thought-provoking writing that Sawyer does at his best and encourages others to do as well can serve an even deeper purpose than pushing the boundaries of science fiction. Like world philosopher Ken Wilber, Robert J. Sawyer may be helping his readers achieve a higher state of consciousness – something which our troubled world needs desperately of all of us.

Valerie Broege
Vanier College
St. Laurent, Quebec

Footnotes

[1] Brooks Landon, *Science Fiction After 1900: From the Steam Man To the Stars* (New York: Twayne Publishers, 1997), 32.

[2] For example, see "Mr. Concept Pulls It Off Again; Thornhill's Robert Sawyer Fashions Another Intriguing Point of Departure – What If Everyone in the World Blacked Out for Two Minutes, Only to Wake with a Clear-eyed Vision of Their Futures Exactly 21 Years Hence?," *Toronto Star,* 4 July 1999, 1, and Tom Flynn, "Science Fiction Goes Anthropic," *Free Inquiry,* Buffalo, 22.1 (Winter 2001/2002): 62.

[3] The Robert J. Sawyer Site, "Robert J. Sawyer Autobiography," 2003, 16 April 2004 <http://www.sfwriter.com/gale.htm>

[4] David Ketterer, *Canadian Science Fiction and Fantasy* (Bloomington and Indianapolis: Indiana University Press, 1992), 136.

[5] Chris Krejlgaard, "Sci-fi Author Dares to Challenge Readers' Views," *Sudbury Star,* 30 September 2000, B9.

[6] Barry Seidman, "Using Science Fiction to Promote Creationism," *The Skeptical Inquirer,* Buffalo, 26.2 (March/April 2002): 53.

[7] Ed Willett, "Sci-fi Author Sawyer Calculates God," *Leader Post,* Regina, Saskatchewan, 9 September 2000, D4.

[8] Robert Price, "Calculating Sawyer: Robert J. Sawyer in Conversation," *Descant* 34.3 (Fall 2003): 191-193.

[9] Robert Price, "Science Fiction in a Canadian Context: Robert J. Sawyer As a Case Study," unpublished final essay for the course Conditions of Cultural Authorship at York University, 13 April 2004.

Valerie Broege's Wonder and Mystery
Cryptic Crossword Puzzle

Those of you who are aficiandos of cryptic crosswords as well as Robert Sawyer's science fiction may want to try your hand at solving this puzzle (next page). Most of the clues are related in some way to Sawyer's life and work. If you are unfamiliar with this intriguing genre of crosswords, please feel free to contact me at broeger@vainercollege.qc.ca for some tips on how to solve cryptic crossword puzzles.

ACROSS

1 Carolyn, hesitations may lead to first-rate things in Britain. (8)

8 Pal, soar into the sky but use a sunshade. (7)

9 Going round and round is not a riot! (8)

10 Electrical disturbances are unchanging. (6)

11 and 17. Hold a letter fast – with the result of going back in time. (5, 6)

13 Door confuses Ponter in the means by which he figures out who Mary's rapist is. (4)

14 It is illegal to give false testimony in an investigation – book him! (5)

15 Is this kind of piece of glass the best for 23 down by far? (6)

17 See 11.

18 Mode of transport's time has come in book of final days. (5)

19 Where Sawyer thinks you'll go to if you have the wrong thought at the wrong time. (4)

20 Send someone to a specialist for treatment of madness caused by so-called reefer. (5)
22 List mu as a letter in the Greek alphabet on your chemistry test. (6)
25 What you can get if you read RJS' thrillers. (8)
26 The impact of a big lance distracted a soldier so that he only looked quickly. (7)
27 Is "dour" an inappropriate description of Dybo? (8)

DOWN
1 Where the ring is is hard to discern. (4)
2 Remove part of a dinosaur to make an engraving. (8)
3 Set of parts to be assembled precedes boss of the cop shop to create what probably is his favorite room. (7)
4 Situation comedy involving Greek letter and prosecutor. (5)

5 Bar is locale of the blue planet. (4)
6 See 21.
7 Choose Hubbard's orbiters. (9)
12 "Stop," said Jag on other frequencies. (2, 3)
14 Insect next to 3-dimensional image gyrates a bit to create tesseracts. (9)
15 One hundred, king, is the profit. (5)
16 Gregor initially investigates a utopian habitat. (8)
17 The Spanish alien swallows men to produce gold. (7
18 Battle of man with cancer. (7)
21 and 6. Fox raid map re theory about lack of intelligent life forms. (5, 7)
23 See 15 across. (4)
24 Russian said, "Pitch around a Pole." (4)

SOLUTION

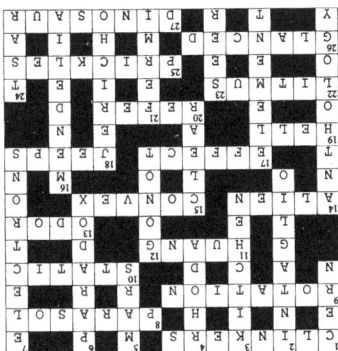

Robert J. Sawyer Bibliography

NOVELS

Golden Fleece. Warner Books (Questar) mass-market original, December 1990. Reprint by Tor, November 1999. Signed, limited edition from SoulWave Publishers, Nashville, TN; that edition with an introduction by Orson Scott Card. A Science Fiction Book Club selection. Aurora Award winner.

End of an Era. Ace mass-market original, November 1994. Reprinted in trade paperback by Tor, September 2001. Seiun Award winner.

The Terminal Experiment. HarperCollins (HarperPrism) mass-market original, May 1995. First serialized in *Analog Science Fiction and Fact* under the title *Hobson's Choice*, Mid-December 1994 through March 1995. Signed, limited edition from SoulWave Publishers, Nashville, TN. "Collector's Edition" from The Easton Press, Norwalk, CT; that edition with an introduction by James Gunn. A Science Fiction Book Club selection. Nebula Award winner. Aurora Award winner. Hugo Award finalist.

Starplex. Ace mass-market original, October 1996. First serialized in *Analog Science Fiction and Fact*, July-October 1996. A Science Fiction Book Club selection. Hugo Award finalist. Nebula Award finalist. Aurora Award winner.

Frameshift. Tor hardcover, May 1997; Tor mass-market paperback, November 1998. A Science Fiction Book Club selection. Hugo Award finalist. Seiun Award winner.

Illegal Alien. Ace hardcover, December 1997; Ace mass-market paperback, January 1999. A "Signed First Edition" selection from The Easton Press, Norwalk, CT; that edition with an introduction by James Gunn. A Science Fiction Book Club selection. Seiun Award winner.

Factoring Humanity. Tor hardcover, June 1998; Tor mass-market paperback, May 1999; Tor trade paperback, January 2004. Hugo Award finalist.

Flashforward. Tor hardcover, June 1999; Tor mass-market paperback, April 2000. Aurora Award winner.

Calculating God. Tor hardcover, June 2000; Tor mass-market, July 2001. Hugo Award finalist.

Mindscan. Tor hardcover, April 2005. Tor mass-market, forthcoming.

The Neanderthal Parallax

Hominids. Tor hardcover, May 2002; Tor mass-market, February 2003. First serialized in *Analog Science Fiction and Fact,* January-April 2002. Hugo Award winner.

Humans. Tor hardcover, February 2003; Tor mass-market, September 2003. Hugo Award finalist.

Hybrids. Tor hardcover, September 2003; Tor mass-market, November 2004.

The Quintaglio Ascension

Far-Seer. Ace, June 1992. A Science Fiction Book Club selection. Reprinted by Tor in trade paperback, May 2004.

Fossil Hunter. Ace, May 1993. Reprint by Tor in trade paperback forthcoming

Foreigner. Ace, March 1994. Reprint by Tor in trade paperback forthcoming.

<hr />

COLLECTIONS

Iterations (introduction by James Alan Gardner). Hardcover from Quarry Press, Kingston, Ontario, 2002. Trade paperback from Red Deer Press, Calgary, Alberta, 2004.

Relativity (introduction by Mike Resnick). Hardcover from ISFiC Press, Deerfield, IL, November 2004.

<hr />

ANTHOLOGIES

Tesseracts 6 (with Carolyn Clink). Tesseract Books, Edmonton, Alberta, 1997.

Crossing the Line: Canadian Mysteries with a Fantastic Twist (with David Skene-Melvin). Pottersfield Press, Lawrencetown Beach, Nova Scotia, 1998.

Over the Edge: The Crime Writers of Canada Anthology (with Peter Sellers). Pottersfield Press, Lawrencetown Beach, Nova Scotia, 2000.

<hr />

SHORT FICTION

* included in *Iterations*

"The Abdication of Pope Mary III," *Nature: International Weekly Journal of Science,* July 6, 2000. *

"Above It All," *Dante's Disciples,* edited by Peter Crowther and Edward E. Kramer, White Wolf, Atlanta, February 1996. *

"Black Reflection," *In the Shadow of the Wall: Vietnam Stories That Might Have Been,* edited by Byron R. Tetrick, Cumberland House,

2002. Modified and incorporated into the novel *Humans* (2003) as Chapter 22.

"The Blue Planet" as "Mars Reacts!," *The Globe and Mail: Canada's National Newspaper*, Saturday, December 11, 1999. *

"Caught in the Web," *White Wall Review 1982*, edited by Denise Coney, Jennifer Harwood, J. Craig Sandy, and Robert J. Sawyer, Ryerson Polytechnical Institute, Toronto, 1982.

"Come All Ye Faithful," *Space Inc.*, edited by Julie E. Czerneda, DAW Books, New York, July 2003.

"The Contest," *White Wall Review 1980*, edited by Lisa Coleman and Ed Greenwood, Ryerson Polytechnical Institute, Toronto, 1980; reprinted in *100 Great Fantasy Short Short Stories*, edited by Isaac Asimov, Terry Carr, and Martin Harry Greenberg, Doubleday, New York, 1984. *

"Driving A Bargain," *Be VERY Afraid!: More Tales of Horror*, edited by Edo van Belkom, Tundra Books, Toronto, 2002.

"The Eagle Has Landed," *I, Alien*, edited by Mike Resnick, DAW Books, New York, forthcoming.

"Fallen Angel," *Strange Attraction*, edited by Edward E. Kramer, ShadowLands Press, Centreville, VA, June 2000. *

"Flashes," *FutureShocks*, edited by Lou Anders, Roc, New York, forthcoming.

"Forever," *Return of the Dinosaurs*, edited by Mike Resnick and Martin H. Greenberg, DAW Books, New York, May 1997. *

"Gator," the lead story in *Urban Nightmares*, edited by Josepha Sherman and Keith R. A. DeCandido, Baen Books, New York, November 1997. *

"Golden Fleece," *Amazing Stories*, edited by Patrick Lucien Price, TSR Inc., Lake Geneva, WI, September 1988.

"The Good Doctor," *Amazing Stories*, edited by Patrick Lucien Price, TSR Inc., Lake Geneva, WI, January 1989.

"The Hand You're Dealt," *Free Space*, edited by Brad Linaweaver and Edward E. Kramer, Tor Books, New York, July 1997. *

"Identity Theft," *Down These Dark Spaceways*, edited by Mike Resnick, Science Fiction Book Club, New York, 2005.

"If I'm Here, Imagine Where They Sent My Luggage," *The Village Voice: The Weekly Newspaper of New York*, 14-20 January 1981; reprinted by Story Cards, Washington DC, in 1987. *

"Immortality," *Janis Ian's Stars*, edited by Janis Ian and Mike Resnick, DAW Books, New York, August 2003.

"Ineluctable," the lead story in *Analog Science Fiction and Fact*, November 2002.

"Iterations," the lead story in *TransVersions: An Anthology of New Fantastic Literature*, edited by Marcel Gagne and Sally Tomasevic, Paper Orchid Press, November 2000. *

"Just Like Old Times," *On Spec: The Canadian Magazine of Speculative Writing*, Summer 1993; commissioned for and also published as the lead story in *Dinosaur Fantastic*, edited by Mike Resnick and Martin H. Greenberg, DAW Books, New York, July 1993. *

"Kata Bindu," *Microcosms*, edited by Gregory Benford, DAW Books, New York, January 2004.

"Last But Not Least," *Be Afraid!: Tales of Horror*, edited by Edo van Belkom, Tundra Books, Toronto, September 2000. *

"Lost in the Mail," *TransVersions 3*, October 1995. *

"Mikeys," *Space Stations*, edited by Martin H. Greenberg and John Helfers, DAW Books, New York, March 2004.

"Motive," *FutureScapes*, Strasenburgh Planetarium, Rochester, NY, Summer 1980.

"On The Surface," *Future Wars*, edited by Martin H. Greenberg and Larry Segriff, DAW Books, New York, April 2003.

"Ours to Discover," *LeisureWays*, November 1982. *

"Peking Man," the lead story in *Dark Destiny III: Children of Dracula*, edited by Edward E. Kramer, White Wolf, Atlanta, October 1996. *

"Relativity," *Men Writing Science Fiction as Women*, edited by Mike Resnick, DAW Books, New York, November 2003.

"The Right's Tough," *Visions of Liberty*, edited by Mark Tier and Martin H. Greenberg, DAW Books, New York, July 2004.

"Shed Skin," *The Bakka Anthology*, edited by Kristen Pederson Chew, The Bakka Collection, Toronto, December 2002, and *Analog Science Fiction and Fact*, January-February 2004.

"The Shoulders of Giants," as the lead story in *Star Colonies* edited by Martin H. Greenberg and John Helfers, DAW Books, New York, June 2000. *

"The Stanley Cup Caper," *The Toronto Star*, Sunday, August 24, 2003, page M1.

"Star Light, Star Bright," *Far Frontiers*, edited by Martin H. Greenberg and Larry Segriff, DAW Books, New York, September 2000. *

"Stream of Consciousness," *No Limits: Developing Scientific Literacy Using Science Fiction* and *Packing Fraction and Other Tales of Science and Imagination*, both edited by Julie E. Czerneda, Trifolium Books, Toronto, 1999. *

"Uphill Climb," *Amazing Stories*, edited by Patrick Lucien Price, TSR Inc., Lake Geneva, WI, March 1987. *

"Where the Heart Is," *Ark of Ice: Canadian Futurefiction*, edited by Lesley Choyce, Pottersfield Press, Nova Scotia, 1992. *

"Wiping Out," *Guardsmen of Tomorrow*, edited by Martin H. Greenberg and Larry Segriff, DAW Books, New York, November 2000. *

"You See But You Do Not Observe," *Sherlock Holmes in Orbit*, edited by Mike Resnick and Martin H. Greenberg, DAW Books, New York, February 1995. Authorized by Dame Jean Conan Doyle. *

About the Author

Robert J. Sawyer is one of only sixteen writers ever to win both a best-novel Hugo Award and a best-novel Nebula Award. The Hugos are the "people's choice awards" of the SF field, voted on by the attendees of the annual World Science Fiction Convention, and the Nebulas are SF's "Academy Awards," bestowed by the members of the genre's professional association, the Science Fiction and Fantasy Writers of America.

In total, Rob has won thirty-two national and international awards for his fiction, including eight Canadian Science Fiction and Fantasy Awards ("Auroras"), as well as three Japanese Seiun Awards for Best Foreign Novel of the Year. He's also won the *Science Fiction Chronicle* Reader Award and the Crime Writers of Canada's Arthur Ellis Award, both for Best Short Story of the Year, as well as the Collectors Award for Most Collectable Author of the Year, as selected by the clientele of Barry R. Levin Science Fiction & Fantasy Literature, the world's leading SF rare-book dealer.

Rob's books are top-ten national mainstream bestsellers in Canada, and have hit number one on the bestsellers' list published by *Locus*, the American trade journal of the SF field. He is the author of the bestselling "Neanderthal Parallax" and "Quintaglio Ascension" trilogies, plus ten stand-alone SF novels. In addition, he edits the "Robert J. Sawyer Books" SF imprint for Canada's Red Deer Press, and is a frequent TV guest, with over two hundred appearances to his credit. He is also a highly sought-after speaker, having given keynote addresses at such varied conferences as the Second International Symposium on Physical Sciences in Space, the 2004 Annual Meeting of the Canadian Association of Science Centres, and BioMedex 2004.

Born in Ottawa in 1960, Rob now lives in Mississauga, a city just west of Toronto, with poet Carolyn Clink.

. For more information about Rob and his work, visit his World Wide Web site — which, according to Reuters, was the first-ever SF author site, and now contains more than one million words of material — at www.sfwriter.com.

RELATIVITY

November, 2004

Relativity by Robert J. Sawyer was pub-
lished by ISFiC Press, 707 Sapling Lane,
Deerfield, Illinois 60015. One thousand
copies have been printed by Thomson-
Shore, Inc. The typeset is Berthold
Baskerville and Digi Grotesk Bold
Condensed, printed on 60# Nature's
Natural. The binding cloth is Arrestox B
Black. Design and typesetting by Garcia
Publishing Services, Woodstock, Illinois.